Soul Support
Spiritual Encounters at Life's End

To Doug— with love and blessings, Joan

Soul Support

Spiritual Encounters at Life's End

Memoir of a Hospital Chaplain

Joan Paddock Maxwell

RESOURCE *Publications* • Eugene, Oregon

SOUL SUPPORT: SPIRITUAL ENCOUNTERS AT LIFE'S END
Memoir of a Hospital Chaplain

Resource Publications
An Imprint of Wipf and Stock Publishers
199 W. 8th Ave., Suite 3
Eugene, OR 97401

www.wipfandstock.com

PAPERBACK ISBN: 978-1-5326-1874-1
HARDCOVER ISBN: 978-1-4982-8642-8
EBOOK ISBN: 978-1-4982-4453-4

Manufactured in the U.S.A. 05/30/17

"Elevator Chaplaincy," "The Little Space," and "Facing an Amputation" were originally published in PlainViews®, the professional journal of HealthCare Chaplaincy Network™, and are reprinted with permission.

The Shalem Institute for Spiritual Formation in Washington, DC (www.shalem.org) gave permission to reprint "Beauty in the ICU" and a revised version of "Surgery & Prayer" (here "The Little Space"), both of which originally appeared in the Shalem News.

Contents

About This Book | ix
Acknowledgments | xi

1. Listening | 1
Great Is Thy Faithfulness | 3
Calling Dr. Paddock | 5
"Do You Feel Different Inside?" | 8
God and Me (1) | 11
Night Anointing | 15
My Call | 21
"Row Your Boat" | 21
Chaplain School | 27
Beauty in the ICU | 28
Handcuffs | 29
About Dying | 33
Hospital Ministry | 39

2. Learning | 43
Patient Teachers | 45
Behind the Scenes | 50
"My Parents' Fault" | 53
Permanent Ink | 56
At the Foot of the Bed | 58
Helplessness | 61
God in the Window | 65
The Palliative Care Office | 66
At the Foot of the Cross | 68
The Grocery Cart | 71
Five Minutes | 73
Ms. Trouten's Pillow | 75

The Little Space | 81
Ophelia Rivers, Trusting God | 84
God and Me (2) | 88
Vulnerability in the Hospital | 91
My Lady with ALS | 97
Deep Diving | 101
Elevator Chaplaincy | 103
Exorcism | 105
Ash Wednesday | 107
Praying, Out Loud | 110
Facing an Amputation | 115
The Crow | 116
Dead Bodies | 118
On the Vent | 122
"Not Me" | 128

3. Loving | 133
Ms. Doka with Shining Eyes | 135
"Useless Old Woman" | 139
Hold the Phone | 142
Bleeding Out | 146
Mr. Rupert's Blessing | 149
The Singing Bowl | 152
Under the Pillow | 155
"I Know that Prayer!" | 158
Expletive Undeleted | 160
Psalm 88 | 161
Silent Night | 164
Witch Doctor | 169
No Family | 175
Peace—Be Still | 183
"We Have a Situation" | 186
Garden Communion | 190
The Holy Koran | 192
Many Mansions | 194
Maria, Full of Grace | 196
Ending | 201

Afterword | 202

Appendices | 205
1. Surviving the Hospital | 206
2. Care Package for a Hospital Patient | 209
3. When Someone You Love Is Terminally Ill | 212

Bibliography | 217

About This Book

This book tells of the holy encounters between the human spirit and the divine that I have been privileged to witness: my burning bushes, so to speak.

For twelve years, between 1999 and 2011, I served in the Washington, DC, area as a chaplain to hospital patients, many of whom were dying. I started as a greener-than-green chaplaincy student, went to seminary for a master's degree in theology, became a hospital chaplain, and finally served for six years in an urban hospital as the chaplain on the palliative care team; that is, my colleagues and I worked with patients with life-threatening illnesses. I was moved by patients' suffering, impressed by their courage and generosity, and awed by the grace-filled encounters they sometimes experienced.

To me, the stories in this book are sacred. They show the beauty of the human soul in travail. They show the scientifically inexplicable presence in suffering of what some call God and others call a Mystery. And they show how that boundlessly compassionate Mystery can make use of the most unlikely creatures—even of me.

This book is based on hundreds of pages of notes that I typed nearly every evening after getting home from the hospital. I began that practice to hone my observations of patients and improve my interactions with them. As time went on, I became convinced that much of what I witnessed was the continuing revelation of the Mystery at the heart of life. The stories I heard and the events I saw were sacred to me, and I attempt here to share them.

These days acute-care hospitals discharge patients as quickly as possible. Thus chaplains working in such hospitals encounter patients over short periods, often only once. But when patients are gravely ill, they sometimes have spiritual experiences they yearn to share with another person, even if that person is a stranger. The stories in this book are therefore both intense and brief. I wish I could have known more about these people, but the fleeting nature of our relationships made that impossible. Instead, I got moments: moments where the beauty of the human spirit in the midst of adversity shined forth in the light of the great Mystery.

Part of chaplaincy training required students to produce what are called verbatims. These included lengthy reports of conversations with patients, family, and staff written in word-for-word dialogue. We reviewed our verbatims in depth with classmates and our supervisor, and from that process we learned that nearly every single word mattered in our interactions. Students were not allowed to take notes in the patient's presence, but with practice we learned to recall with surprising accuracy what was said by whom. Every conversation you read here actually happened and was recorded the same day it occurred.

I believe my patients' stories deserve to be told and honored. Because most of the people I served have died, and I have no way of locating those few who may still be alive, I have not been able to obtain their permission to report what I witnessed. Therefore, patient names and identifying details have been changed to protect patient confidentiality. But the essence of each encounter is as exact as I could make it.

Mixed in with the patients' stories are bits of my own story. I am by nature a private person and not inclined to self-revelation, but friends have convinced me that since I am the only constant in these stories, I must overcome my reluctance. This book tells how I was transformed from being an agnostic for forty years to a serving hospital chaplain. I hope that seeing the impact of my patients and their experiences on me over time will help you understand what it is like to be a chaplain and why I was motivated to serve.

Friends sometimes admired my serving as a chaplain with dying people. However, people who have held similar jobs know that the service was at least as much for me as it was for the patients. Seeing the Mystery at work was worth everything.

Acknowledgments

On a low altar in the room at home where I pray, lies a crocheted shamrock of faded green wool. More than ten years ago a patient, scheduled for a high-risk, "last-chance" surgery, spent what turned out to be her final evening furiously crocheting shamrocks for the hospital staff who worked with her. She poured out her energy on creating and giving, expressing her gratitude and working to leave behind a little mark of her time on this earth. Whenever I light a candle on the altar, I see the shamrock. I think of her spirit and the spirits of the many other patients who allowed me to witness, with them, the actions of the great Mystery in their lives as they came to a close. I am profoundly grateful to them all for that privilege.

This book and its author have been blessed by the help of many generous people. Ryland Swain, Eileen Simon, Beth Norcross, Debbie Little, Dee Miller, Susana Franck, Jane Geniesse, and Madzy Beveridge listened, questioned, and suggested. I was the fortunate beneficiary of the teaching of Gerald G. May, Carole Crumley, Tilden Edwards, Cynthia Bourgeault, Thomas Keating, Barbara Brown Taylor, James D. Nenninger, Beverly Mitchell, Sharon Ringe, and Sandra Wheeler. My colleagues in the three Washington metropolitan-area hospitals where I trained and served were supportive and inspiring. The dissertation by the late Landis Vance, my dear friend and coworker, on sources of spiritual support for non-religious people was a great help to my work. The people of Washington, DC's St. John's Episcopal Church, Georgetown Parish, commissioned me as a chaplain, encouraged me to preach, and responded graciously when I offered some of these stories in sermons.

Barbara Rosenblatt and my classmates in her memoir class and the members of the Cosmos Club's Cosmowriters nonfiction writing group were most helpful and encouraging.

Olga Seaham, Lucian Vaughan, Deborah Smith, and Roger M. Williams provided valuable editorial advice and assistance. Faith Collins helped keep everything together with expertise and grace when deadlines and details seemed overwhelming.

The support and love of my family, especially Tina Foster, Lowell Paddock, and my husband, David Maxwell, made it all possible.

This book is dedicated to David, who has been a rock and a joy throughout the long process of bringing it to birth.

1. Listening

Great Is Thy Faithfulness

"Since he was admitted two days ago, he hasn't spoken. Not a word."

The charge nurse (responsible for staff assignments on the patient floor) was giving me background on the last patient on my list, a Mr. Weldon in Room 854. The list showed that Mr. Weldon was thirty-one, HIV positive, with no known address. Religious preference: unknown. I was halfway through my second unit of Clinical Pastoral Education (part of the training process for hospital chaplains) and I had never encountered a situation like this.

"Is he sentient?" I asked.

"I think so," the charge nurse replied. "He opens his eyes when you talk to him, but you can't be sure. He won't speak."

"Okay. Thanks mucho."

The charge nurse turned to pick up the phone, and I went down the hall to 854. I prayed for guidance and tapped on the open door. A thin, dark-skinned man was lying flat and still under a sheet, his head turned toward the door. He had curly black hair, close cropped, and a short, curly black beard. He was lean, but not emaciated. At my knock, he opened his eyes.

"Mr. Weldon?" No response. "Hi, I'm Chaplain Maxwell, just sticking my nose in to see how your day is going." Again, no response. Looking into his eyes, I sensed that he was understanding my words; but I couldn't be certain.

What to do? Does he speak English? Is he in his right mind? Does he have any faith in God? If so, how does he think of God? Christian? Muslim? Buddhist?

I was completely at a loss as to how to proceed. Suddenly the morning sun flashed on a window pane and caught my eye. *The deer herd.* The hospital bordered a large field, public property, where a dozen or more deer sometimes appeared, safe from humans behind a high metal fence. The window offered a glimpse of a small portion of the field, well away from where the deer usually grazed. But it was worth a chance, and I took it.

"I don't know if you know it, Mr. Weldon, but you have a special room." A flash of interest sparked in his eyes. *So he's tracking what I'm saying.* "If you look out your window, just to the right of the telephone pole—see the pole there? —you can see part of a field. And some days a herd of deer comes into that field, usually a little before the sun goes down."

He turned his head slowly and looked out. "Maybe they'll come tonight. Who knows? If it's okay with you, I'll stick my head in tomorrow to find out if they have. Just keep an eye on that field around five in the afternoon. Take care of yourself—see you tomorrow."

The next day I went back to his room.

"Hi, Mr. Weldon, it's Chaplain Maxwell again. Just checking on those deer. Did you see them?" Silence. *I'm probably just bugging this poor man. He must be lonely—advanced AIDS, no visitors, no speech.* Then a slow, deliberate nod.

"You saw them? That's great! How many were there?" No response. *Stop pushing. Just let it be.* I talked a bit more about the deer and said I would check back the next day.

On Day 3, another nod: he had seen the deer again. On Day 4, the nod was accompanied by a soft, "Yes." *Contact! Bless those deer.* A few probes got no further response, but he had taken the first step. In the hall, I told his nurse, and we high-fived.

On Day 5, as soon as I walked into his room he sat up in bed, vigorous and suddenly transformed. *Hunh?*

"Sit down," he ordered firmly, pointing to a chair. We talked for nearly an hour, moving from the deer, who had come yet again, to a life review. Sometimes directly, sometimes by implication, he told me about his family of origin, his love for the aunt who'd raised him from birth, his pride in his ability to steal cars, his delight as a young man at showing up at his aunt's behind the wheel of a flashy auto. Then his lengthy imprisonment out of state, a walk of several hundred miles after his release back to his home town, his shame at being homeless and destitute. His yearning to telephone his aunt but his resolve not to let her see him as a "failure." His collapse on the street . . .[1]

The dam had broken, and it all flooded out. He talked about his belief in a God who loved him even when nobody else did. We prayed together to that loving God.

When I came back to his room two days later, Mr. Weldon was lying flat under the sheet again, his eyes closed, but his order to sit down was even more forceful than the first time. I sat close to his head.

"Last night," he whispered. "Last night . . . I woke up. It was 3:00 in the morning. It wasn't frightening. There was nobody in the room, nobody in

1. I am sometimes asked *how* a patient contracted a communicable disease, such as HIV. I never asked a question about that or anything else unless I felt that doing so would increase my ability to support the patient. In the case of Mr. Weldon, I speculated that he might have acquired HIV in prison, but I didn't raise that issue. I have often thought that if that were the case, our society essentially extracted a terrible price—death—for what he told me was his conviction for burglary.

the hall, nobody came in. It was so quiet. But there was such joy." His face glowed. "From 3:00 until 4:30—joy. Joy in the room."

He paused, remembering. "Oh, I needed that. You don't know how much I needed that. I didn't dare move. I didn't want it to end. I just laid there. Just laid still. No one in the room," he repeated. "Just joy."

Just God.

As I looked at his profile, his shiny black hair and beard, his warm brown skin and strong nose, I was filled with the memory of an icon I had seen of the Sinai Christ. Mr. Weldon looked very much like the Christ figure in that painting. The biblical parable of the sheep and the goats tells of Christ in his glory speaking of being visited when he was sick (Matt 25:31–46). I had always taken that as a metaphor. Now, as Mr. Weldon talked, I saw that he *was* the Christ.

What he didn't yet know, but what I had learned just before I came into his room, was that in a few hours the doctors would inform him there was nothing more they could do to try to cure him. He was going to die.

We prayed together, I left, and that afternoon he was moved from the hospital to a nursing home where he would receive hospice services. Three days later, he died.

As I think of Mr. Weldon today, I am reminded of the goodness of God, who brought him such joy at the last, and whose deer were so exceedingly faithful.[2]

Calling Dr. Paddock

When I was a child—from about the age of six on—my physician father, Frank Paddock, would occasionally take me with him when he drove to the local hospital in the small town of Pittsfield, Massachusetts. He was an attending physician who made his patient rounds after dinner. These evening trips were my only real opportunity to be alone with him. He parked in one of the doctors' spaces abutting the red brick building and took me into a little room off the hospital lobby, where he deposited me with the telephone switchboard lady.

He would put me in a worn wooden chair behind the switchboard lady, tell me, "Sit still and be quiet until I come back," and stride off to the elevator to go see his patients. A good-looking man in early middle age, with a hefty dose of Irish charm, he was popular with patients and staff alike.

2. Another version of this story was published in *Journal of Pastoral Care*: Maxwell, "Great."

The same lady was on duty every time we went. I knew that her job was very important. Through the switchboard she connected the outside world to the hospital, and the people inside the hospital to one another, using both hands to insert and remove plugs that joined the cords linking the callers; sometimes holding two plugs in each plump hand, she deftly swapped them among fingers without even looking, all the while carrying on conversations with different callers via a curved, black metal mouthpiece hung around her neck. When as an adult I watched a church organist pulling out and pushing in organ stops, I was reminded of the switchboard lady's dexterity.

Sometimes, when my father's medical rounds were unusually long, the switchboard buzzers would still and the call lights remain dark. Then the lady would swivel her chair and talk with me, breaking off mid-word at the sound of a buzz. One such evening, a call came in for my father. With a smile the lady said, "Joanie, do you want to make the announcement? You know what to say: 'Dr. Paddock, telephone call.'"

I had heard her do that hundreds of times, and knew that the announcement would be broadcast all over the hospital, to places where I had never been allowed to go but where doctors and nurses were doing important, grown-up things. At that point, I was seven years old, and I was yearning to do this vital adult task. The lady held the large, silver public-address microphone toward me, switched it on, and I sat up very straight. "Daddy, phone call," I said distinctly, and immediately the microphone was jerked away.

A few staffers waiting for the elevator laughed and smiled in my direction. Mortified at having embarrassed both the switchboard lady and my father, I apologized to her. We sat in silence, other than the occasional buzz, me worrying that I was in big trouble. But when my father came back to take me home, he said something to her about this being "a genuine country hospital." They both laughed. But even though no more was said about the faux pas, I was never invited to make an announcement again.

The hospital was the center of my father's professional life, a scientific temple where he served as one of the high priests. For many other people I knew, such as Marie, the Irish immigrant who cared for my elderly grandmother, it was a place of terror. "You'll never catch me going to a hospital, Joanie," she would say. "You only go to a hospital when you're dying."

At that time—the late 1940s—Marie's perspective had some merit. The complex medical procedures that are commonplace in America in the twenty-first century—robot-assisted surgery, targeted radiation, and a panoply of drugs—were unknown then. Relatively simple surgery, penicillin, and crude diagnostic X-rays were virtually all hospitals had to offer. Thus, doctors relied much more than they do today on their personal presence as a source of healing.

As a healing force, my father's personal presence was remarkable. On those few occasions in my childhood when I was sick enough to warrant his medical attention, he would stride into the sickroom exuding a combination of vigor, calm, and medical authority. The folds of his clothes would bring in the piney air of the New England outdoors, sending a cool wind from the natural world across my sweaty cheek.

His attitude toward his children's illnesses was tinged with scorn. We all knew how hard he worked, the long hours he kept, the frequent emergency house calls he made at 3:00 in the morning. We children were taught that it was our responsibility not to add to his burdens, and mild childhood fevers and stomach upsets were trivial annoyances compared to the cancers and heart attacks that ravaged his adult patients and were featured in his dinner-table conversation. But a "real" illness, a bad case of measles, say, would elicit his therapeutic presence, albeit briefly. Having him by my bedside, taking my pulse, reading the thermometer, would lift me out of the miasma of my illness and remind me of the glowing natural world calling me to come outside.

I admired my father. I admired his skill at bringing solace to suffering people. I envied his ability to go into what seemed to me to be the secret and powerful world of the hospital.

Not surprisingly, then, as a child and teenager, I wanted to be a doctor, an ambition I kept secret. When I was thirteen, I was sent away to boarding school, partly to get a good education (I had always done well in school) and partly to put some space between me and my stepmother. In my junior year, without forethought, I mentioned casually in a letter home that I was taking biology in preparation for medical school. In reply my father sent me a drawing he had made of an open-mouthed man lying on the floor, a knife in his chest, and a pool of blood on the floor next to the man. On the wall he had drawn a sign: "Over my dead body."

As someone who believes in the equality of women and men, I am ashamed today of my response. But at the time and in my family system, I had no power whatsoever. The possibility of going against his decree never crossed my mind.

Many decades later, as palliative care chaplain, I had around my neck a staff ID that made it possible for me to unlock the inner doors to every part of the hospital devoted to patient care. I relished the access to the secret and powerful world I had yearned to enter as a child. And I prayed to bring the same sense of comfort to my patients that my father had brought to his.

"Do You Feel Different Inside?"

She had asked for a visit from a chaplain. She was thin, in her early eighties, with a hospital pallor, a black wig slightly askew on her head, and faded brown eyes. When I introduced myself as Chaplain Maxwell from the palliative care team, she went right to her point.

"Chaplain, when you're dying, do you feel different inside?"

Never thought of that. Better check what she means by "inside."

"Do you mean in your body?"

She frowned impatiently. "No, in your *self*."

Wonderful question. Wonder what the answer is.

"I don't know. No one I've been with who was dying ever said anything about that. Why do you ask?"

"They told me I'm dying, and I feel just the same inside."

"Mmm." I paused to consider.

Oh my. The docs tell me she's going to die very soon, yet she feels the same inside. What should I say?

Most people don't want to talk about death with a dying person. It's the elephant in the room: Everyone knows it's there, and no one is willing to talk about it. Visitors who themselves aren't actively dying often suffer from "magical thinking." That is, they think that if they even mention death, they will help bring it about. And patients, often feeling vulnerable and isolated at the end of life, are generally exceedingly thoughtful of their visitors. They know the topic of death is upsetting and don't want to drive people away, so they usually don't bring it up.

When I first started to serve as a chaplain, I found it extremely hard, even terrifying, to ask people if they thought they were dying. I feared if I did that I might be bringing up a topic they had never considered. Patients soon taught me that nearly everyone who's in the frightening and alien world of a hospital, even for something medically inconsequential, considers the possibility of death. Once early in my chaplaincy training I encountered a young patient recovering from minor surgery for a deviated septum. An overnight hospital stay brought her face to face, for the first time, with her own mortality. She spent a long time talking with me about how terrified she was at the prospect.

And if patients don't want to talk about death, they won't. If they are in denial, they cannot be reached through ordinary conversation. Sometimes the thought of dying is so overwhelming that the terminally ill person is simply unable to imagine it. I have found, however, that this inability is uncommon.

Over time I became relatively comfortable broaching the subject, for one simple reason: If patients want to talk about it, bringing up death is a gift to them. They are grateful to discuss what's on their mind with someone who is compassionate yet totally uninvolved in their lives. The compassion means they can tell me what they're feeling and be gently received; the lack of involvement means they don't have to worry about upsetting me when they're talking about their own pain and fear.

This woman feels just the same inside—so she thinks perhaps that means she's not dying. She hopes she's not dying. Let's go there.

"So you wondered if that meant the doctors were wrong saying you are dying. Do you think they're wrong?"

"I don't know." She avoided my gaze and picked at the top sheet.

Obviously she hopes they're wrong. I bet she's afraid of what I'll say, that I'll look down on her for hoping she's not dying.

"I can see why you would wonder. I never thought about that before. If you're dying, it does seem as if you ought to feel different inside."

Shouldn't such a big change looming in your body cause a big change in your spirit as well? Makes sense to me.

"That's right." She looked up from the sheet to meet my eyes. "And I don't," she said decisively.

"What do the doctors tell you?"

"They say I have cancer in my lung and in my spine, and there's nothing more they can do."

How can the docs keep on doing that?? They tell a patient "there's nothing more we can do" and just walk out. Not true! It may be true for the doctors focused on a cure, but it's not true for the palliative team, focused on comfort.

"What they mean is that there's nothing more they can do about the cancer. But there are more things that can be done for you, and will be done for you. Just different things. That's why the palliative care team is here."

"To treat the cancer?"

Oh, dear lady, I wish it were, but no, no, no.

"We can treat the effects of the cancer. Sarah—the nurse—you met her, right?" She nodded. "Sarah can help with pain relief, and if your stomach gets upset or anything like that. She's good. And Hoshi—the social worker—can help with family stuff, insurance, setting up home care, that sort of thing. She's great. She'll be by in a little while. And if you like I can help with things of the spirit."

She shook her head. "I'm not religious."

People always think a hospital chaplain is just about religion.

I nodded. "Lots of people aren't religious. But do you consider yourself a spiritual person?"

"Yes, I do."

"You know, there are five ways people are spiritual. Religion is only one of them." She looked at me and furrowed her brow. It took me a moment to realize she was raising her eyebrows, but she had no facial hair left after the chemotherapy. "Do you want to know the other four?"

"Okay."

Often I ask people to guess them, but that didn't feel right at this moment. She had enough on her plate just now. I held up my right hand toward her, fingers curled, and raised my thumb. "You've already mentioned religion. Another way"—I raised my index finger— "is through a sense of something inside. Religious people call it the soul. Jungians call it the Self. Hindus call it Atman. Others call it the human spirit. It's something that feels like it's more than just you."

A nod.

Okay, she's following, and looks interested. So continue.

I raised another finger. "A third way is through deep interpersonal relationships: your parents, your children, your partner." I raised a fourth finger. "The fourth way is through nature, like watching a sunset, smelling a flower, being in the woods, being on the water." I raised my last finger. "The final way is through things of beauty created by human hands. Paintings, novels, poetry, dance, music, astronomy, mathematics, science, philosophy."[3]

I paused for a minute so she could absorb what I had said. "Do any of these work for you?"

"I love my grandchildren. And I love being by the lake."

Good. I smiled. "That's two of the ways."

"And I love the piano." She touched her chest. "And I know what you mean about something inside me being more than me."

"So that's four ways you're spiritual. That's great. Those are rich resources you can draw on."

And they'll give her pleasure in the time she has left, however long that may be. She just needs to know how to call on them for support. I can help there.

Hoshi appeared in the doorway. Perfect timing, typical of Hoshi.

"We can talk about that tomorrow if you want. But here's Hoshi, the palliative-care team's social worker. Is it okay if she talks with you now? Or do you need a break for a minute?"

"I need to use the rest room."

"Let me help you," Hoshi said, walking over holding out her arm.

3. The original inspiration for these five categories came from Vance, *Spiritual Experiences.*

"See you tomorrow, okay?" I asked.

She nodded and I left.

A good start.

I wonder, do you feel different inside when you're dying? What a remarkable question. Guess one day I'll find out for myself.

God and Me (1)

Ten days after I was born, America entered World War II, and almost immediately my physician father was called up for military service. Soon he was sent overseas, first to Africa and then to Europe. My young mother was left alone with me. In support of the war effort, she went to work as a welder in a factory making military weapons, taking me with her to the factory floor in a basket on her bicycle. I was later told that as a graduate of Vassar College who had never before done manual labor of this kind, she found the work extremely stressful. The stress, combined with caring for a little child and worrying about her husband at war, proved too much for her, and she committed suicide. I was three. It was terrible.

After my mother died my Gran—my father's widowed mother—took me in to live with her. That continued for a couple of years. After my father returned from the war, he remarried, and when I was five I was taken to live with him and his second wife. But my heart belonged to my Gran. Since my father and his mother lived in the same town, about a mile apart from one another, I got to see Gran every week, though never as much as I wanted. And no living arrangement could make up for the reality that my mother was dead.

When I turned six, a new opportunity arose for me to be with my grandmother—accompanying her to the Sunday morning service at the local Congregational Church. I didn't know anything about church, and my father was an atheist, so presumably the original idea was Gran's. The church building was clad in grey stone, the inside was dark wood, the service was highly intellectual and in my recollection utterly joyless; but I would have gone anywhere and done anything to be with my grandmother, so I didn't care. I got to sit next to her, and before the sermon began she always gave me a mint LifeSaver to encourage me to be quiet.

Because of living with my Gran and then not having any siblings until I was six, I was a precocious little girl. I whiled away the endless sermon time by trying to understand the message enough to come up with a question for the minister when we shook his hand at the end of the service. I can't recall anything he said, nor any question that I asked, but I can still see the burgundy color of the cushions on the pews, the open-topped wooden containers on the back of the pews in front of us where hymnals were kept, and the huge space over our heads that lifted to the roof high above.

Congregationalists did not kneel in church. When it came time for prayer, my grandmother clasped her hands in her lap, bowed her head, closed her eyes, and leaned forward. Of course I imitated her. The minister would pray for a while, which meant he did more talking. Then he would stop praying, and Gran would sit up straight again. When I felt her move, I sat up too.

Finally the service ended, we walked together to her parked car, and I became the happy beneficiary of her undivided attention during our much-too-short drive back to her house, where the family gathered for Sunday dinner.

I didn't think about God but accepted his existence (God was definitely male) in the same way that I accepted that the sky was blue. Marie, the Irish Catholic maid who kept house and cared for my grandmother, had taught me that prayer was something humans said *to* God. You were supposed to recite either the Lord's Prayer or, "Now I lay me down to sleep/I pray the Lord my soul to keep/And if I die before I wake/I pray the Lord my soul to take." I disliked that prayer since I didn't want to imagine that I could die before I woke again.

Marie taught me that you could begin or end your prayer with requests. They could be general ("Please bless Gran") or specific ("Please let me pass the spelling test tomorrow, and help Kay find her lost dolly") but that was all: requests only. It seemed that God was a very busy, very important, and very invisible old person who would sometimes listen to you and sometimes not. If he did listen, occasionally he would decide to give you what you asked him for. There was no particular reason why he made those decisions, but he did, so it was wise to keep your wishes active, near the top of the pile on God's desk.

When I was about six, I learned that Santa Claus was made up and didn't exist. I felt very grown up to be in on the secret. Then when I was twelve, I learned that God was also made up and didn't exist. Here's how that happened. I had gotten in trouble at school. In trying to convince the teacher that I was unjustly accused, I told her that I "swore to God" that I didn't do it (which was the truth). When she reacted scornfully to my protestations, I realized that for her God was just another version of Santa Claus. I checked this realization out with my father, who confirmed it. Since he was the final authority in my family, I gave up on God.

I was sorry that God didn't exist, because I had liked having an invisible force to which I could turn for help in what was to my childish understanding rather like a game of chance. Chance with the possibility of winning was better than no chance at all. But something of the sermons I had endured for so many years must have stuck as well, because my sorrow at God's non-existence went deeper than losing access to chance. If God had existed, life and the universe would somehow have a deep inner order, coherence, and *meaning*.

So even though I'd come to know there was no God, I kept my eyes and ears open just in case I was mistaken. All through high school and college, I took courses and read books, went to lectures and visited all kinds of places of worship, and talked far into the night with all sorts of people about the possibility of the existence of God. Whenever I met someone who believed in God, I would ask them,[4] "Why do you believe in God?" Most people were startled by the question. But once they assured themselves that my question was genuine, they would graciously spend considerable time trying to answer. Although their answers showed me they were sincere, I never found them personally convincing.

I continued my search through my single years living and working in New York City and then afterwards when I married my husband David. Almost without exception, every single week I did or read something relating to the question of the existence of God. Occasionally I attended a religious service, but nothing I encountered felt meaningful to me and I remained a seeker but nonbeliever.

Then one autumn, when I was well into middle age, I heard that the *daughter* of a man I knew had become an Episcopal minister and was leading a little church on the Maine island where David and I had a vacation home. By this time in my life, I was a dyed-in-the-wool feminist, but I had never seen a woman lead a church service. I went to the Sunday worship. To me, there was nothing special about what unfolded except for one thing she said in her sermon. "Belief in God is a matter of choice," she said. "You can say yes to God or you can say no. It's up to you."

How about that? I thought. *I can make the choice and there it is? Sounds kind of crazy, but I'll give it a try. I'll say, "Yes!" What have I got to lose?* I sat there in the pew, silently saying *yes, yes, yes!* Nothing happened.

When I went home after the service David asked me how it went—"Okay," I said—and if I was going to go back. I didn't know if I would, but the following Sunday I decided to give *yes* another try. I spent a good deal of the service silently saying *yes*, but once again nothing happened.

4. To avoid the tiresome "him or her" and "she or he" I am using "them" and "they" throughout this book, grammatically incorrect at times but gender neutral.

By the third Sunday, I was cross. I had spent a fair bit of my life on this God business, and it was clearly a waste. But like a good baseball fan, I believed you deserved three strikes before you were out. *This is it,* I decided. *I'll go one last time, and if nothing happens—and it won't—I'm just going to drop the whole thing. It's time to give up.*

Back to church I went. I sat in the pew saying *yes* for much of the service, nothing happened, and I resolved to give up.

At the end of the service, there were a few brief announcements from the congregation. Out of courtesy I waited in the pew for them to be over. One rather strange item was about a "quiet prayer" group, which was going to meet at six that night at someone's house. An address was given. It was a few miles from where I lived.

What's "quiet prayer"? I asked myself. Sounded rather weird—praying "quietly," whatever that meant, with strangers in a stranger's house. *I'm sure going to give that a pass.* But then I thought of how much I would like it if God did exist, and how the service just now concluding marked the end of my search. *If I don't try* everything *I'll never know if I missed God.* Of course there was no God, but I wanted to leave no stone unturned, even a truly weird stone like quiet prayer.

That evening I drove from our house to try to find the stranger's house, which was in a sparsely inhabited area I'd never been before. The sun had set; there were no streetlights and no road signs. This was well before GPS, so I was on my own, and I got lost quickly. I found myself driving through a dark, woodsy area, peering for a light. (The symbolism of this was entirely lost on me at the time.) Just as I was about to give up and turn toward home, I saw a yellow glow in the woods. I pulled my car off the road and stumbled through the trees to a porch light over the door to a small wooden cabin.

I knocked, and the woman priest opened it. I had no idea she would be there. She greeted me and invited me to choose a seat in the small, spare room. There were two other women present, one my age and one about ten years older. The older woman looked like she knew what she was doing, but the woman my age looked befuddled, so I went and sat by her. "I don't know what quiet prayer is, do you?" I whispered to her.

"Nope," she said, shaking her head.

"Do you want me to teach you?" The priest had overheard our exchange.

I was put off by the intimacy of the tiny gathering of strangers and by what I was convinced was a waste of my time. But I'm polite, so I said, "Yes, please."

The priest explained that quiet prayer (sometimes called silent prayer) was a way of listening to God rather than speaking to God. You were supposed to sit in a comfortable fashion, upright but relaxed, and still. You closed your eyes and silently, in your heart, as you breathed in and out, you repeated a single word that symbolized your desire to hear God. "You could use the word 'God,' or 'love,'" the priest suggested. "You'll have distracting thoughts, but just let them go. Simply return to the word you are saying in your heart."

She smiled.

"We'll be silent together for twenty minutes," she said, and went and sat on the floor in front of a lighted candle.

Twenty minutes? This is crazy.

Through the window, in the faint post-sunset glow, I could dimly see a forest and a glimpse of the ocean. As I was looking a seagull flew close by. Beside me the other woman breathed gently. I could hear a refrigerator in the little kitchen. There was no other noise.

I can't leave, it would be rude to these nice people. What to do? Twenty minutes is an incredibly long time to just sit and not move. My nose itches. Guess I can't scratch it. May as well try what she said—pick a word and say it in my heart while I breathe. I'll pick 'God' since that's why I'm here. So. . .God. . .God. . .God. Wonder what David's doing. He'd never believe what I'm doing. Oops. . .God. . .God. . .God. Wish I could scratch my nose. God. . .God. . .God.

Imperceptibly my body changed. Although I didn't change my physical position, it felt as if the very molecules forming my body started to slow down. Instead of interacting busily with one another they seemed to be less intense, calmer, quieter. The refrigerator hummed. My companion breathed, shifted once in her seat. *God. . .God. . .God.*

I heard the cry of a seagull.

The refrigerator turned off and an immense stillness overtook the room. And in that stillness, I became aware that we were not alone. A living presence was with us. *God. . .God. . .God.*

Ting. Ting. Ting. The priest was ringing a little bell, letting us know the time was up. The four of us sat silently for a moment, and then the priest rose. The other three of us stood, gathered our coats and went to the door. We shook hands with her and left, one by one.

And my entire life was changed.

Night Anointing

One evening when I got home after work, I discovered that one of the hospital's geriatric physicians had left a message on my answering machine asking me to see Stephen Harwa. An eighty-one-year-old Egyptian visiting his daughter in the US, Mr. Harwa was on the palliative list and was dying. The message said the patient would almost surely not last the night, and the daughter had requested last rites. The physician added that the family had its own priest, but would like me to see him as well.

As it happened, I had already visited the patient and family twice that day, one visit brief and one extended. During the visits, I had learned that Mr. Harwa was Egyptian Orthodox. They had the image of their Patriarch pinned to his pillow, and the prayers they were intoning were Roman Catholic in form, consisting of long rosaries and other formal litanies.

For a moment, I confess, I was tempted to ignore the message, since I had just begun my vacation. That evening David and I were going to see a play, and the next morning we were leaving early for our house in Maine. But I realized that I could go see the patient after the play, if David wouldn't mind the inconvenience of having to wait in the car. (He didn't mind.) I decided I should go.

I had no idea what the physician had told the family about my coming (he might have promised a visit that night). Moreover, when I had visited the man earlier I had not asked them if they wanted me to lead them in any sort of ritual but had simply joined in their prayers. Clearly they now wanted more.

After seeing the play, we drove to the hospital, arriving at about 9:30. I put on my badge and hospital ID, left David reading a book in the car, and went into the building through the emergency department, dodging a few drunken people weaving about in the hot and already jammed waiting room. In the palliative care office I picked up my holy oil and my copy of *Ministry with the Sick*, an Episcopal prayer book that has all the rituals I might need, including "Prayers for a Person Near Death," which can be made into an excellent little bedside service. I didn't know if the patient was still alive, but it was good to be prepared.

I put my ribbon marker in the book at the start of the service and trotted up to Mr. Harwa's room. On the way I passed a few medical staffers looking unlike the way they do in the day: more intense, more focused, a little more tired. I knocked on the door, paused for a second, and let myself in. There were three Egyptians around the bed, one woman and two men. I had seen them briefly during my second visit earlier that day. The three or four other people who had been present then were no longer there.

I went up to the woman, who, by her appearance, was clearly the patient's daughter, and said, "The doctor told me you would like a service. I'm sorry to be late; there was confusion with the message." Understandably, when someone in the family is dying, grieving family members are totally unaware of short staffing, vacations, and the like.

She smiled gently and gestured toward her father, who was in the fetal position and breathing through his open mouth. "I think it's a good time," she said.

Just then the patient lifted his arms into the air. "Is he doing that a lot?" I asked.

"Yes," said the younger of the two men.

"Good," I said. "That means somebody is coming for him."

"That gives me goosebumps," the young man said, crossing his arms over his chest and looking both interested and uncomfortable.

"It's quite common," I replied. "And it's a good thing for the patient." I am strongly committed to "normalizing" these deathbed realities in the hope that people encountering them for the first time will not be afraid but instead moved and comforted. It's a tough line to walk.

He looked at me, expressionless, and grew quiet. Clearly he had some pondering to do.

I turned to the daughter. "What can I do to support you?"

The young man answered instead: "We want him to go to Jesus Christ, we want Jesus for him."

"Would you like a service?" I asked, eyes still on the daughter. "You should know that I am Episcopal. We are close to Catholics, but we are not the same."

"That's all right," she said.

Some people believe that only their own branch of their religion is legitimate in God's eyes. I am happy to serve anyone but always careful not to offer services to someone who would find them offensive, which is more common than I realized when I first started hospital chaplaincy.

"Are you sure?" She nodded. "There is an Episcopal service that is good for this time." I opened my book and showed her the service. People need to see what a service will say before it starts. I don't want anyone to find themselves in the position of being expected to say words they don't believe.

We stood side by side while she looked at it for a minute. Then she asked, "Do you want me to say this with you out of this book?"

"Oh, no, if the service is all right with you I can go make copies for everyone. That will be easier for you, and then you'll have copies you can keep if you'd like."

"Could you do that? That would be nice."

"Of course. And, if you want, after we do the service I can anoint him. I have holy oil with me. But it is Episcopal holy oil." Holy oil, because it is a physical thing that touches and remains on the body of the dying person, is in some ways even more intimate than a bedside service.

"That's fine," she said, and the two men nodded agreement.

When I made the copies and returned to the room, the daughter mentioned that three more people were coming. I offered to make more copies, but she said they would share.

"Okay," I said and went to the head of the bed. "Before we start I need to talk with the patient."

The three of them nodded and drew back a little.

I squatted to put my face on a level with Mr. Harwa's. His eyes were closed. It is always hard to know what to call a person in these circumstances. I don't like to call someone who is eighty-one and dying by their first name when I first speak to them. I believe it is important both to the patient and the family to show great respect. Unsure how to pronounce his last name, I settled on "sir."

"Sir," I said, "I'm Chaplain Maxwell, the palliative care chaplain. Your family is here with me and we are going to stand around your bed together and pray for you. Is that all right?"

I always ask a patient's permission before praying for them, unless they're comatose, but I could tell this man was actively dying and doubted he could speak.

He opened his eyes and looked into mine.

Dying people have a quality of looking that is like no other. Staring into his eyes was like looking into the darkness of deep space. I saw stillness, no fear, no curiosity, but a sense of presence. You could almost say I saw his soul. He was still alive and still conscious, looking out at me from a place very near death. There was a clearness, a simplicity, and at the same time an enormous "otherness." Even though our faces were close together, I was aware of an immense distance between us.

Only my awareness of the germs living on the floor kept me from falling to my knees. This was the first time we had connected; when I had visited him earlier, his eyes had always remained closed.

I knew nothing about his condition. Clearly he was gravely ill, but did he know he was dying? I didn't know what his culture preferred in this respect. Some cultures consider it a breach of privacy to talk with a dying person about death. Some consider it forbidden, as if talking about it will hasten their demise. But by virtue of the prayers we were going to say, we were about to make it clear that he was dying. I needed to tell him one-on-one just in case he didn't already know.

I spoke slowly. "Sir, you know you have been very sick. Soon you will see the face of God, and when you do you will see the face of a friend, not a stranger. You are safe, your family is here, and it is all good." I kept my eyes locked on his, which remained open and focused while I was speaking. Then his gaze shifted to expose blood-shot whites. I looked at his chest to make sure he was still breathing. He was. I stood up.

I discovered that while I had been talking to Mr. Harwa, three other young people, all Egyptian, had entered the room and were standing around the bed with the others. I looked at them and said, "For those of you who don't know me, I'm Chaplain Maxwell. We're going to do this service together. As you probably know, the person who is leading the service says the words in regular type and the congregation says the words in the slanted type."

"In italics," the daughter said. The new arrivals smiled knowingly, and I blushed at my mistake; their English was fine.

I nodded. "Before we begin, let us take a moment and remember that we are in the presence of God, which is always true, but especially true at a time like this. Let us open our hearts to the Creator of the Universe. Let us surround this man with our love."

I let a little silence arise, then asked: "What does he prefer to be called? Stephen?" The hospital chart had two first names for him, one "Stephen" and one an Egyptian-sounding name. I needed to know because in the service one refers to the dying person by their first name.

"Yes, Stephen," replied the daughter, and I began the service. The family followed along without difficulty, and said the responses strongly and clearly. No one wept, which was unusual during a bedside ritual for a dying person. No crying. Not even a misty eye. Earlier that day two of the people who had been with him had been weeping. From their stoicism I got the sense that this was a proud family and they were demonstrating their pride and strength now.

After the spoken service was over, it was time for the anointing. The holy oil I carried for anointing was kept in a small round silver container, about the size of a fifty-cent piece in diameter, and half an inch thick. In it I kept a small wad of cotton moistened with consecrated oil. I took the container out of my pocket, slipped the safety ring over my middle finger, unscrewed the cap, placed my thumb on the oil-soaked cotton, and said to Mr. Harwa, loudly enough to let everyone else in the room hear as well, "This is an outward and visible sign of an inner spiritual grace, for when you were baptized you were marked as Christ's own forever."

I made the sign of the cross on the patient's forehead, saying "In the name of the Father" when I put my thumb on the center of his forehead, then "and of the Son" as I moved my thumb down in a straight line, then "and of the Holy Spirit" as I made a horizontal line bisecting my vertical one.

I repeated the words and gestures on the backs of each of his hands, first on the hand nearest me and then on the other, which was quickly lifted toward me by his daughter.

Whenever I anoint someone, I find that the others present watch the act closely, almost as if it is magical. Something about the physicality of it seems very meaningful. I am careful to move slowly so that people can see the little container and its undramatic contents and everyone knows what's going on.

When the anointing was complete, I screwed the cap back on and put the container back in my pocket. No one moved. The room was silent except for soft chanting, in what I presumed was Arabic, coming from a laptop in the corner. The stillness felt holy. I was glad that Mr. Harwa was making the transition to the next world in such a calm and respectful setting.

I said to the daughter, who still had the printed service in her hand, "You can keep those copies if you like. And when the time comes, you might want to say those last two prayers together." I pointed to the section headed "Commendation at the Time of Death." I noticed that no one, including me, had used the word "death," but everyone knew what was happening. It seemed to me that the prayers the section contained might offer considerable support to the family when Mr. Harwa died.

"'Depart, O Christian soul, out of this world'?" she asked, looking at the copy.

"Yes. I think that's the most beautiful prayer in the whole prayer book. And you might want to say the last one as well: 'Merciful Savior, we commend to you. . .'" She looked a little doubtful about the propriety of my suggestion, since the prayers are introduced by the instruction "*The minister may introduce the commendation. . .*" I continued, "We are all ministers by virtue of our baptism." I tapped my red "Chaplain" badge. "This doesn't matter. What matters to God is what is in our hearts."

She nodded gravely. I ran my eyes around the bedside circle of faces. "Is there anything more I can do for you?" Heads were shaken. I waited for a moment and then took my leave by going around the circle, shaking hands with everyone, and saying, "God bless you" to each.

"God bless you," the daughter responded. I thanked her and left, stopping to chart the visit and only then returning to my husband who didn't have a word of complaint about the long wait in our car.

When I got back from vacation I learned Mr. Harwa had indeed died that night. And then I reflected on something else I'd learned. A "doula" is a woman who helps other women when they are giving birth and after they deliver. This was one of the times I felt I was a "death doula." It probably sounds creepy, but in fact it was a great privilege to help Mr. Harwa and his family go through his dying. And as a doula eases a person's passage into this world, I helped, in my small way, to ease my patients' passages out.

My Call

From time to time during my life, I've heard someone say they "had a call," whether to the priesthood or to some other spiritually oriented profession. I wondered what "a call" could be. Did some mighty voice speak to that person out of a thundercloud? How did they *know* it was a calling? It all seemed mysterious, and rather hard to believe.

But then *I* had a call. No thundercloud, no single event, just a series of whispers that became undeniable.

When people ask what drew me to become a hospital chaplain, I usually answer in terms of a farmer catching a chicken. Imagine that you are in a barnyard and want to get a wandering chicken from one side of the yard to the other. If you run at the chicken to catch it, it will squawk, flap its wings, and scamper away as fast as it can. It's much more effective to take a few corn kernels and slowly drop them, one by one, first in front of the chicken and then behind you as you walk slowly toward the other side of the yard. The chicken will focus on the food, pay no attention to where it's going, and end up just where you want it. Such was and still is God the Farmer's way with me the chicken.

What happened was that over the course of a year, during which I was working full-time on a social action project, five people who were dying asked me one by one to spend time with them. Each relationship became increasingly intimate. The first was a nursing home resident I didn't know, but whom I sometimes drove to church. The second and third were a terminally ill couple who lived down the street from me. The fourth, a professional colleague who had become a friend many years before. And the fifth, a teacher named Lauren who also became a friend. The next story is about Lauren.

"Row Your Boat"

The Bone Marrow Transplant Unit at University Hospital was hard to find. When I finally got to the plain grey doors and the small white sign at the entrance, I stopped and took a deep breath, trying to calm down. I had never been to a bone marrow transplant unit before, and I didn't know what to expect; but I was sure it would be a difficult experience.

Lauren had been admitted two days earlier in preparation for a transplant to try to cure her leukemia. She had asked me to visit, telling me she would be in the hospital for some time before the procedure and expected to be extremely bored. I didn't understand what she would be doing in the hospital before the transplant, but it had something to do with preparing her bones to receive the new marrow. I did know that her resistance to infection would be extremely low both before and after.

Her mother was in Michigan and wouldn't be coming until closer to the time of the actual transplant. Her second husband—Ray, a fireman she'd met online, whom she had married only a few months before—didn't like hospitals and was outraged by his willowy new wife being gravely ill.

Lauren taught Pilates, a physical fitness system helpful to many, including people like me with bad backs. She had been my instructor for several years, and we had developed a friendship. Devoted to her teaching, she was otherwise shy, and she didn't have many friends. Because I was one of them, and because she seemed very alone, I felt responsible for her in a way.

I reminded myself that I was there to keep Lauren company and that if she could stand to be in this place for weeks, I certainly could stand to visit it for half an hour. Then I pulled the door open and found myself in a corridor with a solid wall on the left and a series of strange small rooms on the right. The walls of these rooms facing the corridor were made entirely of clear plate glass, floor to ceiling, plus a glass door giving access from the corridor to the room itself. All the doors were closed. And each room was the same: a hospital bed in the middle with a couple of small tables beside it, a plain chair, a wash basin in the far corner, a television mounted on the wall, and one hospital-gowned patient.

As I recall it now, there was something odd about the patients. Most weren't moving around much. Most were white and remarkably pale. Most heads were bowed. They didn't seem to be reading or watching TV, just still. It felt like going into a laboratory where scientists were running experiments–not on white rats in cages, but on human beings in little glass rooms.

I took another breath and went down the hall to a counter opposite the glass-walled rooms. Yes, the clerk told me, Lauren was in Room 27–81. She could have visitors. I should be careful to wash my hands at one of the sinks in the corridor before I went in.

Lauren was sitting in her chair and grinned when I tapped on her glass wall. I mimed washing my hands, she nodded, and I went to the nearest sink. Over the sink was a sign saying hands should be washed for at least sixty seconds, including under the fingernails, and suggesting that a good way to tell how long sixty seconds lasted was to sing, slowly, the song "Row, Row, Row Your Boat" six times. Obediently, I bent over the steel basin and sang under my breath:

Row, row, row your boat
Gently down the stream,
Merrily, merrily, merrily, merrily,
Life is but a dream.

In this strange place where patients were so sick, I felt uncomfortable singing, even very softly, the words "life is but a dream." I wondered if the people who put up the sign had thought about that.

When I went, clean handed, into Lauren's room, she hugged me, which seemed odd given the hand-washing instructions, but I trusted she knew what she was doing. We had a long talk, mostly about how upset her husband was about the demands of her illness. "He says he didn't sign on to this when we got married in May," Lauren said, waving her hand at the hospital room.

Lauren's first marriage had ended in divorce after her alcoholic husband had turned violent. Now her new husband was showing worrisome signs of not "being there" for his wife. My heart went out to her.

"This leukemia is really serious," Lauren said.

I couldn't think of what to say. I knew nothing about her chances of surviving or how sick she was. But I certainly didn't want to encourage her in negative thinking. She was only in her late thirties, was an ex-dancer, and was physically fit.

"You'll be fine," I said heartily. "You look great."

Or at least not as pale as most of the other patients.

I glanced at her.

But you haven't been in this hospital very long.

"And you've got a great attitude," I continued. "This is a first-class hospital and I'm sure everything is going to work out."

Important to stay positive.

Lauren nodded politely, and we moved on to talk about other things. When it came time for me to leave, she asked me to return soon, and I promised I would. After I left the unit I found my way to the hospital's chapel and prayed for Lauren. As I was leaving the chapel a plump, black-clad nun who looked about sixty was just coming in. She smiled and introduced herself as Sister Helen, explaining that she was a hospital chaplain. I asked her to look in on Lauren, whom I knew was Catholic. I told Sister Helen that Lauren was afraid and alone and a truly nice person. Basically I was trying to do a sales job to encourage a visit to my lonely friend. Sister Helen seemed like a nice person too, and I thought they might get along.

I continued visiting Lauren for two weeks. Each time I came, she was a little paler, a little skinnier, a little more depressed. Each time she'd mention how serious her illness was, and each time I would assure her that she looked well and was going to be fine. At the time I had no idea how unhelpful it was for me to say that. Then she said to me, "I don't know if I'm gonna' make it."

She's talking about dying. *Of course she isn't going to die. It just isn't possible. She's young, she's super fit—or she was until she got in here. I've got to keep her spirits up.* I worried that if I even mentioned the word "death," she *would* die. For sure I didn't want to let that terrible word into the room. In my ignorance and fear I told Lauren again how great she looked, she nodded briefly, and we talked about other stuff.

Afterward I went to the chaplains' office and found Sister Helen there. I told her how worried I was about Lauren. "Is she going to die? Do you know if she is? I'm scared, and I don't know what to say."

Sister Helen replied that she didn't know how serious Lauren's situation was, but said she had already visited her once and would go again. "If she wants to talk about dying," the sister continued, "It's all right. It's okay for you to say 'death' or 'dying.' That won't make her die."

I smiled in embarrassment. Was it that obvious?

"I know that's silly of me," I said. "But it is scary to talk about dying with her. I don't want her to die, she's too young. I don't know how to talk about death with someone who's sick."

We talked for a few more minutes, until Sister Helen said it was time for Mass. Would I like to attend with her?

"I'm not Catholic," I said. "I'm Episcopal."

"That's all right," she replied. "You're welcome to participate as much as you want."

We went back to the chapel, which was so crowded with visitors, staff, and a few bathrobe-clad patients that we had to squeeze into the back row. I was familiar with the Catholic Mass—fairly similar to the Episcopal service—and when it came time for Communion I stood to allow Sister Helen to get out of the pew and go to the altar.

"Come if you wish," she said. I was surprised. I knew that according to Catholic doctrine only Catholics were supposed to receive Communion, but she smiled and nodded. I figured a nun should know what she was doing, and decided I'd do it for Lauren. With the rest of the Communion seekers, we walked up the aisle and were each given a wafer by the priest. No wine was offered.

After the Mass was over and we walked back to the chaplains' office, Sister Helen gave me a hug. "Thank you, Sister Helen," I said.

"Call me Helen," she replied. "'Sister' is too formal." I agreed.

When I returned to the hospital a couple of days later, Lauren was sitting on the side of her bed, her face drawn, her skin ashen. I sat next to her on the bed.

"I'm really scared," she said.

"Oh, Lauren," I replied. "I'm so sorry."

She started to cry and I put my arm around her. She cried more loudly, and out of the corner of my eye I saw a nurse start walking quickly toward the room, looking to see what was happening. But when she saw us, she turned and went back down the corridor. It was just the two of us, and I didn't know what to say.

"God loves you, Lauren," I whispered. I knew she was a believer, and I thought that reminding her of this might comfort her.

She pulled away from me. "God doesn't love me, Joan!"

I was horrified. "What do you mean, God doesn't love you? Of course God loves you!"

"I'm divorced and remarried," she replied. "That's a mortal sin. I can't receive Communion. God doesn't love me."

I had forgotten the Catholic doctrine against divorce. Looking at Lauren's tear-washed face, I was filled with anger. *What religion would deny the sacraments to this precious young woman? Her husband beat her up. Of course she had to leave him. Here she's terrified she's dying, and in the midst of her suffering, with no support from her new husband, she tells me God doesn't love her.* I wrapped my arms around her and inwardly raged while she sobbed on my shoulder.

In time she stopped crying and said she needed to sleep. I tucked her in and said I would be back the next day. She nodded her thanks and curled up on her side, her back to the glass wall.

With smoke practically coming out of my ears, I marched off toward the chaplains' office to seek Sister Helen. To get there I had to cross the hospital's main lobby—and in the middle of the crowd, there was Helen, accompanied by another chaplain. I walked up to her and erupted.

"Do you have any idea what's going on up there?" I shouted, pointing in the general direction of the Bone Marrow Transplant Unit. "What kind of church teaches a dying young woman that God doesn't love her? Just tell me that!"

"Joan, Joan, tell me what's going on," Helen replied, remarkably calm considering that several people in the lobby had turned to see what the yelling was about.

I continued yelling. "Lauren just told me that God doesn't love her—because she got a divorce. And she thinks she's dying! Can you imagine what it's like for her all alone up there on that unit and afraid she's going to die and scared of what will happen when she does? Can you imagine? What is wrong with your church?

"I've been given Communion in several Catholic churches, and I'm not even Catholic! Why can't Lauren be given Communion? She left her husband because he beat her up! And she married Ray rather than live with him unmarried. How can you accept a non-Catholic and keep out a dying young woman who *is* Catholic? That is so not of God! Jesus fed Judas at the Last Supper—what's so bad about Lauren?"

I inhaled to continue my tirade and for the first time really looked at the faces of the two chaplains standing before me. They were clearly listening to my yelling, yet they were relaxed, not angry, not getting ready to fire back. I sensed that they were letting me yell myself out. In that moment I realized I was being completely unfair. These women didn't make the rules. I liked Helen, and there I was shouting at her.

A small crowd had gathered to watch what was going on. Before I could start to apologize, Helen moved a little closer to me and said, softly, "I'll get a Jesuit."

"Huh?" *What does a Jesuit have to do with anything?* I knew a Jesuit was a kind of Catholic, but that's all I knew.

"It'll be fine, truly. I'll get a Jesuit today. They know how to work these things. You come back tomorrow and see." Helen put her hand on my arm. "Don't worry. Go home and get some rest."

I thought of Lauren and how sad and alone she was. But Helen's kind face and gentle touch gave me hope. "That would be wonderful if you could fix it," I said quietly. "It's awful for her."

"It'll be fine," she said again. "Go home. Sleep."

I did.

The next day I went back to Lauren's room. She was sitting up in bed, still thin, still weak, but glowing. "This wonderful priest came," she said. "We talked. And he gave me Communion."

"God loves you . . ." I said tentatively.

"God loves me. Yes." She laid back on her pillows, drained but smiling.

That was the last time I saw Lauren. That night I came down with a huge cold, and people with colds were forbidden to visit the transplant unit because everyone there had compromised immune systems. Colds could kill. When I called the unit, the nurse said Lauren was off having a test. I called Helen and asked her to tell Lauren why I wasn't there.

The next day Helen called and said Lauren was dying, and the day after she died. I yearned to go see her, but it was forbidden. Helen told me that before Lauren died, the same Jesuit priest gave her the sacrament that Catholics prize at the end of life, known at the time as the Last Rites.

A week after Lauren died, Helen called to see how I was doing. I told her my cold was much better, and while I missed Lauren I was glad she was at peace, and thanked Helen for making it possible for her to reconcile with the Catholic Church.

"That was really you who made it possible," Helen said. She paused. "I wonder if you've ever thought about becoming a chaplain?"

It had never crossed my mind. Yet when she asked me that question, I felt a little ache of yearning in my heart. I quickly dismissed it. I was in my late fifties and didn't know anything about being a chaplain. Silly idea. It might have been worth considering had I been younger. It would have been worth considering had I been younger. . .but I wasn't. The thing to do was just forget about it.

But I couldn't.

Chaplain School

There is no recognized school for hospital chaplains, or at least there wasn't one that I could find when God the Farmer's kernels called me, God's chicken, to be a hospital chaplain. But the kernels didn't stop with my awareness of the call. Just at the right moment, something completely unexpected would happen, and I would respond to a new piece of proffered corn.

I was led through a series of small and then more complicated experiences. After several false starts I found myself attending seminary as a day student seeking a graduate degree in theological studies (Master of Theological Studies, or MTS) and at the same time taking a series of formal trainings in hospital chaplaincy (Clinical Pastoral Education, or CPE), one after the other, at two area hospitals.

I chose to seek the master's degree because I felt a need to be more deeply grounded in Christianity, both through studying the Bible and through in-depth instruction in religious creeds, history, theology, and liturgy. I considered seeking ordination, but my local bishop told me I was too old. In retrospect I'm glad of that, because in fact I *was* too old to go through many years of training and apprenticeship for parish ministry in addition to the training and apprenticeship necessary to serve as a hospital chaplain.

I learned that there were many hoops through which people had to jump before being accepted as hospital chaplains, including faith group commissioning and endorsement, graduate education, professional certification, and on-the-job training. All of them added up to a process known as *formation*. The best explanation of formation I heard came from one of my on-the-job CPE teachers, a superb chaplain named Jim Nenninger. One day in class someone asked him, "Jim, how will I know when I'm really a chaplain?"

"Well," he replied with a little smile. "You'll know the day you're walking down a hospital corridor and a voice calls, 'Chaplain!' and you turn immediately because you know they're calling you."

It sounded rather pat at the time, but he was right. One day it happened to me. Someone called "Chaplain!" and I turned, because I was a chaplain and I was being called.

After six years I shifted from being a regular "floor" chaplain, meaning I visited all the patients on the floors to which I was assigned, to being the palliative care chaplain, meaning I visited all the patients receiving palliative care in the hospital. I was particularly drawn to patients at the ends of their lives and to the intensity of the work involved in dealing with them. The stakes were so high, and spiritual matters were often of prime importance in the foxholes of the dying. Most important of all, it seemed to me that the actions of the great Mystery were clearest in the refiner's furnace of dying.

Beauty in the ICU

A hospital's Intensive Care Unit (ICU) is a place of suffering, transformation, life, and death. Machines beep, whir, and sometimes cry out; patients are frequently comatose; nurses tend to trot rather than walk from one task to the next. Flowers are banned; red bins labeled "medical waste" provide the only touches of color. In this strange world, high technology seems to overwhelm the humans lying flat under white sheets. The one thing an ICU is *not* is a place of beauty. But one day, amid all these machines and medical tasks, I was surprised by beauty.

Here's what happened. As the chaplain on call, I got an urgent request from an ICU nurse, asking for a chaplain to visit Ms. Thompson, a patient the staff believed to be actively dying. When I asked about Ms. Thompson's faith tradition, the nurse replied, "All I know is that the patient said she was 'hanging on to Jesus.'" I grabbed my Bible and went to the ICU.

The patient was a middle-aged woman, eyes closed, lying very still, her body swollen from IV fluids. I took her hand and noticed there was no flexion in her wrist; when I lifted her hand slightly, her whole bloated arm rose with it, stiff as a tree trunk and nearly as heavy. I prayed for guidance, and it came to me that it would be appropriate for me to read a few Bible verses and see what happened.

Since Ms. Thompson was "hanging on to Jesus," something from the Farewell Discourse of the Gospel of John seemed like the right place to turn.

The Bible fell open to Chapter 15 in that Gospel, and I read a few of the verses:

> As the Father has loved me, so I have
> loved you; abide in my love. If you keep
> my commandments, you will abide
> in my love, just as I have kept
> my Father's commandments and abide in his love.
> I have said these things to you so that
> my joy may be in you, and that your joy
> may be complete. (John 15:9–11)

Then I stopped, and after a little silence Ms. Thompson's eyes opened. And although she didn't speak, she smiled at me with her eyes.

"I'm Chaplain Maxwell," I said. "I understand you're hanging on to Jesus. I hang on to Jesus too, so I came to be with you. Is that okay?" She gave me assent with her eyes. "Would you like me to pray?" I asked her. Again she silently agreed, and I prayed. She closed her eyes during the prayer.

When it was over, I stopped, and after a little time she reopened her eyes and again smiled at me. Then she opened her mouth—for the first time since I had come into her room—and began to *sing*. In a lovely, soft voice she sang a beautiful hymn to Jesus, one that I had never heard before but clearly a hymn, with a simple tune and words that rhymed. I could follow the melody and hummed along with her. It was an astonishing moment, this hymn rising out of her dying body, the two of us singing in the middle of the ICU with life-sustaining machines beeping in the background. She was getting in voice before joining the heavenly choir.

When Mrs. Thompson finished, I reminded her that (as her nurse had told me) she had family due to visit in about twenty minutes, and asked her if she wanted to get a little sleep before they came. Once again she smiled, then closed her eyes, and fell asleep. I tiptoed out.

She died the next day.

Handcuffs

The hospital often housed prisoners as patients. Every prisoner, no matter how debilitated, had two uniformed and armed police officers with him always, day and night. (I never saw a female prisoner, although I imagine there were some.). There was no indication on the charts or the floor census lists that a patient was a prisoner; you only learned that when you saw one or both guards sitting in the hall outside a room.

As I became more experienced as a chaplain, I found myself drawn to prisoners. No one gave me any special instructions about how to serve them; so as much as I could, I treated them like all the other patients. I had no idea what their crimes were and made it a point never to ask. That information had nothing to do with why they were in the hospital—or why I wanted to offer chaplain support. I imagined that a few of them were not guilty of whatever crime they had been charged with, since our justice system is human and thus imperfect. I knew that some probably were guilty of violent, even horrific crimes. But my job was to support their spirits, which had already been tested both by serious illness and by imprisonment.

Because of the extraordinary difference in power between free health-care workers and seriously ill persons under armed guard, I was extra careful and tentative in asking if they wanted a visit from a chaplain. They always said they did. I asked about the course of their illness and about how they were coping with it spiritually. Often one of the guards stood in a corner of the room, apparently listening and observing as we talked.

At the end of the visit, the patient would invariably request prayer. Usually I would invite both guards to pray with us if they wished. When they accepted, as they always did, we stood in a circle around the bed, all four of us holding hands together, and I prayed for them as well as for the prisoner. The power of the state over individual humans, both prisoners and guards—and over me as well—seemed to suffuse the room.

I was always keenly aware of the presence of the great Mystery in these encounters. I believe that God is present always and in all places, and especially so when people are helpless and suffering. Something about prisoner + guards + serious illness + prayer seemed to cry out especially powerfully to God.

It took me a while to even begin to appreciate just how complete these patients' imprisonment was. Every prisoner was handcuffed to his bed. Sometimes the other bracelet of the handcuff encircled the wrist of the arm that was not hooked up to the IV line. In such cases the man's nurse usually had placed an unfolded towel over the handcuffed wrist, hiding the manacle in such a way that it looked as if the towel just happened to be tossed there. This kind gesture made the fact of the patient's imprisoned status a little less glaring. Sometimes the restraint was on the prisoner's ankle, and you only knew it was there if you noticed its firm, curved outline under the thin sheet.

But a handcuff was always present, somewhere, even if the patient was unconscious or on a ventilator. A guard told me that prison protocol used to require manacling female patients giving birth, even during the final stages of labor; but apparently this is no longer done.

The handcuffs restricted the patient in and of themselves. They were also a visible reminder of a much deeper helplessness. Prisoners didn't have visitors, so they were isolated, with only the guards for company. There was never anything personal in the room: no flowers, no photographs, no stuffed animal, no magazines or books, just a suffering human in an unattractive, institutional room. Consequently, in my visits I tried to spend a little extra time just being sociable, encouraging the patient to chat about whatever he wished.

One prisoner-patient, a Mr. Hebb, in his early forties, black, had been in the ICU for several days and now was back on the general-medicine floor. When I asked him how he was doing, he told me he was dying, and soon. He confirmed that the doctors had given him that diagnosis, and that his own sense of his body seemed to bear out their prediction.

So what does he need?

"Mr. Hebb, that's tough news. I'm so sorry." I paused and took a breath. "I'm wondering: Is there anything you'd like to do before that happens?" *Other than get out of this hospital and go home, of course.*

"See my family. See my mother."

That shouldn't be very hard. Surely a dying man has the right to see his mother.

"What seems to be the problem?"

"My mother doesn't know where I am, or how sick I am."

"How come?"

"I've got no way to get in touch with her."

A little warning bell went off in my mind. I had heard of prisoners taking advantage of credulous prison visitors and delivering coded messages in the guise of contacting their family. I had no way of knowing if that was the case with Mr. Hebb. He *was* dying, or so it seemed. And even Jesus got to see his mother before he died. How to deal with this in a morally sound and safe way?

There was no guard in the room. And the only one I could see in the hall outside was a middle-aged black woman talking on her cell phone. "Mr. Hebb, can you give me a phone number for your mother?"

He knew it by heart. I scribbled it down on a card.

"And, Mr. Hebb, I have to ask you a few legal questions: May I have your permission to call your mother? To tell her you are in the hospital? To tell her your diagnosis? To say that the doctors have told you that you are dying? To say that you would like her to visit you if she can?"

He nodded assent to each question.

"Okay. I'll see what I can do." We prayed and I left.

When I got back to the office, I called the number he had given me. A woman answered, and said she was Mrs. Hebb.

"Mrs. Hebb, I'm Chaplain Maxwell, a chaplain at City Hospital. Your son Curtis asked me to call you."

"Curtis? Is he alive?"

Oh, Lord help me. "Well, Curtis is alive. . ."

She interrupted me before I could finish the sentence. "Thank you, Jesus! Thank you, Jesus! Praise the Lord! I didn't know if he was alive or dead!"

"You didn't? How awful that must have been for you."

"They told me he was sick and going to have an operation. But I've been calling and calling, and they wouldn't tell me nothing more. They wouldn't tell me where he was or what the operation was or nothing."

"Why not? I don't understand."

"It's that major, he's the man in charge, and he told them not to tell me nothing."

What? "Mrs. Hebb, I don't know what the problem is."

"They won't tell me nothing."

"Well I don't know if they'll tell me something, but if you want I'll see what I can do. Do you want me to?" I had to obtain her explicit request before doing anything to try to help. Sometimes families were so broken that they didn't want to see one another again. And I didn't want to give her information about her son's location and condition before seeing if we could work out a way to do that within the system. She would never see him again without official sanction.

"Lord, yes, Chaplain. Lord, yes."

"I'll call you back as soon as I can. I'll call you back by tomorrow night, even if I haven't learned anything."

"God bless you, Chaplain."

"God bless *you*, Mrs. Hebb. Talk with you soon. Goodbye."

Me and my big mouth. Now what am I going to do?

I walked back down the hall, praying for a way forward. Outside Mr. Hebb's room the female guard was off her cell phone and writing in what looked like some sort of official log book. The other guard wasn't there. *Ask her.*

"Excuse me, officer," I said. She looked up from her writing and I introduced myself. "Kind of a boring job, I imagine. At least you hope it's boring."

"It's boring, you got that right." She nodded toward the patient's room. "He's no trouble."

"Guess not."

"Poor guy." *Aha. She feels sorry for him.*

"It does seem pretty tough. He was telling me he can't even see his mother."

"She have to get permission to see him."

"How can she do that? He asked me to call her. . ." *Oops, OK, cat's out of the bag on that one.* ". . .and she said they're not telling her anything."

"Who she talking to?"

I gave the major's name.

"He say 'no,' that's no."

"Oh, but officer, under the circumstances, isn't there anyone who can help her?" Confidentiality rules prohibited my saying anything to her about his dire diagnosis; but from her sympathetic manner, I intuited she knew.

"Well. . .." She frowned.

I moved a little closer to where she was sitting and asked in a soft voice, "Is there anything you can do to help?"

She looked over her shoulder. No one was in sight. She opened her log book to the inside front cover, where there were several hand-written names and phone numbers. "He dying," she said. "His mama got the right to say goodbye."

She pulled a slip of paper from her pocket, and wrote a name and number on it. "You call his mama and tell her to call this man. Don't you tell her where you got this number. Don't tell her nothing about me. You tell her to tell him her son real sick, and she need to see him."

"Officer, may God bless you for your kind heart. Thank you." I smiled at her, but her face stayed serious.

"The right to say goodbye," she repeated.

I called Mrs. Hebb again, and two days later she came to visit her son and say goodbye.

About Dying

Both suffering and grace can be part of dying. Because I am a chaplain, I'm mostly writing about suffering from the mental and spiritual perspective, not the physical. What I write here does not apply to people who die suddenly, perhaps in an accident or from a fatal heart attack. It applies to people who die over a period of time, whether a long time or a short one. And there are exceptions to everything I'm going to say.

People usually enter the ministry for personal reasons. Often they have to do with a death or deaths that have affected them personally. That was certainly true in my case. My mother's death when I was a little girl made death not an abstraction but a searing reality—from the earliest days I can remember.

But a subsequent personal experience, some fifty years later, also played an important role in my becoming a hospital chaplain. I was joining David at the end of a long day for a business reception. At the time, I was the head of two complex and demanding social-action projects. I was passionate about my work and under a great deal of stress. As I walked down a short flight of stairs to where David was waiting, I was suddenly struck by a tremendous pain in my head that was different from and more powerful than any I had ever experienced. Somehow I managed to walk to my husband, and he and a friend brought me to the emergency room at a nearby hospital, where I was admitted.

I don't remember anything more until about fifteen hours later, when I suddenly "clicked in" and found myself lying in a hospital bed listening to two physicians who looked extremely somber. They were just finishing telling me that they were going to operate on my brain because one blood vessel had burst and another one was about to do so. They said that the operation was extremely dangerous and that I had a strong possibility of dying or sustaining major brain damage, but it was my only chance.

I'm embarrassed to say what happened next, but people who are very ill can regress emotionally and mentally, and I certainly did. I found myself trying to explain to them that I lived in my brain, that my brain was very important to me, so they needed to be extremely careful. They both looked at their shoes. Suddenly I realized that what I was saying was absurd. Each person's brain matters tremendously to that person, and of course the doctors would be as careful as they could. I apologized and they said they understood. They said that I would be operated on in an hour, and left me alone in the room.

There was a clock on the wall, and the big hand was pointing at 12. I had regressed, very much so. I looked at the clock and realized that I might have just sixty minutes to live. I remember thinking a corny but powerful thought: *This is it.* One hour to go. For a few of those minutes I thought about how I didn't want to die, about how I didn't want to be a vegetable. Then I remembered I had a living will, which was quite stern about how I did not want to live on a ventilator.

But that means they may let me die! I briefly considered revoking the living will. Contemplating death in the abstract is quite different from contemplating death coming right at you. But then I realized that I definitely did *not* want to live on a ventilator and was flooded with gratitude that I had a living will. That knowledge liberated me from my fear of becoming completely incapacitated because of the surgery. If that happened, they'd let me die naturally rather than artificially prolong my life. That realization gave me a tremendous sense of freedom.

By this time nearly twenty minutes had gone by, and my husband David came in the room to be with me until the operation. It seemed that I might have only forty minutes left to live. I had just one thought. I knew David loved me very much, and I was seized with the fear that if I died he might not remarry out of respect for my memory. I spent most of my "last" forty minutes lecturing him. I told him how much I loved him, that he was too fine a man not to be married, that to remarry would be a testimony to the goodness of our marriage, and that the day he remarried would be a joyous day for me—that I would be looking down from heaven and blessing him and his new bride.

As I trust you can tell, I recovered, thanks to my surgeon and the staff at the hospital, and David and I are happily married to this day. But the experience of nearly dying was something I frequently drew upon in my work as a chaplain.

In working with people who *were* dying, the single most powerful source of spiritual suffering that I saw had to do with what we might call the human heart. By "heart" I do not mean that vital physical organ behind our ribs, but rather our inner sense of self, of personhood, of who we actually are. Consider this psycho-spiritual heart. When we were born, our heart was one with our mother. It lived absolutely in the present moment. It was completely open and completely vulnerable to what is.

Drawing on the work of Ken Wilber, Kathleen Dowling Singh describes brilliantly in her outstanding book *The Grace in Dying*[5] how in our minds we divide up reality bit by bit, placing boundaries that we then defend passionately. After we're born we draw our first boundary, separating the world into self (me) and not-self (everyone and everything else). This boundary creates space as a dimension of consciousness. Our second boundary separates the world into life and death, being and nonbeing, creating time consciousness.

Later we shrink from knowledge of our body's vulnerability and finitude. Creating a third boundary, we identify our sense of who we are with our mind rather than with our fragile and mortal body. And the fourth boundary we create splits our *persona*—our acceptable self-image—from our *shadow*—all those parts of ourselves that we hide and deny, the beautiful parts that we feel unable to claim as well as those about which we feel shame.

5. The material in this and the next two paragraphs is quoted and paraphrased from Singh, *Grace*, 35–41.

At this point the open human heart which we had as an infant is encased, metaphorically speaking, in stone. We do not live in the present. We do not inhabit our essential selves. We are ideas about ourselves. We believe we are the roles we play—child, partner, parent; outfitted with such-and-such education, such-and-such job, such-and-such pastimes and concerns. We think those roles are who we really are.

Sooner or later we have an experience that brings home to us the reality that death is not an abstraction: WE are going to die. And the stone that surrounds our heart is cracked, and eventually shatters. Everything is changed. We are stripped completely naked, brought back to just one thing: our fragile and vulnerable human heart. This is the essence of ourselves, an essence we have hidden from our consciousness since early childhood.

I cannot overemphasize how difficult it can be to be "stripped" in this way: It is enormously painful, depressing, and frightening. We wonder if our core essence has any value at all. We wonder if there's even anything there. The key questions now are: Who am I? What is the meaning of life? The search for meaning becomes central.

That is a lot about suffering. But what about grace? There can be some mighty grace in dying. Not everyone who enters difficult times becomes awakened by them. But the shattering of the stone around the human heart can be an initiation when it occurs, unleashing a process of metamorphosis. With the release of the lifelong repression surrounding our own mortality can come the strength and desire to do the inner work that needs to be done for our wholeness. As the theologian and priest Henri Nouwen has said, we need to keep remembering that we "are mortal and broken, but also that with the recognition of this condition, liberation starts."

I cannot count the numbers of patients who said to me in one way or another, "Chaplain, I'm grateful for my cancer" or some other serious disease or condition. The people who said this were facing their deaths, in very difficult circumstances, yet through their suffering they discovered primal and vital truths about themselves and about existence. They changed their lives, sometimes literally, sometimes just in the privacy of their own being. But however they changed and were changed, they realized they were moving toward truth and a kind of terrible beauty.

During this change, people almost always developed or increased some form of spirituality. By spirituality I mean that which connects us with the transcendent. I do not necessarily mean "religion" or even "God." As I described earlier in 'Do You Feel Different Inside?' (page 8) people find the transcendent in at least one of five ways, and usually in a combination of more than one of these ways: within themselves, in deep interpersonal relationships, in nature, in beauty made by human hands (anything from mathematics to paintings to performing art), or/and in a formal religion.

When I asked patients what they found the most difficult part of being hospitalized, they almost always said, "The lack of control." As the dying process progresses, the sensation of not being in control becomes more and more pressing until, at the last, the person surrenders. Paradoxically, in this surrender lies peace.

I found it particularly difficult to work with families who said, "We don't want her [or him] to 'know'"—that is, about the patient's true situation. The physicians may have believed the patient only had a few days to live, yet the family insisted that they not be told. Often, at some level, the patient already knew, but some of the goodness that is possible at the end of life was not realized because people were all hiding the truth in the name of kindness. I honored this request when it was made. In fact, I never told a patient they were dying because that was a medical assessment I was unqualified to make. But, as some of these stories show, when a patient wanted to talk about their sense that they were dying, I always tried to give them freedom and support to do that.

If you are supporting someone coming to the end of life, there are some key features that may be helpful to keep in mind. The first is what is known as a "life review." Virtually everyone who is close to death has a powerful need to tell their story one last time. Be on the alert for this possibility. If a dying person chooses to tell you their story, their life review, drop whatever you were planning on doing, sit down, shut up, and *listen.* This is a final chance for the dying person to make meaning of their life, and your listening is a vital part of that. Don't try to "fix" it, don't offer your opinion while they're talking, just be present, be still, and let them do their inner work.

Sometimes a life review will include a good deal of regret and even self-hatred. Don't comment while it is underway, but when the patient is truly finished with their story, see if they talked about one or more things that you can honestly praise. If you can, do so, shortly and simply, and perhaps add a little more honest praise if you see that what you're saying is comforting. Even if said to bolster a dying person's self-esteem, I believe it is wrong to lie about intimate matters, and never more so than at the end of life. The stern and yet liberating reality of death should not be violated by well-meaning falsehoods.

A second important feature of the end of life is the opportunity it offers for reconciliation. Broken relationships can be acknowledged and sometimes repaired. Against the backdrop of eternity, wrongs committed can be forgiven. Over time I learned that often it is much harder for a dying person to forgive than to ask for forgiveness. Many patients said to me, "After what he did to me there is no way I will ever forgive him!" Often I responded that to forgive does not mean to forget, nor does it mean that what was done was acceptable.

Sometimes I pointed out that not forgiving gives the offender greater power, not less power, over them. And sometimes I reminded them that on the cross Jesus said about those who betrayed and crucified him, "Forgive them, Father, for they know not what they do." As one of my teachers said to me, that was because Jesus couldn't forgive them himself, but he knew that the great Mystery could.

A third feature is the opportunity to say thank you to people who have been important in the dying person's life. Relatives, friends, teachers—whoever has been important to the person—all can be thanked, in an exchange that can be powerful and rich for both the person thanking and the person being thanked. Similarly, oncoming death offers the opportunity for the dying person to tell someone—perhaps for the first time— "I love you."

And it is important, if time permits, for people to say goodbye. This is good for the dying person and for those left behind. This is sometimes referred to as "closure." Of course that's not true; when someone you love dies, you don't achieve closure by saying goodbye; but after that person has died, it is a comfort to be able to remember generous last words.

Sometimes a dying person will be joined by figures who are invisible to anyone else, but clearly visible to the patient. These figures seem to come to provide support to the dying person and guide them into the next life. (See, for example, "At the Foot of the Bed" on page 58)

People sometimes seem to know when they are going to die. This knowledge is usually expressed indirectly, often in terms of a trip. For example, a patient will talk about a train to be taken next Tuesday morning at 10:00. Death will often come around the time when they have said they need to start on their journey.

People seem to have some control over the time of their death. Sometimes they will not die until after the arrival of a loved one who is coming from a distance, or until after a major family event, such as a birth or a marriage. And sometimes they will die when a loved one has left the room, as if to spare them the pain of seeing the death. Once a grieving new widow said to me, "I was with him every moment for the last two days. I just went down the hall to get a hot cup of coffee, and when I came back, he was dead."

At the very end of life, in the last twenty-four hours or so, the patient's appearance will often change. A strange beauty will overtake them, almost as if their essence is shining through the body that is failing them. The last time I was with a patient at the time of her actual death, her face was quite transformed by beauty. In her final moments she apparently saw something or someone, raised her arms in an embrace, smiled, and then fell back on the pillow, seemingly at peace, and died. One, two, three, just like that.

Hospital Ministry

The theologian Marcus Borg has written about how the human spirit is rather like a hen's egg. The fragile egg yolk needs to be protected by a hard shell, or it will die. But at some point the hard shell must break, or the egg inside will rot. The breaking of the human shell— "the opening of the self to God, the sacred"[6]—can occur in many ways, but one of the most common is through serious illness.

Hospital beds are, in my opinion, filled with cracking shells, and the tender souls that are thus being exposed urgently need support as they revise the meaning of their lives and wonder about the presence and action of a higher power. This support is what I believe a chaplain is called to provide.

In some ways seminary is poor preparation for hospital ministry. While you're in seminary, you are surrounded by generally like-minded people who are going through the same classes, supervised work experiences, and spiritual challenges as you are. But once you graduate, you are remarkably alone in the world. Seminary is over, your classmates are scattered, and your family is understandably disquieted by stories of how you spent your day amid death and the dying.

Chaplaincy is a lonely profession. Even if you are fortunate to be part of an interdisciplinary palliative-care team, as I was, you are the person specifically responsible for giving a patient spiritual support. When a hospital patient is first enrolled in palliative care, the team works together for his or her medical, social, psychological, and spiritual welfare. But when the patient nears death, the rest of the team is often called elsewhere, leaving the chaplain alone to comfort the dying person and console the grieving family. The chaplain must turn away from memories of seminary groups and support sessions, and stand unaided, sometimes surrounded by large groups of shocked and unhappy strangers, facing life's ultimate mystery, praying for divine guidance and strength. Not only for herself, but for everyone else as well.

Hospital ministry—at least in the three hospitals where I worked—differs from ministry in a typical religious community in several significant ways. The chaplain's "congregation" is not self-selected. Instead, it is anyone in the hospital—patients, their families and friends, staff, and volunteers.

6. Borg, *The Heart*, 154.

Unlike most congregants, patients and their companions almost invariably do not want to be present, and typically are frightened, disoriented, and upset. And while churches, synagogues, and mosques are nonprofit organizations, more and more hospitals are for-profit enterprises; further, virtually all hospitals are under extreme financial pressure, sometimes putting the needs of their administrations sharply at odds with the needs of their patients.

The role of a congregational leader is fairly well defined, at least in theory and usually in practice. The role of a chaplain, by contrast, can often be ambiguous, depending on hospital policy and on the religious and spiritual views of the individuals with whom the chaplain interacts. Given that hospital medical care is based on the scientific method, some people, both patients and staff, find a chaplain anachronistic. People who go to a place of worship are usually interested in talking with the religious leader; some people in the hospital actively reject the opportunity to talk with the chaplain; others are in close touch with their own religious or spiritual communities and are not in need of additional spiritual support; others are quite unfamiliar with the concept of a chaplain and need to learn what one can offer; others suddenly find themselves in a time of crisis and are grateful for the presence of a chaplain; and still others eagerly seek out and welcome spiritual care.

A defining characteristic of my particular chaplaincy was that I served people who were gravely ill. In many cases, they were in the hospital to try one last course of medical treatment. Sometimes this treatment held the possibility of halting their disease, at least for a while; sometimes it was simply to relieve pain or otherwise stabilize them before discharge to hospice care. In either case, it often happened that patients became attentive to spiritual matters in a way they had never been before. This put a great deal of responsibility on me as chaplain, because sometimes my spiritual counsel was the last the patient received.

In my experience, human touch in the form of holding hands was greatly appreciated by most patients, not only during spoken prayer but also in times of physical and emotional pain. Consequently I held hands with the great majority of my patients—although I was very careful to make sure that this contact was something they welcomed. When someone was dying I would sometimes simply sit by their bed, hold their hand, and pray in silence. I often offered sips of water, or fetched a blanket, although in my early training I was taught not to do so because such assistance was viewed as time-wasting and incompatible with a chaplain's role. My experience told me otherwise, told me that a small act of physical kindness established a valuable connection with the patient.

In addition, I was personally incapable of *not* helping gravely ill patients who were cold or thirsty. Hospital patients nearing the end of their lives were sometimes not given water very often, and were too weak to lift their paper cups for themselves. I had dying patients drain a full cup with one long, urgent sip through the straw.

2. Learning

Patient Teachers

What's *your* idea of a professional hospital chaplain? Do you think of a harbinger of death? Do you envision a black-clad religious person entering a dying patient's room, intent not on that person's welfare but on "saving" a helpless soul according to the chaplain's particular religion, collecting another convert for the chaplain's idea of God?

If you do, you have lots of company. I'm glad to say that, at least in my case, you are also wrong.

Let me try to unpack the reality behind these ideas. Hospital chaplains vary widely in their approach. I can only talk about my own, which changed over time and which was shaped by the training I was given in seminary and in hospitals, and most of all by patients.

The hospital where I worked as the palliative care chaplain was in the city, serving people of all ages, nationalities, religions, levels of education, and socioeconomic groups. As a person who is fascinated by the infinite variety and splendor of the human species, I took great delight in the range of my patients, from a homeless person to a high government official, from a non-English-speaking visitor from Cambodia to someone who collected trash for a living. All these people were my patients—and my teachers.

As the science of medicine has evolved, scientists have developed many ways to treat life-threatening diseases, sometimes curing them, sometimes delaying death. Hence people today often live a long time with grave illnesses, many more people than did so in the past. A specialized form of medical care has arisen to help people with such illnesses. I've mentioned it above: It is known as "palliative care." Such care is typically provided by a team: physicians and nurses to relieve physical pain and uncomfortable side effects of treatment; social workers to help with temporary or permanent life changes that may be required; and chaplains to help with spiritual matters. The group works as a team to support patients and help them understand the benefits and burdens of various forms of treatment so they can choose among complex medical options in keeping with each patient's own core values.

Patients can seek palliative care themselves, or their physician can make a referral. If someone is diagnosed with a life-threatening illness, it can make excellent sense to seek out palliative care right then, although at this point in our history it is unusual for patients to do so. For one thing, in many places there are not enough palliative care providers available to meet the need.

Many people confuse palliative care with hospice care. Hospice is a service to help people whose death is expected in a matter of weeks or months. To receive hospice care, the patient and the patient's medical care providers acknowledge that a cure is no longer believed possible. The goal of hospice is to make each patient's day the best day that it can possibly be, given the disease burden they are bearing. By contrast, people can be on palliative care for years as they seek a cure. There is a helpful saying: "All hospice care is palliative care; not all palliative care is hospice care."

Spiritual care is an integral part of palliative care. Therefore, when a patient is assigned to the palliative care service, a visit to the patient by the team's chaplain is part of the service.

That was where I came in as I was the palliative care chaplain.

Let's start with two important and closely linked questions. The first is: What was my purpose when I visited a patient?

The image I held in my heart when I asked a patient's permission to come into their room was of a candle burning in the center of that person's being, a candle representing the deepest inner self, which some call the spirit, some the soul. My job, as I saw it, was to gently cup that candle flame with my hands, helping it withstand the challenging winds of a hospital stay and, as was often the case for my patients, the inexorable approach of death. Each human being has a particular view of the world and his or her place in it. My job was to respect and support that view, putting my own beliefs entirely aside.

When time permitted, which is to say when the patient's death was not imminent, my job was also to help people die "well" spiritually. I have talked about this in "About Dying" (see page 33).

This brings up the second question: Who is in charge? The official answer, as is true of all interactions between staff and patients, is that the patient is in charge. This is because he or she is seen as having made a positive choice to come to the hospital (not true, of course, of patients brought in because they were found unconscious, were in an accident, or came by way of an involuntary psychiatric commitment). Patients have the right to decline services and to leave the hospital if they wish, even against medical counsel.

Fifty years ago, the doctor and other medical professionals were presumed to know best, and staff-patient relations were paternalistic. Staff told patients to do such things as have this surgery, or take that medicine, and patients usually did so with little discussion. But over the years this approach has changed radically. Now the patient decides whether to take the professional's instructions, regarding them as advice rather than orders.

This means that every hospital staff member wishing to interact with a patient first needs to gain the latter's consent to do so. For routine services this usually is easily accomplished.[7] In the case of chaplain services, however, it is sometimes not easy. For me, the biggest barrier arose when the patient did not know the services a chaplain offered. For example, many people assume that a chaplain is only concerned with "religious" matters; so if the patient is an agnostic or atheist, they will decline to see the chaplain. The chaplain therefore needs to find a way to let the patient know that a chaplain may have something more than "religion" to offer. And the chaplain, visiting a patient for the first time, must do this fast, because if a patient tells you to leave, you must leave promptly.

Word choice is important. The term "chaplain," to most people, connotes not just religion but Christianity, making the idea of a chaplain's visit unwelcome to many people of other religions as well as to non-believers. The chaplains tried to counteract that association by naming our department "Spiritual Care" rather than "Chaplaincy Care." But the job title was "chaplain," no matter whether held by a Christian, a Muslim, a Jew, a Buddhist, or a humanist.

At the start of my onsite chaplaincy training, which took place in a small, relatively unsophisticated hospital serving mostly well-to-do suburbanites, I was assigned to patients who were hardly ill at all. The patients were polite, and so was I. I would knock on the door and, after verifying the patient's identity—a necessary step since patients are often moved from one room to another—I would say something like, "Hi, I'm Chaplain Maxwell, how are you?" I became increasingly dissatisfied with this socially accepted greeting. If they were "fine," they would not be in the hospital; yet almost always they'd reply with something like that—"I'm fine, thanks"— and the conversation would often stay at the level of polite chatter.

Part of the problem was that as a chaplain-in-training I was greener than grass, scared and uncertain, and I'm sure patients picked up on that. Nonetheless, I decided I had to change my initial greeting. But what to say?

In my mind I played with lots of alternatives, from "Would you like to talk about God?" (I didn't even test that one) to the more informal "How's it going?" but nothing seemed right. Then, by happy chance, two lively young women in their twenties were assigned to a two-bed room on my floor. Admitted for minor gynecological "fixes," they had bonded with one another, were wildly bored by their enforced inactivity, and were eager to chat. I decided to ask their advice.

"How do I start the conversation?" I asked. "If I say, 'How are you?' they say 'Fine,' and we're nowhere."

7. But not always. For example, patients can take a strong dislike to a specific physical therapist or a tech assigned to take blood pressure readings and refuse to allow them into their room.

"You bet," they agreed with a discouraging degree of enthusiasm. "Nowhere indeed." *All those wasted greetings.*

"Then why did you two talk with me?"

"We're bored, we have nothing better to do"—*Oh great!*— "and we've never met a chaplain before you."

"Well, I need your help with starting a conversation with people who are sicker than you guys, a way to be inviting. . .."

"And not scary," one of the young women interjected.

So easy to forget that, for many people, a chaplain is associated with bad news.

"And not scary," I agreed. "Low key. Okay, that's your assignment, if you're willing to help." They grinned their assent. I said I'd come back at the end of the day to see what they had come up with.

Late that afternoon I went back to the young women's room. "We've got it," they chorused. "We spent all afternoon talking about it. Like you said, 'How are you?' is a stupid question in the hospital. We think you should say this: 'How is your day going *so far*?' No matter how sick you are, some days in the hospital are better than others. Thus, 'so far' makes it a question that will work for anyone, even for people who are really, really sick."

They're right! Not only is the "so far" very good, it takes the patient right to the present moment, the here and now.

"And," one of the women continued. "you need to start by showing you're not there to say the patient is dying or something. So start with some sort of a casual opening."

"Well, I have to say my name and my job," I said.

"How do you do that now?"

"I just say, "Hi, I'm Chaplain Maxwell."

"That could be very scary right there." *Oops.* "Let the patient know you're just dropping by—if that's what you're doing."

"Okay, I can say, 'Hi, I'm Chaplain Maxwell. I'm just stopping by to see how your day's going so far.'"

"There you go!"

I've used that phrase ever since, and when I do I always think of the two kind young women who thought it up for me.

Anton T. Boisen, a Protestant minister who was a founder of one of the training programs for hospital chaplains known as Clinical Pastoral Education, taught that "the patient is the living human document," and as such should be consulted and studied as a source of wisdom for chaplains. That first experience I had with those two young women spurred me to continue to ask patients for advice and assistance in pastoral matters and to pay close attention to the rich variety of helpful responses I received to my questions and my actions.

For many people, one of the frustrating aspects of being hospitalized is the inability to be of help to another person. Consequently, many patients are delighted to teach their chaplain something about the disease they suffer from or other aspects of their existence. I learned that all I had to do was ask.

Over time, based on patients' positive responses, I got bolder about what I asked—*after* I gained the patient's permission to have a conversation and then only if I sensed that they might be open to my questions. Encouraged by people's generosity to me, I moved from asking about the details of illnesses to matters of the heart and spirit. I always tried to speak softly, to be slow and calm. I never asked a question just to satisfy my own curiosity ("Why did your daughter run off with that deadbeat, anyway?"), but only if I sensed that there was something on the patient's mind or heart that they might wish to tell to a caring person. And if I encountered any resistance, I backed off immediately.

I never had any fixed line of questioning, believing that it was my job to stay entirely in the present moment, however things were going for the patient right then and there. To start things off, after explaining the purpose of my visit I might say, "You've been in the hospital for a while. I wonder, what have you been thinking about as you've been lying here?"

Or, "You look like you feel sad. Are you? Would you like to tell me what's wrong?"

If a patient cried, instead of politely ignoring their tears, as is the socially accepted thing to do, I would gently say, "What are those tears about?" To my initial astonishment, people were usually eager to answer.

If a patient was a religious believer, I would often ask, "What role do you think God has been playing in your illness?"

If a believer mentioned a personal problem, I might ask something like, "Have you been able to pray about that?" or, "What has God said to you?" or, "Where is God now in all this?" Believers generally welcomed this sort of question and the conversation that would result.

Over time I learned that for many people, a hospital stay is in certain ways like a religious retreat. They are entirely removed from familiar surroundings, stripped of their usual daily activities, forced to be continuously aware of their mortality, deprived of their privacy, fed unappetizing food, made to endure physical privation and pain, and subjected to almost total loss of control. Hospital stays usually involve a huge amount of time spent waiting: for someone to come to take you for a test; for the nurse to give you your medicine; for a doctor to tell you how your body is doing;

for a meal to be brought; for help getting to the bathroom; for a visitor; waiting. . .waiting. . .waiting. . ..

Television often loses whatever attraction it once had, and becomes background noise. Magazines and books can be too heavy to hold and too hard to read. There can be nothing to do but lie back on the uncomfortable plastic mattress and worry. A chaplain who is genuinely interested in you often becomes a most welcome visitor. And a conversation about matters vital to you becomes a true godsend.

Behind the Scenes

It was important to let patients and staffers understand my profession as clearly as possible. All hospital workers had to wear a staff badge hung around their neck or pinned to their coat giving name, professional degrees and affiliations, and department; mine said "Joan Maxwell, MTS, AC" and "Spiritual Care." MTS meant Master of Theological Studies, the degree I earned in seminary, AC meant Associate Chaplain, a designation from a professional group of chaplains, and Spiritual Care was the department to which I belonged. In addition I wore a small red plastic badge on my right shoulder that said "CHAPLAIN."

I could have worn a formal long, white hospital coat—the other chaplains did—but I chose not to because I wanted to show, in my clothing, that I was not a physician or nurse but something different. Seeing a gaggle of white-coated people come into the room can be intimidating for a patient, and I liked to be the *non*-intimidating one.

I chose my clothing carefully to look clean, neat, and mildly conservative so I was ordinary looking to my patients, many of whom were homeless and only a few of whom were well to do. To mask possible stains, I wore black—corduroy in winter and cotton in warmer weather. On top I usually wore a white tee shirt with a colorful short scarf around my neck to give patients something cheery to look at. A long scarf would inevitably have brushed up against various surfaces during a hospital day and gotten full of hospital germs; I wore a short scarf for the same reason doctors wear bow ties rather than long ties. I invariably selected one of several "civilian" jackets that I had specially chosen for hospital use, each with huge pockets for the patient-index cards, pens, book of religious services, holy oil for anointing of the sick and dying, tissues, and anything else that seemed called for.

My appearance included three other characteristics that were helpful in developing relationships with patients. The first was age. During my active chaplaincy career, I was in my fifties and sixties. I believe that even in our youth-obsessed society, age is an asset for a chaplain. Illness and dying are viewed as the special province of the old, so an older chaplain might be thought of as more likely than a young one to know the nuances of these conditions. Being an older woman made me non-threatening to younger people; often they treated me as a respected grandmother.

Moreover, my age signaled to the elderly that I knew some of the secrets hidden from the young, who sometimes view older people, particularly sick older people, as essentially finished, without strong feelings and without interesting inner lives. My wrinkles showed older patients that I knew older people have the same sorts of feelings as younger people do, often with the same or even greater intensity.

Second, although I'm physically fit, I am moderately overweight, a condition I have struggled with all my life. I think this obvious sign of my fallible humanity was comforting to people who were struggling with their own fallibility.

Third, people tell me that I have an infectious smile. If so, that's fortunate, since humor is something that delights me and can be a welcome relief to people in times of stress.

On my feet I wore Mephistos—black clodhoppers, heavy but comfortable, necessary for someone on her feet for most or all the work day. The hospital had eight floors and a basement, and sometimes I found myself called to all nine levels during one shift. Given that the elevators were slow and crowded, it was often easier and faster to take the stairs.

Somewhat like Waldo in the *Where's Waldo?* children's books, the stairs were a secret world hidden in plain sight. They were utterly utilitarian, unheated, not air conditioned, and surrounded by concrete-block walls painted a dreary grey. Their main purpose was to serve as fire escapes in case of emergency, but they were heavily used by staff and a few of the more knowledgeable visitors to get around the hospital in a hurry. Stair-walking often yielded the opportunity for a quick encounter with a physician or nurse, where we could briefly exchange patient information in privacy.

Considerable space above each floor's ceilings was required for the complicated equipment needed in a medical facility. Thus, going from one floor to the next involved at least two flights of stairs, sometimes three. Staff members appreciated the opportunity to be off the patient floors for a few moments and collect themselves between visits.

Although the stairwells were a little like a featureless no-man's-land in the endlessly war-torn hospital world, the landing on each floor was surprisingly spacious. Landings were where I would encounter a few staff members having a chat, or someone huddled up against the wall talking quietly on a cell phone to take advantage of a little privacy–not much, but better than standing in the corridor with patients, visitors, and supervisors walking by. And when someone, generally a nurse or other patient-care worker, needed a sympathetic ear and a shoulder to cry on, the stairwell was sometimes the best available place.

The floor corridors were different. Corridors on "regular" patient floors were always busy during the day, with, for example, visitors trying to find a patient's room or the elevator or a rest room, usually looking uncomfortable in this alien and perhaps-frightening environment. Frequently I saw patients trying to take a walk, sometimes with painful slowness, or being pushed in wheelchairs or on rolling beds with IV poles rattling beside them. Staffers strode along singly or in a gaggle. They often talked loudly to one another, more loudly than they would in the stairwells, which could be troublesome for patients trying to rest.

Each patient floor had several supply rooms that only staff members could access. Some contained bed linens, some patient supplies and medical equipment. If you needed to have a private conversation with another staffer, you could slip into one of the supply rooms and huddle in a corner, surrounded by urinals or bed sheets. Other staffers would usually honor your privacy, knowing that you would afford them the same respect when needed.

A special refuge was the employee john. The one for our office floor—unisex and a one holer—was in a little room right next to the copying machine. Often a line of nurses stood waiting to use the facility, even though other, public bathrooms were available on the floor. Its restriction to employees accounted for its popularity, since most users were nurses who were careful to keep it clean. (The public bathrooms, by contrast, were occasionally disgusting and at best unkempt.) Besides, going into the staff section of the floor to use the staff toilet allowed us to shut the door on the public corridors and patient rooms, relax for a moment, share a joke, nibble a cookie or candy from the gifts received daily from grateful patients and nursing-supply salespeople, or buttonhole a colleague for a quick word about a patient we were both dealing with. Perhaps most important, this john was the only place in the hospital where a staff member could be alone for a moment behind a locked door.

The employee toilet itself was small and unadorned. The toilet paper, a huge industrial-sized roll probably a foot in diameter, usually ran out at least once a day, testimony to the john's heavy use. A hulking white wastebasket, often filled to overflowing, was always placed next to the door. As an infection-control procedure, after you wiped your hands you used the paper towel to open the door before tossing the towel in the basket.

The john's proximity to the copying machine sometimes produced surprising moments. While using the toilet you would overhear private conversations between staffers—usually gossip, occasionally whispered spats, and, rarely, shouts. The stress direct patient care put on nurses was enormous, made worse by the fact that most worked twelve-hour shifts. Occasionally a nurse went into the bathroom to cry, a practice frowned upon by colleagues as a long line of people waiting for the facilities would develop. Its central location and thin walls made the john an unsatisfactory refuge; but there was no other private space in the hospital where these overworked caregivers could go to grieve.

In the stress and fear associated with serious illness, patients and their families sometimes forget that hospital staffers are human beings like themselves. And staffers are trained to conceal their humanity and vulnerability. Their professional clothes, badges and IDs, technical knowledge, and use of seemingly endless abbreviations are all tools that set them apart from patients and their suffering. Without a certain amount of distance, hospital workers would burn out even more quickly than they do ordinarily. What I saw in the refuges of the hospital—stairs and back offices—were little bursts of ordinary humanity released for a moment from behind the professional veil.

"My Parents' Fault"

"Thanks for coming by, chaplain, but I'm not religious." Ms. Pomfret was tall, thin, white haired, erect against her bed pillows. Her chart said she was eighty-three, suffered from colon cancer that had metastasized (spread beyond her colon), and was due for "debulking" surgery tomorrow. This was an operation to reduce the size of the tumor, making her more comfortable but not eliminating the cancer.

"That's okay, Ms. Pomfret. I'll leave now if you wish, but sometimes people who aren't religious still enjoy talking with a chaplain."

"Just chatting?"

"If you like. I can also offer various relaxation exercises, or a listening ear, or silent companionship. I can help answer or get answers to any questions you have about how things are going for you in the hospital."

"They're going as well as can be expected," she said.

"Sounds like they're not going great. I'm sorry." She nodded. "How are you dealing with that within yourself?"

"You mean that I'm dying?" she said sharply.

"Is that what the doctors tell you?"

"Yes."

"Do you think they're correct?"

"What do you mean, 'correct?'"

"I'm wondering if you agree with them, if you think you're dying."

"They've shown me the scans. I think they're correct."

"It must be very hard."

"I'm eighty-three. I've had a good run. I'd like to see my granddaughter marry, though."

"Is she engaged?"

"No, Zoe's only fifteen."

"Who knows, perhaps you'll see her marry." Ms. Pomfret's forehead wrinkled in disbelief. "I don't mean you'd be at the ceremony in your body, but perhaps in spirit."

"I'd like to believe that, but I don't. I wish I could believe in God. But I don't."

"Did you ever believe in God?"

"No, never. I never had any religious training as a child. Both my parents were atheists."

"It's never too late to learn about God."

"No, chaplain, you don't understand. I don't have any receptors in my brain for that kind of information. I wish I did. It's my parents' fault. I'm angry at them about that, but there's nothing I can do at this point."

"If you'd like, we could do some exploration together. Or I could give you something to read." I kept a neutral tone, not wanting to pressure her in any way, but wanting to offer her assistance if she wished.

"No. Thank you, but no. It's too late." She pulled the bed sheet higher around her chest. "I'm so angry at my parents."

This incident happened early in my chaplaincy. I respected her wishes, but if I had been a better chaplain I might have been able to help her discover that she did not have to be limited by her parents' views. Since then, when talking with young parents about baptism, I've passed on Ms. Pomfret's story as an example of the importance of early religious training.

But God does not depend on early religious training. I have a dear friend who is now a gifted Episcopal priest. She was born to committed atheists scornful of people who needed what her parents viewed as the illusory comfort of religious belief. Yet somehow, as a little girl, my friend was drawn to God. She has no memory of being exposed to a Communion service as a child, although she must have been.

"I used to line up all my dolls behind the skirts of my dressing table and pretend to give them Communion," she says. It charms my heart to imagine this powerful preacher as a little girl ministering in the flowered catacombs under her dressing table.

I didn't know this story when I met Ms. Pomfret, and I don't know that it would have been of any help to her. She's long dead now, and has experienced for herself what lies beyond the grave. I wish I could have been a better companion during her last illness.

Conflicts between patients and children over religion were relatively common. In contrast to Ms. Pomfret, consider Ms. Beck. When I responded to her request for a chaplain, I learned she was a seventy-two-year-old lady whose middle-aged adopted son had killed himself just five days earlier. She had a lot to say and many tears to shed, and I listened. She told me about how their relationship had been a difficult one and how her son had not had any religious faith. A devout Christian who believed that every word in the Bible was literally true, Ms. Beck had tried and tried to bring him to belief in Jesus Christ, but had not succeeded.

Given her strict religious convictions, I wondered if she might believe he was now in Hell. Such a belief would make her distress at his death even worse. To find out, I asked her where she believed her son was now.

"I believe he is with God," she answered, speaking matter of factly.

"And how do you think it is for him?" I continued.

"Well," she replied. "I think he's learned I was right about at least one thing."

I roared with laughter and so did she.

Our shared laughter was an encouraging sign that she would be able, as she herself said to me, to get through what is one of the most devastating losses anyone can experience—the death of a child.

But a shared religious belief was no panacea. Once I was called to the bedside of an eighty-year-old gentleman who was literally in the midst of dying. His devoted daughter and son-in-law were at his side, and wanted a bedside service for him before he died. They told me that he was an extremely devout Episcopalian and they were as well. It was important to all three of them that he die surrounded by holy ritual. They were concerned that everything be done "right." Theirs was a military family (US Marines) that wanted to do things by the book.

I therefore proposed a service based on "Ministry at the Time of Death," from the Episcopal *Book of Common Prayer,* and the family added three of his favorite psalms. Everything had to be according to the King James Version of the Bible, a translation completed in 1611; no more recent translation would do.

I always found it deeply moving to lead a service around the bed of someone who might die before the ritual was finished. In this case, while we were praying, a nurse was holding the patient's head, giving him air by compressing a bag connected to a mask over his mouth to help his breathing; a second nurse hovered in the doorway. He lasted through the service, and the family seemed to find it helpful.

When we were finished and the nurse removed the breathing mask, which had been keeping him just barely alive, they gathered lovingly by his head. I stood at the foot of the bed and prayed for them all in silence. What was important was that during his final moments, the family seemed to have a sense of the presence of the Mystery.

After the patient died, the son-in-law told me that his wife had no life other than with her father: He had been living with them for the last several years, and she had spent all her time caring for him. Now that he was dead, the son-in-law feared she would feel her life had no more purpose. Such a fear was not uncommon among family members who had spent vast amounts of time caring for an ill member, and was often warranted. I gave him the name of a highly regarded facility where they could meet with a grief counselor (though, as usual, I later had no idea as to the outcome). I wondered about the couple's relationship and why she couldn't find meaning in caring for her husband; but he was young and seemingly healthy; I imagine he was not sufficiently needy.

Permanent Ink

When I got home from work late one night, despite scrubbing my hands half a dozen times, I had four names written in ink still visible on my palm: a mother, a father, and the mother's two sisters. That's something I learned from my first chaplain supervisor. When you're in a situation full of high emotion and you absolutely must remember the names, write them on your palm. In this case, involving a dead fetus, I *didn't* write the name the parents had chosen —partly because the parents hadn't decided whether they wanted me to use it and partly because, when they did decide, I knew I would be able to remember it if necessary.

The fetus, at twenty-two weeks, the nurse had said, was strangled by the cord in the womb, already dead when this was discovered. Labor was induced, the fetus was delivered, and the nurse called saying the parents wanted some sort of service. When I got to the labor and delivery room, I found both parents glowing with health—beautiful young people, remarkably different from the usual hospital patients. The mother looked tall and strong, wide hipped, built to bear children. The father was tall, muscular, shaved head dripping with sweat in the hot room, able to speak only in an incongruously tiny voice because of his sorrow.

When I first responded to the call, the father left to go home and shower (and, I expect, to weep). Both sisters stayed there with the mother, and we talked about the service, what she would like, what prayers she wanted, whether she might favor Psalm 139 as a sort of frame for the service. When I returned an hour later, as agreed, the sisters had gone, the father was back, and it was just the parents and me.

The nurse brought in the body wrapped in a tiny blanket and put it on the mother's lap. The father sat on the bed, thigh touching his wife's thigh, not looking at the baby, nor at her, just staring at the floor. I stood on her other side and she grabbed my hand with a grip of steel, her other hand on the little blanketed mound. When the nurse came in, we were talking about the service, and after she left I suddenly found myself praying with no prefatory time of silence or invitation to prayer, just swept into it by the Spirit. At least that's how it seemed. The most powerful sense of the Mystery, together with the baby's spirit, overwhelmed me.

The prayer went on for a bit, and then we read together the first seventeen verses of Psalm 139. I introduced the reading by saying that the psalm expressed something of what the baby might feel if he were in this life and able to speak, but that we knew he *was* with us both in body and in spirit. The room was hot, and I was sweating and then crying—not sobbing, just tearful. After we finished praying, the mother grabbed me and gave me a big hug. I said, "I'm sorry I'm all sweaty" and she replied, "That's okay."

And I looked at the mound in her lap and said, "Do you want to keep him for a while or would you like me to take him away?"

"Take him," she said.

I looked at the father, who was utterly stricken, and said, "Do you want to hold him before I take him?"

He nodded yes, and she gave him the blanket. He looked down at the baby, his face ravaged by sorrow, and the mother peeled back the blanket to show a tiny, tiny head with a tiny, tiny knit cap on it (bless the volunteer who knitted it and the nurse who put it on). I patted the father's shoulder and again gripped the mother's hand. Then he gave the bundle back to her, and she gave him to me. The body was a feather, just a feather, still flexible, no rigor mortis yet, and still a little warm, although perhaps that was from the parents who had been holding him.

I blessed them and went out in the hall, carefully not covering the body until I got in the hall but then covering him at once so no happy parent passing by would see this tiny dead creature. My face was red and streaming water and a nurse saw me and gave me a look of immense compassion. I found the baby's nurse and said, "Here."

"Are they through?" she asked.

"Yes, they're through. Where can I go to wash?"

She told me and I washed. But when I got home the names were still on my hand. Permanent ink.

My prayer group met that night. I took the whole experience there and gave it to the Mystery.

At the Foot of the Bed

Sometimes my visits with patients or their families were so deep that time became elastic. We would exchange relatively few words, spend most of the visit in silence, and, in a way I don't understand, seem to go into another space, another world.

One such instance involved a Dr. Burton Newell. A physician at the hospital called me and said she thought it would be helpful if he saw a chaplain. He was not expected to live for more than another day or two. She added that Dr. Newell was a famous planetary scientist who had taught for some decades at a nearby university. The hospital didn't often get excited about "VIPs," but my informant let me know that Dr. Newell was a major VIP.

I confess that made me a little uncomfortable. Typically, VIP patients had an unusual number of people coming in and out of their rooms, making it hard to have a private conversation. Furthermore, most scientists I encountered in the hospital made it clear that in their opinion spiritual matters were not scientifically provable and hence not credible.

When I went to Dr. Newell's room, one of the few large singles on the floor, the door was ajar. I tapped lightly and pushed it open a little more. A thin, handsome man in his early seventies lay flat in bed in the center of the room, eyes open behind horn-rimmed spectacles, looking at the ceiling.

Happily, the television was off and the room quiet. To his right, on an upholstered sofa that looked considerably more comfortable than the plastic chairs normally available to visitors, two attractive women in their forties looked up from their magazines at my knock. "I'm Chaplain Maxwell," I said. "I'm just stopping by to see if Dr. Newell would like a visit."

"Oh, good," the older woman replied. "We'll go to the cafeteria and get some coffee." The other woman nodded.

I was amazed. Close family members, which presumably these women were, never leave a gravely ill relative as soon as a strange chaplain enters the room. Usually I must chat for a few moments to establish how non-threatening I am before inviting the relative to *consider* going for coffee while the patient and I talk.

Do they know Dr. Newell has something he needs to discuss with a chaplain, or do they just need a break?

"That's great. I'll keep him company until you come back." *I don't want you to worry that he'll be alone while you're nursing your coffees in that noisy cafeteria.* They nodded, picked up their purses and magazines, and turned to the patient.

"We're just going for a coffee, Dad," the younger one said. "The chaplain's here. We'll be back in about twenty minutes."

Thoughtful of her to let me know how long I'll have for the one-on-one visit.

Dr. Newell nodded, the women left, and I went to stand beside the bed, next to his head so it would be easy for him to see and hear me. When I introduced myself, he looked up at me, frowning. "There's a woman standing at the foot of my bed."

There was no one there that I could see.

What's this? Is he hallucinating? Is he referring to me? Or. . .?

"I'm not at the foot of your bed. I'm standing here beside your head."

His frown deepened. "I know."

This could be tricky. I have no relationship at all with this man and I have no idea what he knows about dying. But he should know what's happening.

"Perhaps she's someone who loves you who's coming to be with you as you go to the other side," I ventured.

"There's no one who would do that for me."

Oh my. What a thing to feel.

"Really," I said noncommittally. I stood silent for a bit, and then said, "What about your mother? Did you have a good relationship with your mother?" *Where did that come from? I guess I know. It's such a cliché. But there it is.*

"Oh, yes," he smiled, his voice changing, a little wave of relaxation flowing through his body. "I certainly did. But she's been dead for so many years."

"That wouldn't stop her from coming to be with you now." I paused, then continued: "Perhaps it is your mother. Does it look like her?"

"She could be," he replied, peering at the foot of the bed. Then he looked up at me again, suddenly scowling, and growled, "Do you know who I am?"

Here's the skeptical scientist part coming out. Well, there's nothing I can do but tell it like I see it. I took a deep breath. "Yes, sir, I do. But you're also a human being. This is a very human experience. It's perfectly normal, you know, to see someone at a time like this."

"It is quite an experience," he replied with a little laugh. He reached out his hand and I took it. "Oh, it feels wonderful to hold your hand," he sighed, a smile on his face. "Wonderful."

"I'm so glad." *What a lonely person.*

He looked at my ID tag and asked me what he could call me.

"'Joan,' or 'Chaplain,' or 'Chaplain Joan.' Whatever you like."

"Chaplain," he replied softly, seeming to find pleasure in saying the word. Then, "I see a car," he said, looking up at me questioningly.

Since I had an idea about the woman, he thinks perhaps I'll have an idea about the car. At least he trusts me enough to be interested in what I *see.*

"I don't see it, but I'm glad you do."

"I do."

I paused. I knew that dying people sometimes saw trains or planes or some form of transportation shortly before they died, but I saw no advantage to him in saying that.

"What kind is it? Sedan or limousine or. . .?" I asked.

"Sports car," he replied. "Very nice one."

That made me think that indeed the car was coming for him, as divine transportation is usually of high quality.

Since I couldn't think of anything more to say, I shut up and pulled up a chair. We sat together in silence, holding hands the while. This was one of those elastic times. I wasn't praying, he wasn't sleeping; we were simply together in a wordless holy communion. It felt as if the two of us were contemplating his impending death in a deep calm. As I think back on our shared reverie, it was as if we could see his death coming like a cloud floating slowly over the sky. He was peaceful and accepting.

After some time, I have no idea how long, we heard the "clack-clack-clack" sound of high heels walking briskly toward the room. Dr. Newell dropped my hand just before the two women came back through the door, one carrying a paper cup of coffee. I rose and told them I had to finish my rounds. Dr. Newell asked for my card.

"You've caught me with my cards down," I replied with a smile. "But I can get you one in a flash. My office is on this floor. Would you like me to get one?"

"Yes, please."

I told him I'd be right back.

"I'll be watching for you," he said.

When I returned with a card, he reached out his hand for it and held it upside down, unable to read it even though he was wearing glasses. I turned the card right side up and read slowly, pointing to each word: "'Chaplain Joan Maxwell, Department of Spiritual Care, City Hospital.' Do you want me to put it on your bedside table?"

He shook his head and pulled it to his chest, covering it with both hands. A talisman of our time together.

"I'll be back tomorrow afternoon," I said, and we parted.

I came back, but he wasn't there. He had died that night. I like to think that he drove away with his mother in that very nice sports car. I was grateful he wasn't alone at the end.

Helplessness

Early in my training I asked a mentor who was an Episcopal priest of long standing, "Who am I to go into a patient's room? What on earth can I do? What use am I to someone who is suffering?"

She replied, "Joan, what makes you think God can't make use of anything, even you?"

I was jolted by the question, which showed me my lack of trust in God.

But trusting God in little, specific things, in what to say to a patient, in discerning what the patient most needs—I'm supposed to trust God? I'm supposed to trust God will guide me?

In a word, yes.

Each day in the hospital was different. Indeed, that was a significant part of its appeal for me. I like change, adventure, surprise, and the hospital offered that every moment. Every day I walked into rooms where I knew little or even nothing about the person I was visiting. At times the chart offered some help, giving a scrap of family information. I always looked at the "next of kin" listing to see what kind of helping relationship, if any, existed for the patient. A few read "none." Marital status, a spouse, kids? I usually checked the home address, if one was given. City, country? A "good" neighborhood, a "bad" one? A religious preference other than "nondenominational"? That was a meaningless entry embracing everything from Roman Catholic to atheist. Harried admitting clerks sometimes clicked "nondenominational" without asking; and if a comatose patient was admitted without family present, there would be no way to tell. Since the hospital would be given demerits by regulatory agencies for recording religion as "unknown," "nondenominational" was the preferred selection. Hence a good regulatory intention—to require the medical system to note and respect a patient's religious convictions— gave birth to a bad result.

Often the chart answered *none* of these questions, because the patient had been brought in unconscious. Sometimes all I knew would be the medical diagnosis, if that had been made. Often it was cancer, but sometimes heart disease, and sometimes a gunshot wound or kidney failure or occasionally a disease of which I had never heard. And occasionally I didn't even have a name to start with, for the patient would be "John Doe" or "Mary Doe"—or a more fanciful pseudonym when they were the victim of a crime and the police wanted to conceal the person's identity for their protection. (In such cases the nurse would usually alert me that the patient was listed under a pseudonym and give me their correct first name.)

Of course I rarely had the slightest information about what was most important to me: Did they believe in some form of something generally called God? If so, through what lens did they *view* God, not just via a religious denomination, if any, but through what emotions—love, fear, anger, hope? If they did not believe in God, what did they believe in? What did they think and feel about their current condition? If death was likely to come soon, did they know that? Were they accepting? in denial? praying for a miracle?

All of this meant that when I walked into a patient's room, I was entering a total stranger's complex and usually frightening situation, surrounded by a firestorm of emotion and with zero prior knowledge.

But despite the handicaps it imposed, this ignorance offered a vital spiritual component. For me, and for most of my colleagues, one of the hardest things about being a chaplain was the desire to fix things. Compassion drew me to chaplaincy, but chaplains, compassionate or not, must endure being completely helpless in the face of great physical, emotional, and spiritual pain. I did not possess the skills of physicians, nurses, physical therapists, or any of the other physically oriented healthcare workers. I yearned to make illness and pain go away, but I could not.

It took me a while to realize that this very helplessness was what I offered and, paradoxically, was a good thing. It served the community with which I was engaged. If necessary, sometimes I would "do something": give a cup of water, straighten a pillow, call a nurse; but such tasks were not always needed, and even when I did one, it didn't take long. When I stopped doing, when I was still and open, when there was less of me, I found there was a whole lot more of the Mystery.

This may seem odd to you, as at first it did to me. All my reading, training, and experience were not my most important attributes. My helplessness and my ignorance were what was needed most. In time I learned to rely on the Mystery to guide my words and actions in each moment with each patient. Human spiritual needs are too particular, too complicated for anyone to identify them immediately at any one point in time. Thus, whenever I went into a patient's room, I put what you might think of as my mental automobile in neutral, free to roll around the patient's landscape with the Spirit leading.

It became my practice, when I went to the hospital, to begin my day in the little room called the interfaith chapel. I would sit on a bench in silence and offer myself to the Mystery. My prayer usually unfurled to this effect: I knew I would see people about whom I knew nothing; the people I would see would be suffering; I couldn't fix their problems; but I trusted that the Mystery would be present.

I therefore threw myself on the Mystery to guide me to do and be whatever was best for each patient. My mantra was, "Make me a blessing." Jews will sometimes say about someone recently deceased, "May his name be a blessing," and I like that prayer. By praying to be a blessing, I was praying to be available to the Mystery on behalf of the patients in any way they wanted and needed.

In chaplaincy training I was shocked when I was told I must always go into a patient's room empty handed. No pen, no notepad, no list, *nothing*. My supervisor said this was an absolute requirement. At first I was horrified. I had nurtured an image of myself carrying a little clipboard with a list of patients plus a pencil to check off names and jot a few notes. This image seemed "professional," and was rather comforting to me. What on earth was I going to do with empty hands, no list, no *thing* at all? What use was that?

My supervisor said my empty hands were to remind me, and to show the patient, that I came to see them without an agenda and that the patient was in charge, not me. It took me years to fully accept and adjust to the wisdom of that instruction. I came to learn that the Mystery was in charge—if I could get myself out of the way, and, indeed, even when I couldn't.

In time I also learned there were in fact a few things I needed to have, not in my hands but in my pockets. I wrote out a three-by-five card on each patient assigned to me so that, before walking into the room, I would know a few key elements. Most important, and indeed essential, was the patient's name. That let me make sure the person I saw in the bed was the person I had come to visit.

Sometimes I found that the woman I thought was Ms. Jones was actually Ms. Smith; and instead of having Stage 4 cancer, she had diabetes. A note on the patient's gender was also important, because many patients had lost their hair because of chemotherapy; in addition, their bodies often swelled up if they'd been given intravenous fluids, so there was no way to tell whether the round body under the white sheet was male or female. Imagine how unpleasant it would be for a bald female cancer patient to be addressed as "Mister." I did this a few times, much to my distress.

Age was important, because it told me how much life experience the patient probably had, and the information helped alert me to the family dynamics that might be at play. For example, elderly people were more often concerned about their grandchildren than their children.

I recorded religious denomination or preference, if any, on the card only after I had confirmed it with the patient or a close family member. If someone was Catholic, for example, it could be extremely important to them to receive Catholic Communion. If someone was an atheist, then as a rule it would be offensive to ask if they wanted prayer (although on occasion a self-professed atheist did request just that).

It was also helpful to know how long the patient had been in the hospital, because a "new admit" usually had different concerns than someone who had been in the system for a while. The card also indicated whether I had visited them previously. On occasion a patient would return to the hospital after some time away, and would be hurt if I didn't remember that we had visited together before. But the truth is that I saw so many patients—all clad in identical hospital nightgowns—that I sometimes couldn't remember if I had already seen someone that week, let alone that year.

(Once I encountered a former patient in the hospital waiting room. He rose from his seat and greeted me warmly, but I couldn't recall him. When he reminded me of his name, I blurted out, "I'm so sorry, I didn't recognize you with your clothes on." The entire waiting room burst into laughter. Fortunately, he laughed as well.)

I had a pen to check names from the list of people I needed to visit that day and to jot notes on key spiritual issues that had surfaced. But I did my jotting in the hall, not in the patient's room.

I carried two religious tools: a container of holy oil and a copy of *Ministry with the Sick*. When I needed a Bible, I went back to the palliative care office to get one. I nearly always carried a couple of tissues, usually for my own use but sometimes to offer to someone else. I kept these resources in my pockets, never in my hands, and over time built up a small repertoire of generously pocketed jackets exclusively for hospital use.

But despite all this stuff, useful as it sometimes was, my empty hands and blank agenda were the most helpful gifts I had to offer. That was a lesson I learned and relearned at deeper and deeper levels over the years. I found that if you keep on praying "Make me a blessing," sometimes you are.

God in the Window

Mr. Newton was a tall, thin, eighty-eight-year-old African American who had been in and out of the hospital over several months. A nasty oral cancer made the side of his face puff out. He lived alone in an apartment somewhere in DC and had no family. He had a quiet dignity that I greatly respected. He started off a little skittish about me but soon figured out that I was harmless and that I liked him; he liked me, too, I believe.

He called me "Reverend," even though I told him more than once I wasn't ordained. I think he stuck to the title as a sign of respect; he was a very polite gentleman. We visited and prayed together several times during his hospitalizations.

I saw Mr. Newton's name on the palliative care list after he had been out of the hospital for a couple of weeks. When I went into his room, I found him seated in a straight chair close by the window, his bony knees almost touching the glass. He had an excellent view: It was a two-bed room, and he had the bed by the good-sized window. The view was of two side streets that merged in a V. At the base of the vee was a tiny park with several large trees.

Something about the way Mr. Newton was looking out at the view was immensely peaceful. He was completely still, yet I could tell that he was keenly involved in what he saw. I greeted him and he turned to me with a smile, saying he was glad to see me. When I asked him what he was looking at, he pointed out two squirrel nests, one in each of two adjacent trees; he told me the squirrels competed for food on the ground, but banded together when a human walked near one of the trees. He talked about the people he saw walking by, how he watched them and felt he could tell a great deal about them just by how they walked. He told me he spent a lot of time looking out of his window, rejoicing in what he saw and saying prayers of thanksgiving for the world.

He asked me if I had ever noticed that the leaves at the top of a tree were often greener than the ones underneath. I said I had not noticed that. He explained that leaves at the top turn when it is raining and cup the rain in their undersides, perhaps to absorb a few drops, and when they are through slowly turn and let the water run down the stems and branches and trunk into the ground. I said I had never noticed that about tree leaves. "You don't really look at a tree, do you?" he said in a matter-of-fact way, not judging, just observing.

"I thought I did, but after what you've told me about the leaves I guess I don't," I replied, resolving to check this out the next time I had a deciduous tree in view for a while.

There was something compelling about this man's gentle appreciation of what he saw.

"You know, Mr. Newton, listening to what you say about the view, I have to say you make me think of God." *Wow, what a thing to say. But it's true.* "You remember how in Genesis on the seventh day God rested and saw that the creation was 'very good?'"

He looked at me for a moment, then replied, "I guess you could say I am like God that way. What I see is very good." He paused. "I've been thinking about Jesus. If he were down there today I wonder what he'd be wearing. He wouldn't be wearing no suit. . ."

I'd never considered what Jesus would be wearing if he were walking down a side street in Washington. A suit seemed unlikely, I agreed.

"He wore a dark robe," Mr. Newton continued.

I gave him a surprised look. *Has he been seeing Jesus in a vision?*

"Back in the day," Mr. Newton explained. "Back in the day he wore a dark robe. He couldn't wear no light robe. A dark robe hides the dirt. It was patched."

All at once I could see this dark, patched robe, deep brown with perhaps a reddish tinge, careful stitches making the patches. We sat quietly together, me contemplating Jesus' robe. I don't know what Mr. Newton was contemplating, but he was clearly a contemplative soul. Then we prayed together and I got up to leave.

"I like seeing you," he said.

"I'm so glad," I replied. "I like seeing you too." We smiled and parted.

I spent much of the rest of the day thinking about Jesus' dark robe and God watching the world from a window through Mr. Newton's eyes. Nearly every contemplative teacher encourages their students to be aware of what is before them. Mr. Newton's example fit squarely in the heart of that tradition. I wondered if he had been taught to pay attention by some spiritual teacher, but when I went back to his room the next day, I found he had been discharged, and our paths never crossed again. I think he just figured out for himself how to live in the present moment.

The Palliative Care Office

The palliative care office was the size of two narrow closets, one next to the other. There were no windows, just one door that typically banged into one of us in the office when it was opened. We four regular inhabitants sat side by side on rolling chairs at a long, waist-high, wall-mounted shelf that served as our desks. I sat between Hoshi, the social worker, and Alyssa, the junior palliative-care nurse practitioner. Sarah, the senior palliative-care nurse practitioner, was at the end nearest the door.

Each of us had two open shelves above our work station, a two-drawer filing cabinet mounted underneath the desk surface, and a few feet of desk surface for a phone, a computer, and papers. The complete lack of privacy served to benefit the patients. All phone calls and all visitors were community property, so each of us could—and did—weigh in when we had a piece of information to add about a case.

As palliative-care nurse practitioners, Sarah and Alyssa were responsible for patients' bodies. They were experts in pain relief and in adjusting medications when organ systems began to shut down as lives drew to a close. They helped patients and their families make difficult treatment decisions. They didn't tell them what to do, but could and did ask questions that revealed patients' values and then supplied them with information about the consequences of the possible options.

For example, if a patient prized life over everything else, trying a form of chemotherapy with difficult side effects that offered only a tiny chance of success might make sense. If a patient prized quality of life over duration, avoiding that chemotherapy might be more in keeping with their desires.

As the palliative-care social worker, Hoshi was responsible for helping patients deal with family and personal responsibilities as their lives were ending. She helped place young surviving children in foster care; helped find patients appropriate post-discharge settings (for example, a nursing home with hospice care if no family support was available for a patient who was expected to die soon); and helped assess the safety of possible at-home placements. If, for instance, a patient's only offspring was a drug-addicted daughter, Hoshi might have to find an alternative living situation, since addicted relatives often divert patients' pain medications for their own uses.

Lunch time was the best opportunity during the day to check on patient progress and catch up on hospital gossip. Around 12:30 we usually found ourselves in the office, charting morning visits and planning our afternoons, and someone would ask, "Anyone else hungry?" We were hungry most of the time, perhaps because of spending so much time with deteriorating bodies. One invitation was all it took for the little refrigerator tucked under the office printer to be opened and a series of plastic Baggies and storage boxes hauled out for inspection and sharing.

Our mealtime conversations in the cramped office ranged from spouses to children to hopeful developments with Alyssa's long-term boyfriend, who was proving recalcitrant when it came to the question of marriage. Often Sarah showed off a new pair of astonishingly high heels, which made her well-muscled legs look sexy, but which the rest of us found completely impractical for the daily miles of walking along hospital corridors. I took advantage of the group's presence to get the inside scoop on patients newly added to the palliative list, paying particular attention to suggestions from Alyssa as to which should be seen first. Even though she was the youngest and least experienced team member, Alyssa had a remarkable sensitivity to unarticulated spiritual need. When she said, "You might want to see Ms. Jones," I put Ms. Jones near the top of my list.

Sarah and Hoshi were more likely to report who was nearing death and the resulting emotional state of family members. At first it seemed unfeeling to be enjoying a seaweed-wrapped bite of carrots, cucumbers, and rice while talking about how the pressors (medications) were becoming less and less effective in raising a dying patient's blood pressure. But in time I barely noticed the contrast.

Lunch lasted only about ten minutes, sometimes considerably less. Then Sarah would get up, roll her chair back into the corner, and say, "Well, time to get going." The rest of us would respond by chewing a breath mint to save the patients from a blast of lunch and return to the patient floors.

At the Foot of the Cross

One morning I had an idiotic fight with David over nothing, but it included angry words and even some shouting. I left late, still feeling angry as well as stupid and full of self-doubt. When I finally arrived in the hospital, Hoshi asked me to see a Mr. Fenton who had been "found down" (meaning helpless on the floor) in his apartment and was very weak. They wanted to contact his daughter; but the phone number he had given Admitting wasn't correct, and he could not remember the right one. Feeling distracted, I went to see Mr. Fenton—and was just about as ham handed as it is possible to be. Of course he didn't want any part of me, and I thought that showed excellent judgment.

I left his room feeling terrible and wondered if I should just go home. But not wanting to give up quickly I went to see the second patient on the palliative list. To my shame, I was pretty ham handed with him too. Clearly I had totally lost it and should stop trying to be a chaplain, at least for the day.

As a last gasp I went to see a man I had visited twice the previous week and with whom I had made what seemed to be a good connection. (I looked at this as one of those times when I visited a patient more for me than for the patient.) He was a senior real estate executive, overwhelmed by nausea because of experimental chemotherapy, yet elaborately courteous to me. He greeted me with his usual graciousness, told me how terrible he was feeling and how bad the nausea was, and asked for prayer. I prayed from the depths of my own unhappiness with myself, feeling able to cry out in the name of this poor man, and from his reaction the prayer went well for him. Thanks to him I could climb back on my chaplain horse, hollow though it was.

The most noteworthy encounter that day was with a relatively young man from Brazil, a Catholic in the throes of kidney failure who had a wife and three kids aged eleven to twenty-one. The man was in the ICU, attached to more tubes than I had ever seen, on a breathing machine, eyes closed. When I went to meet the family in the ICU waiting room, the patient's wife said she knew her husband would soon be seeing God. As she said it she looked scared—scared, I could tell, on her husband's behalf about the impending divine-human encounter.

"Do you know how God will look?" I asked.

She blinked at me in surprise at the question and didn't say anything, but looked even more nervous.

I spread my arms again and repeated: "This is how God will look. Arms wide open to welcome your husband into his immense heart." She seemed uncertain. "Jesus saved us, you know. That job is done. We don't have to worry. That's the good news."

The wife perked up at the mention of Jesus and said she had asked her husband to open his eyes if he had seen Jesus, and he had done so. She added, "Of course, I don't know if he truly did see Jesus . . . "

I said, "I know one place where he saw Jesus for sure—when he saw you."

"Me?" She pointed to her chest in astonishment.

"We're all the body of Christ, so Jesus is in each of us. We're broken, human, fallible, but he's there."

After this the family members wanted prayer, so of course I invited them to pray around the bed with the patient and me. They had not done this before; the mom was worried about letting the kids in the ICU without official permission, which fortunately I could provide. The mom and I took them to the germicide dispenser and showed them how to clean their hands, then escorted them into their dad's room. We stood around the bed, me on one side of the dad, the mom on the other side, and the three kids standing at the foot of the bed, holding hands with one another and with us.

I could not begin to imagine how horrible it must have been for them to see their husband and father helpless, grey faced, and woven into fearsome medical machinery. I thought how agonized I would feel if the patient were my David, and how stupid our morning fight had been.

We prayed together, and after the prayer had finished we went back to the waiting room. It came to me to ask the mom if the kids had had any private time, one on one, with their dad. She said they had not. I told her that if she wished I could take one or all of them back to the ICU so they could talk to their dad in their own ways. I had seen how even people in vegetative states seemed to sense what mattered: the presence and the voices of loved ones. Although their father couldn't reply, I said, I believed he would be able to hear what his children said to him.

Being able to say whatever was in their hearts might be something these children would treasure all their lives. It is hard for a child not to have been able to say goodbye.

I added that I did not speak any Portuguese (the Brazilian family's primary language), so although I would be nearby in case they needed support, I would not—could not—understand anything they said. Their time would be completely private. The mom thought it was a great idea and started pressing the kids to do it. I could see that in her excitement she was coming on too strong and scaring them. Intervening, I said to the kids they didn't need to do this, that it was just an option for them to consider. They sat in a row, three young, black-haired heads bowed, considering.

Finally the son raised his head and said he would like to do it. I looked him in the eye, saw that he was afraid but also eager, and took him back to the room. I showed him both where to stand (near his dad's head) and the one place on his father's body where he could safely be touched, relatively free of the tubes, and sat in a chair as far away from the two of them as I could be without leaving the room.

I prayed for them in silence with the soft murmur of the son talking to the dad providing the background to my prayer. When he was done I took him back to the rest of the family, and the two girls separately took advantage of the offer. All three of them maintained great poise, although one of them broke down upon leaving the room.

Sitting there listening to these three young people say goodbye to their dad, understanding only the words "Papa" and "Mama," took me to the story of Jesus on the cross. The similarity was overwhelming. A beloved man dying, leaving bewildered followers utterly helpless and in pain in a public place with strange officials standing around watching while they tried to say goodbye. I felt I had a sense as never before of what it must have been like for those at the foot of the cross.

When I went home that night, I was prepared to make up with David, but, typical of his generous spirit, he had already forgotten our silly fight. That was just as well. After the day's experiences I couldn't even remember what we'd argued about.

The Grocery Cart

Only a few weeks into my first year of chaplaincy training in the hospital, I went to see a Ms. Hixon on the orthopedic unit. After having had a knee replacement four days earlier, she was tired and in pain, but wanted a visit. I didn't know it at the time, but bone pain is particularly brutal, and orthopedic patients who are basically well but hurting terribly can be depressed and difficult.

Ms. Hixon was a good example of this. She told me she was depressed ("I'm just so down today"), described the pain she was in ("When they made me stand on my feet less than five hours after the surgery it was so terrible I nearly fainted"), talked about what she viewed as the poor care she was receiving ("When I ring the call bell the nurses take a quarter of an hour to come"), told me about her daughter who had moved to San Diego ("I can't understand why she wants to live so far away from her father and me"), told me about her mother who was ninety-four ("She is in assisted living and is mad at me for not coming to see her today—I told her I'm in the hospital, but she doesn't believe me!"), and on and on.

As a truly green newbie, I was grateful that this patient was willing to talk; most of the patients on my list seemed to sense how little I had to offer them and thus declined to talk with me for long. I listened intently for any signs of spiritual commitment or interest, but heard none. At this stage of my training, of course, I had no idea how to broach spiritual topics in an appropriate way. After about twenty minutes together, however, Ms. Hixon said, with what looked like a genuine smile, "You know, chaplain, I feel much better. I really do. Thank you for listening!"

After we said our goodbyes, I felt pleased that as a brand-new chaplain-in-training I had been able to be of some small service to a patient, but I noticed that I also had a headache, was tired, and felt plain depressed myself.

Another thirty minutes remained before my shift was over, but I knew I was done for the day; no one would benefit from a visit from me in my sorry state. I told Amy, our training supervisor's assistant, that I thought I might have a cold coming on—automatically excluding me from the hospital—and dragged myself home.

The next day I made an appointment with our supervisor. "Jim," I said to him, "I told Amy yesterday I had to leave because I thought I was getting a cold. That wasn't true. I had to leave because I felt so depressed." Then I described my visit with Ms. Hixon.

"So she said she felt fine when you left?" Jim asked.

I nodded.

"Of course she did. She gave you her depression. And you took it away from her."

"What? You can give someone else your depression?"

"That's right."

"So what can I do? Just see one depressed patient a day and then go home? That doesn't sound right to me."

"Nope. You've got to learn how to take it but not keep it. When you go see a patient, they have a lot of garbage they want to get rid of. They want you to take it away, and that's part of your job."

"Yuck."

"You have to protect yourself while serving the patient."

"How can I protect myself and still be open to them?"

"You know the homeless people you see on the streets pushing a grocery cart? And how carefully they guard it? They've usually got the grocery basket covered, but if you took the cover off it you'd see that it's full of junk. They're just pushing their junk around. Every time you go into a patient's room, imagine you're pushing an empty grocery cart. And when they give you their junk—depression or anger or whatever—just put it in your grocery cart. Remember to say 'thank you,' because their junk is precious to them. When you leave, empty the cart and go on to see the next person."

I loved the metaphor, so much so that I left Jim's office happy and ready for the day. *Did I give him* my *depression? Guess he put it in his cart.* But I never asked him how to empty the cart.

The grocery cart metaphor was a huge help to me. In my early years as a chaplain, when a patient started to unload a big pile of "junk," I would imagine my grocery cart by the side of their bed, ready to receive whatever they needed to discard. That simple mental image somehow put just enough distance between me and their pain that I could take it away—but not keep it. I learned to empty the cart by passing the junk on through me to the great Mystery. I couldn't fix whatever the situation was, and I hadn't caused it, so it was something that needed to be handed off to the source of all healing.

Over time, because I *had* to count on God's presence and healing love—nothing else could help—hearing patients' stories became a bit like playing football. The patient would pass the ball to me and I would pass it on to God. While I had the football in my hands it weighed me down, but when I passed it on I passed on the whole heavy thing.

Of course that's not entirely true. As you can tell from the stories in this book, parts of patients and their stories have stayed with me since I met them. They changed me. I know that a few months after I retired, friends volunteered that I looked considerably younger. And I know that my heart is a little larger and a little softer because of all that I was privileged to receive.

Five Minutes

I only spent five minutes praying with Shirin Kazemi, but I've never forgotten her.

The palliative care list showed that she was twenty-six, had cancer, and was Muslim. When I put my head in the open door of her shared room, where she was in the bed next to the door, I found one of the psychiatric residents, a young European woman, talking with her, or trying to. From the body language it was clear that things weren't going well. The resident, sitting on a chair with clipboard and pen at the ready, was leaning forward intently, but the patient, a beautiful, dark-eyed, dark-haired young woman, was curled on the bed in a fetal position, her eyes looking down at the sheet. Both quickly turned and looked at me.

"I'm Chaplain Maxwell," I said. "I'm making my rounds, sorry to interrupt. I'll come back when you're done."

"Oh, no," said the resident, getting up from her chair. "Do come in now. It's fine."

For a psychiatric resident in the middle of an interview to do this was truly remarkable, and it told me that things between her and the patient were going poorly indeed. In the hospital pecking order, most physicians made it clear that what they were doing was more important than what anyone else was doing, and I usually tended to agree with that assessment. Certainly a chaplain's first call should wait in line behind an ongoing psychiatric interview.

"Are you sure?" I said doubtfully, but the resident gestured at the empty seat. I turned to the patient. "Ms. Kazemi, I'm a hospital chaplain, and I just came by to see if you'd like prayer." *Now where did that come from? I never, never say that to a patient I haven't met before.*

Ms. Kazemi locked her eyes on mine. "Oh yes, yes please," she said eagerly. Her pronunciation indicated she was not a native English speaker.

I took the seat, still warm from the resident. "I am not Muslim. I'm Christian, but I have a few Muslim prayers. Is that all right with you?" I spoke slowly to make it easier for her to understand me.

She nodded.

I pulled from my pocket the little book of interfaith prayers I had brought with me and turned to the page of Muslim prayers for the sick. The resident stood beside me, immobile. I could feel how intently she was observing our interaction. I held the book in my left hand and tentatively offered my right one to the patient. She grabbed it and held on tight.

Praying with people of another faith is a tricky business, theologically, personally, and practically. From the theological perspective, different faiths teach different things about the God of their understanding. I disagree with some of the things other faiths teach. But I also disagree with some of the things that my own faith tradition teaches. My understanding of my role as a chaplain was that I should support each patient's faith. (The only exception was if their faith was endangering their survival, as you'll see a little further along in this book.)

Therefore, I decided that I should always make it clear to every non-Christian patient that although I was Christian, I was willing to pray formal prayers from their own tradition if they wished. As a practical solution, I always brought with me set (formal, written) prayers from other traditions that I had reviewed to make sure they were potentially encouraging to a sick person and were words I felt comfortable praying.

The most important part for me was the actual praying. That is, I wanted to encourage the patient's own personal prayer in their relationship with the God of their understanding. Because I cared about every patient, no matter what their personal faith tradition, I wanted to be in a state of genuine prayer myself when we prayed together.

Attending various silent retreats, I had shared silent prayer with many strangers, people whose faith traditions were completely unknown to me. For me, the shared silence transcended whatever religious differences were present—at least during the silence. Yet when we talked about religion, as sometimes happened at retreats, the differences remained.

So how was I to pray with Ms. Kazemi, the Muslim patient, whose faith tradition I knew only superficially? Although I had done some reading, attended several lectures about the Muslim faith, and was friends with a few people who were Muslim, I had no real understanding of the religion. Reading set prayers I had reviewed ahead of time meant that what I said were words that I could in conscience say. But where was my *spirit* in that process?

When I pray in silence I sometimes think of myself as a radio trying to tune to a particular station. You might call it the "God Station," although I would never actually refer to in this way. But there is a mysterious place for which my heart yearns, and that yearning is my prayer. The interaction between myself and the mysterious place is totally out of my control. At times my yearning seems met and returned, and sometimes the station seems totally off the air.

Spiritual teachers tell us that how one feels in prayer has nothing to do with the prayer. They say that prayer in what is known as "dryness," when the station seems silent, can actually be profound. In my personal experience with dryness over the years, I've come to believe that is true.

To my amazement, however, my prayers in the hospital nearly always felt strongly tuned to that mysterious place. The religious tradition didn't seem to matter. I would simply turn to the yearning in my heart and seek a sense of divine Presence. Again and again and again that sense would be granted. I turned to that place of yearning with Ms. Kazemi.

"O Allah," I began, "Prince of peace, protector of the poor and the sick, we come before you in prayer." She squeezed my hand so hard it hurt. Then I slowly read a prayer favored by the Prophet Mohammed: "'O Allah, remove the hardship, O lord of mankind, grant cure for you are the healer. There is no cure but from you, a cure which leaves no illness behind.'"

Ms. Kazemi began weeping silently, tears flooding from her open eyes that seemed to express her love and yearning for her God. Her face was completely calm, so much so that if I had not seen her tears I would not have known she was weeping. What I witnessed in her appeared to be what in the contemplative tradition is called "the gift of tears." Spoken words seemed totally unnecessary, and we sat in silence together, hands clasped, sharing the sense of connection with the great Mystery.

The psychiatric resident stood as still as stone, but I was aware that time was passing and I had to respect the many demands she had to meet each day. So in order that the resident could complete her interview, after a few moments I said, "Ms. Kazemi, I should leave." But she increased her pressure on my hand still further. I glanced quickly at the resident, wanting to make sure she saw the patient's fervent response to our shared prayer. Then, after another bit of silence, I gently disengaged my hand.

"Thank you for praying with me, Ms. Kazemi. Peace be upon you."

She smiled wistfully. "And upon you." I nodded to the resident, and left.

As often happened in the hospital, I never saw Ms. Kazemi again, but the memory of her intense silent prayer has stayed in my heart to this day.

Ms. Trouten's Pillow

Many of our palliative patients were homeless. One of the most interesting of them was an African-American patient in her late forties named Coral Trouten. Diagnosed as a paranoid schizophrenic with terminal cancer, Ms. Trouten was angry, aggressive, mostly uncommunicative. Nevertheless, there was something about her that commanded extra respect.

We tried to figure out what that something was and finally concluded that it was her own sense of her intrinsic self-worth. If you've been homeless for a good while, as Ms. Trouten had, you have experienced a level of vulnerability that people like me, with roofs over our heads, can hardly imagine. If you survive, it's at least in part because you've learned to stand up for yourself in the most difficult of circumstances.

When she was first admitted, she got into a dispute with Alyssa, the junior palliative-care nurse practitioner, and told Alyssa to get out of her room and never come back. Alyssa obeyed, as we all did if a patient told us to go away. Hearing how difficult Ms. Trouten was made me want to see her and, if possible, forge a relationship with her.

I was always drawn to difficult and isolated patients. I suspect some of that attraction was egotistic on my part; I liked the challenge and wanted to see if I could succeed in gaining a patient's trust where others had failed. But I think it was also because I found that I was good at doing so. If I visited a patient once or twice and was meticulous about not pushing, I became a familiar figure in the strange and frightening world that is the hospital, and the patient accepted me.

I began with brief daily visits, during which I learned that Ms. Trouten had no small talk. She was polite, and believed in a Christian God, but also believed her relationship with God was too private to talk about with anyone else. When I asked if she cared to have prayer together, she declined. Each day I stuck my head in her room, asked if a brief visit was okay, was usually told yes—though often rather grudgingly—said about two ordinary sentences, and left. She quickly recognized me as a familiar figure, but we barely advanced beyond that point. In my experience, that was unusual.

Ms. Trouten's conscious isolation continued to intrigue me. I even did something I almost never did: I gave her a little gift, a tiny and plain wooden cross stamped "made in Jerusalem" that I had been given by a merchant in Israel. I told her it came from Israel and had been made there. She accepted it, at first with surprise, then with pleasure, and thanked me politely, but nothing more. I kept up the drop-by visits every day I was in the hospital, but there was no change in her response.

Indeed, the whole palliative team was fascinated by Ms. Trouten. We were all drawn to her by her self-possession, her clarity as to what she wanted and didn't want, her intelligence—we learned she had completed two years of college—and her sense of her own self-worth. Perhaps it was easier for us to identify with her, a homeless person, because of these characteristics, and we all wondered what it took for a woman like her, in her terrible state of advanced breast disease, to survive on the streets of Washington. She told Hoshi, our social worker, who was extremely good at asking basic questions and getting answers, that she lived in a shelter at night and walked the streets during the day. How she could do this day after day, how any homeless person can do this day after day, is almost unimaginable.

Then, at one weekly palliative care team meeting, Sarah said she thought Ms. Trouten was probably going to die within a week. I couldn't see her that day because she was being treated, but when I got to the hospital the following day, I went right to her room. Ms. Trouten was sitting slumped in her chair, leaning forward over a pillow on her lap, not resting on the pillow, just hunched over it. She had extensively metastatic breast cancer. Her right breast had been removed, but there was a suppurating wound there, and a huge tumor, which was impinging on a major artery and her lung so that she had trouble breathing. She couldn't breathe at all when she lay down, so she sat up twenty-four hours a day, making sleeping very difficult.

The tumor could not be removed, and chemo had not helped much. Apparently the mere presence of the pillow in her lap helped her endure the endless hours she spent curved over her burning chest.

I greeted her and asked if she wanted water, and she did. I got some in a cup with a straw and held the cup so she could drink. She continued to curl over her pillow as she drank. It was hard to see her in such obvious pain. I always thought of Jesus when I gave a patient water. Scripture says (Matt 25:40) that if we give to another in his name, we give also to him. Sometimes I imagined that it was not me, but rather Jesus, who was *giving* the patient water, since it was Jesus' words that particularly inspired me. I also knew that a person close to death was often very thirsty.

I asked if I could sit in the guest chair, which was placed in front of and at right angles to hers, near but not overly close, and she said "You can," so I did. This was only the second time that I had sat in her room. While I was normally a very physical chaplain, holding patients' hands, sometimes straightening their sheets, accepting embraces when they were offered, I knew intuitively that she did not want to be touched, so I carefully kept my distance.

There isn't much to chat about when a person is reserved by nature and in pain. I asked her about her pain and she said, "I'm all right," which was her way of saying "Don't talk about it," so I dropped the subject. I offered her more water, and she drank it in the same hunched-over way. Then she said, pointing to the covered water container given to patients, "I let it sit out all night. That's dangerous."

I knew that she had been diagnosed as paranoid, and her remark seemed paranoid; but I did not get into debates with patients about things like this. Instead I said, softly, "Dangerous?"

"Yes," she said sharply.

"Would you like me to get you fresh water and ice, and a fresh cup and straw?"

"I trust you."

"Thank you." I didn't know if that was a "yes" or a change of subject, so I waited, and she twisted her head while keeping her body in its same hunched position over the pillow, and looked up at me.

"I'll go do that," I said, and did. Then I resumed my seat.

"I like to sit in silence," she said. I smiled inwardly because of my own taste for silent prayer, and said that I did too. We sat together in silence for perhaps thirty minutes.

During the silence I found myself praying in a way that was different from my usual practice. Normally when I was in silence with a dying patient or a patient in pain, although my eyes were closed, I moved my inner awareness to the patient's spirit. I sought to sense what the patient was sensing or feeling, and tried to respond through prayer. It was as if I looked at the patient through night-vision goggles, scanning for signs of need and offering that need to the Mystery, together with my prayer for its relief.

But in this case I was so aware of her desire for privacy that I didn't feel I had permission from her to pray in that way. We had never prayed together out loud, and she had always declined to talk about God. I felt I had not been "let in." It seemed inappropriate to attempt what I suspected she would consider an intrusion.

So I prayed in a strange way that I can only think of as restricted. I offered my awareness to the Mystery as a way of praying for Ms. Trouten, but in my spirit there was an almost physical line between me and her, and I never crossed that line. I didn't think about what she might be feeling, didn't try to probe her spirit, didn't even try to send her blessings, all of which was my usual practice. I sat in the chair in silence in a way that I suppose could be thought of as being on her behalf. But I was entirely given to God with no specific request on her account. I was simply present, no more, no less.

Then Ms. Trouten began moving her legs in small, restless ways, movements that told me her pain was increasing. With her permission I went to her nurse to ask that she bring pain relief. The nurse agreed; but first she had to take her blood pressure. Ms. Trouten resisted that at first; the blood-pressure cuff can be uncomfortable when it is inflated around a swollen arm. When I explained that pressure must be checked because a low level can make morphine dangerous (one of morphine's effects is to lower blood pressure), she consented. Her blood pressure was dangerously low. The nurse paged the medical team, and I went back to my chair.

In a matter of minutes several physicians came into the room in a flurry of white coats. Ms. Trouten stayed bent over her pillow and some of the staff looked at her curiously. The lead doctor told Ms. Trouten they couldn't give her morphine until her BP went up, and raising her BP required more fluid in her body. She consented to a needle stick to put in an IV drip, an expert vein-finder came, failed to find a vein, and the doc said they therefore had to put a line in her groin. Ms. Trouten had trouble understanding what he was saying. He was an Indian with a heavy accent and used medical terminology. After some back-and-forth between them, I interjected a translation in colloquial language, and she understood.

As Ms. Trouten was considering the question of a line in her groin, Sarah came in, ascertained what was going on, and gently but firmly took over the conversation. "Coral," she said, using Ms. Trouten's first name, "this is what we've talked about, is this what you want to do?" Sarah explained that the IV, if started, might not help her BP that much, that the fluid might simply swell up her body, making her even more uncomfortable. Sarah added that this lowered blood pressure was part of the progression of her disease.

Patients in a weakened state and without medical training often have no idea of the possible downside of medical actions. One vital question for a patient to ask about any medical procedure is, what are the benefits and what are the associated risks? Out of respect for the expertise of the medical staff, or out of fear, or out of a desire to get a problem resolved quickly, patients often do not ask that question. On the one hand, the patient was in pain. On the other hand, she had earlier told Sarah she prized quality of life over quantity of life. By alerting Ms. Trouten that the line in her groin might end up causing her more discomfort, Sarah's intervention was an example of how the palliative care team helped inform a patient making decisions about proposed medical interventions.

"I need to talk to my brother," Ms. Trouten said, and Hoshi, who had slipped into the room at some point, said that her brother was on his way and would be there in twenty minutes. In view of her deteriorating condition, the team had already telephoned him.

Everyone agreed to delay further discussion until after her brother arrived. The white-coats (including Sarah and Hoshi) rose as one, like a flock of startled egrets, and Sarah said, "Shall we leave Chaplain Maxwell here with you?"

"Yes," Ms. Trouten said.

"I guess you're talking about a lot of things?" Sarah said, looking at her expectantly. Ms. Trouten kept her head down and didn't reply.

"We're just sitting quietly," I said. Sarah shot me a quizzical glance, and she and everyone else left.

The room returned to stillness. After a moment Ms. Trouten looked up from her hunched position and smiled at me. It was a beautiful smile, wide and glowing, lighting up her eyes, transforming her face, the first (and last) smile she ever gave me. "Thank you," she said.

I smiled back and said she was very welcome. She put her head back down and we sat in silence for another half hour until her brother arrived. I introduced myself and quickly left so they could be alone together.

The team told me they would have a family meeting once Ms. Trouten and her brother had talked together. A "family meeting" is when the medical team reports to family members about their loved one's current physical state and tries to ascertain whether they wish to continue aggressive physical treatment. Typically, such a meeting is called when team members believe that nothing more can be done to slow the progress of a disease.

In about fifteen minutes the brother came out of her room, and we walked with him toward the stark, windowless space where we held so many family meetings. On the way, he wiped his eyes with a paper towel. I was glad to see signs of warm feeling between him and his sister. I went up behind him and gently put a hand on his back—a risk, perhaps, but seeing his lonely sorrow impelled me to try. I didn't say anything; he didn't move for a bit; then he threw away his towel and we walked together to the meeting room.

Sarah and the physician briefed him on the situation: If we didn't run the line into her groin, she would probably die very soon; and if we did put the line in she still would die very soon. The brother asked if we could control her pain without the line, and Sarah said they could. As I'd heard earlier, with her current low blood pressure, the morphine might hasten her death by lowering her blood pressure still further. But Sarah felt that the dosage needed did not present much of a risk, and at this point it was a risk worth taking. He said he would discuss it with his sister. We walked him back to her room, where we left the two of them alone again.

When I returned an hour later, I learned from her nurse that Ms. Trouten and her brother had decided not to allow the doctors to insert the line. She had been given more morphine without any negative effects and would be taken to hospice the next day. This meant that she was accepting and consciously moving toward her death. Re-entering the room, I found Ms. Trouten transformed, sitting up in her chair, radiant.

"I'm glad you and your brother worked out everything," I said to her. Looking past me to the nurse, she asked for a second pillow. The brother looked at me, distressed that Ms. Trouten had ignored my comment, and said, "Thank you so much for all your help."

Realizing that she was focused on moving on and didn't need me anymore, I said they were most welcome and left. She moved to hospice the following morning and died that night.

Sitting for some hours in silent companionship with a relative stranger is an intimate and challenging act. I'm reminded of a story commonly told at

Washington, DC's Shalem Institute for Spiritual Formation (which teaches contemplative prayer). A woman attended a silent prayer group that met at the institute every week over a period of six months; at the end, she said to the group, "I don't know any of your last names. I don't know how any of you spend your time when you're not here, but I feel I know you better than almost anyone else I've ever met."

I completely agree with that assessment of the intimacy fostered by shared silent prayer. But I did not have that feeling about Ms. Trouten. She was just as much an enigma to me at the end of our time together as she was the first day we met.

Nonetheless, I am grateful that she let me sit with her during all those hours the day before she died. It allowed me to experience a new kind of prayer. Chaplains talk about "the ministry of presence" as being what we offer, but up to that point my own ministry of presence had often included a good deal of *me* in it: my helpful suggestions to God as to what would be good for this or that patient, my silent probing of the patient's spirit, my aching desire to *fix it*. With Ms. Trouten, no fixing was possible, medically or emotionally. I had no choice but to leave everything in the hands of the Mystery, something you might think that after many years as a chaplain I ought to have done anyway. As this experience with Ms. Trouten taught me, I still didn't do that. Thanks to her, I think I was able to do so more fully the next time.

The Little Space

Hundreds of patients have told me that many people are praying for them. Some boast about the number of people and religious institutions doing so. Even unbelievers sometimes mention they are being prayed for. Several years ago I took to asking them if they had felt anything particular that they attributed to the prayers being offered on their behalf. Sometimes they had no answer, in which case I invited them to think about it and let me know the next time I came by. For other patients, an answer came quickly. My two favorites are: "I feel as if I'm being held by an invisible hammock" and "I am floating on clouds of prayer."

One special experience gave me the opportunity to expand my research into what it's like to be prayed for—by becoming what is known in science as a participant-observer. I was diagnosed with cervical radiculopathy, meaning that a degenerating disc in my neck was crushing a couple of nerves, resulting in considerable pain and increasing weakness in my right (dominant) hand. After trying several alternative approaches—acupuncture,

Reiki, osteopathy, physical therapy, and denial (my favorite)—I decided to undergo a surgical procedure medically known as cervical laminectomy, fusion, and instrumentation. Translated into more easily understandable language, this meant the surgeon would make an incision in my throat, work his way around my esophagus and other body parts, find his way to my neck bones, cut off and remove various parts of my spine, shove in a wedge of cadaver bone, add two pieces of titanium, screw it all together, and sew me up.

The thought of what was going to be done to me was frightening. But I decided to treat the experience as a research opportunity. Now was my chance to see for myself, in the moment, what it was like to be prayed for while hospitalized. I had been the fortunate beneficiary of considerable prayer over the years, but never—consciously—around a surgical event.

The surgeon was highly recommended, the surgery was viewed as routine but "major," and it was *my* neck they were going to cut. I asked everyone I knew to pray for me. And I asked people who were not believers to "send positive thoughts." When the specific date and time of the surgery were set, I put the word out, encouraging people to pray for me and the surgical team, especially around the time of the operation.

I found that I increasingly enjoyed asking for prayer. I had asked for it in the past, but never in such a focused way, and never from so many people. I grew used to saying, "I'm scared" and "Please pray for me." I was touched by the softness that would come over the other person's eyes, often accompanied by a touch on my arm, and the eagerness with which they would promise to hold me in prayer. I noticed that the more people I asked, the more other people would volunteer even before I had a chance to ask them. It was as if I had created an invisible field around myself, silently asking for prayer support.

At last the day came when I had to go in for the surgery. It was in a hospital where I had done some of my chaplaincy training, and a seminary classmate was now one of the senior chaplains. I asked her, if her schedule permitted, if she would please come by and see me in pre-op, and happily for me she did. It was a powerful reminder of the greater Reality to see her smiling face amid anesthesiologists, surgeons, and nurses. I asked her to read me whatever psalm it was that she usually read on such occasions, and she picked my favorite, Psalm 63:

> O God, you are my God, I seek you,
>   my soul thirsts for you;
>   my flesh faints for you,
>   as in a dry and weary land
>   where there is no water.

So I have looked upon you in the sanctuary,
 beholding your power and glory.
Because your steadfast love is better than life.. . .(Ps 63:1–3a)

Hearing those words, which had been prayed for thousands of years, gave me a vital chance to catch my spiritual breath.

After my chaplain friend left, the stream of medical people continued coming in and out of my room. Bolstered by the psalm, I tried to monitor my inner state as I answered questions, had an IV line inserted, and saw the time of the surgery coming rapidly closer. I found my fear, which had been intense, so much so that I hardly slept the night before, had ebbed away. Wondering if I had been given a tranquilizer, I looked at the IV pole: The only drug there was an antibiotic. Yet my blood pressure, which had been unusually high when I first arrived (a sign of my anxiety), was now chugging along at its usual normal level.

Shortly thereafter a tech came and said, "Are you ready?" It was a powerful question, giving me the awareness that I could say, "No," if I wanted to. I took a deep breath and said, "Yes." I kissed David and was rattled down a long corridor to the OR (operating room), where my arms were strapped to boards in what seemed like a crucifixion position . . . and I woke up in the post-surgery acute care unit. After wiggling my extremities to see whether there had been an "oopsie" on the table, and finding to my great relief that there had not, I was flooded by a wave of pain, hot, increasing, total. Total . . . and yet not absolutely total. Somehow there was a little space between me and the hot pain. I turned my attention to that space, fell back to sleep, and woke up as I was being rolled into a hospital room.

My hospital stay was medically uneventful. I did a good deal of sleeping, but when I was awake I spent a lot of time observing my inner state. What I noticed, consistently, was that little space. It took the edge off anything unpleasant. It stayed between me and the pain, between me and the dizziness when I first got out of bed, between me and the techs who shouted their way down the corridor at two in the morning. I myself wasn't able to pray in any focused way, but that little space seemed to be alive with silent prayer.

From time to time I had flashes of different people who I knew were holding me in prayer. I would become aware of a dear face in repose—for some reason, almost always seen in profile—and my heart would open in gratitude and love. And the little space abided.

I got out of the hospital and returned to work, my "research" accomplished, at least for the moment. I believe that scary surgical experience made me a better chaplain. That little space accompanied me into many hospital rooms and often evoked a similar space for the patients I encountered.

Ophelia Rivers, Trusting God

One of the many pieces of wisdom in the Jewish tradition is the ban on naming what other religions refer to as "God." In Hebrew, "God" is referred to as YHWH, a word made up entirely of consonants and hence unpronounceable as written. Moreover, Jewish tradition forbids any attempt to pronounce the four sacred letters as a word. When writing in English, many observant Jews write of the deity not as "God" but as "G–d." Behind these practices lies the belief that to name something or someone is to understand it, and the Almighty cannot be named by his/her creatures because our minds cannot grasp the immense Mystery that is G–d.

Some patients from a variety of religions differ wildly from this perspective. They believe they understand God and all God's rules, and anyone who diverges from their understanding is at best in error and at worst doomed to eternal torment. Often the God of this passionately held understanding is an angry, cruel deity who demands total obedience at any cost. The source for this concept among Christians is often given as the crucifixion of Jesus, where God the Father is understood to be demanding of God the Son dreadful torment in expiation of human sin. If that's what God requires of his beloved Son, these folks believe, then from time to time God requires of the rest of us suffering at that same intensity.

As a young minister, one of my seminary professors, the distinguished Bible scholar Sharon Ringe, used to teach Sunday school in a poor neighborhood. She tells the story of a boy in one of those classes who asked, "When God got home at night, did he beat Jesus up?" Further conversation revealed that several children thought this a likely event, and more discussion exposed their belief in a fierce, punishing God who closely resembled their own fathers. Sharon encouraged the children to explore other neighborhood characters for possible alternative images of God. The class finally settled on a nearby grandmother with an ample lap and a generous hand with cookies.

In light of this view of a harsh God, consider the case of Ophelia Rivers, thirty-eight years old, who came to the hospital with advanced AIDS and a bad case of drug-resistant tuberculosis. This form of TB can be fatal and is highly contagious. Consequently Ms. Rivers was put on strict isolation in a single room.

It was disquieting, to say the least, to go into a room where it was possible (unlikely, but possible) to contract a fatal disease. All staff and visitors who entered had to wear a pale blue face mask, numbered N95 and known as a "duck bill" for its duck-like profile. The N95, which covers your face from the bridge of your nose to your lower chin, is so tightly woven that no liquid can enter from the outside, protecting you from inhaling any infectious droplets resulting from another's coughs and sneezes. The weave also prevents any liquid or vapor from exiting, so the humidity from your breath slowly creates a pool of saliva that sloshes annoyingly around your chin.

Far more serious from a chaplain's perspective is the way the N95 conceals your facial expressions from view. When I was mask-free I often formed a wordless relationship with patients, my sympathetic and understanding facial expressions helping forge the bond. An unchanging, Donald Duck-ish mask conveys nothing in the way of human sympathy. Moreover, the mask's tight fit over your face, and its thick weave muffle your voice. So the effectiveness of a second tool in the chaplain's repertoire—little "mm's" and "un-hunh's" of understanding—is also sharply reduced.

Ms. Rivers was an unusually challenging patient. She had a history of heroin and alcohol abuse, and was homeless and unemployed. Her highest level of education was fourth grade, and her chart showed no next of kin. A psychiatric consultation yielded a diagnosis of paranoid schizophrenia. She was wild haired, emaciated, and intense. Because of her social isolation, she was probably in acute need of spiritual support.

When I knocked and went into her room, swathed in my duck-bill mask, blue plastic gown, and green plastic gloves, the first thing I saw was a large and worn Bible on her night table. An open backpack lay in the far corner under the window, with a crumpled green sweatshirt spilling out from it onto the floor. The TV was on, loud and abrasive.

I took as deep a breath as the N95 permitted and looked at Ms. Rivers, who sat cross-legged on her bed, dressed in a faded blue and white hospital gown, her stick-like arms projecting abruptly from its wide, short sleeves. I did a brief spiritual assessment and learned that religion was important in her life. She regularly attended a local church called the Church of the Heavenly Light, but did not want me to let her pastor know she was in the hospital. "It's a big church and he doesn't know me," she explained.

I found myself wondering if Ms. Rivers' reluctance stemmed from her diagnosis—many churches stigmatize people with AIDS—but I couldn't ask such a personal question at this early stage. As we talked about her church, she kept her eyes on mine, leaned forward, and gesticulated forcefully. For her this topic was clearly sacred ground.

After about eight minutes, the pool of saliva from my exhalations had begun to rise around my chin. It was tempting to go to the sink, pull the bottom edge of the mask off my chin, just for a second, so I could spill out the collected liquid. But doing that would let in all the germs the mask was keeping out. During long visits you had to go outside the isolation room to get rid of the saliva safely.

That was one reason to bring this visit to a close. Another was that I try to keep first visits short so the patient has time to reflect on our interaction. Then, the next time I come, in the patient's mind I have often morphed from "a chaplain" into "my chaplain," and the conversation can go deeper.

In the hall, I asked Ms. Rivers' nurse if there was anything special I should know about the case. The patient, she said, was highly mercurial—sometimes completely unresponsive to a visit and sometimes eager to engage in passionate conversation. The medical team was concerned that her AIDS had not responded at all to the HAART (anti-AIDS) medications they had put her on, a protocol that normally was effective in reducing the virus in the bloodstream.

Later that week, before I had a chance to visit her again, the intern assigned to her case told me that earlier that morning Ms. Rivers had been sent for a scan. The housekeeping staff had decided to administer an extra-thorough cleaning while she was out of her room. In the process, they turned her top mattress and to their astonishment discovered a large hoard of pills under it. Examining the collection, the nurse quickly determined that the pills were all anti-AIDS medications. It seemed that when they were given to her, Ms. Rivers had pretended to swallow them and then, as soon as the dispensing staff member left her room, spat them out and stuffed them under her mattress.

When Ms. Rivers was brought back from her scan, several members of the medical team went to her room together and quizzed her. Why had she not taken the pills? Did she not want to feel better, not want to get out of the hospital?

Of course she wanted to get well, Ms. Rivers assured them. She knew she was seriously ill and needed God's help if she were to recover. Therefore, if she took the pills, that act would show that she doubted God's power and was relying on human power, which would anger God. By not taking the pills, she was demonstrating her total trust that she would be miraculously healed of AIDS and TB by God.

This was a classic example of a deeply held religious belief imperiling a patient's life. Such beliefs usually aren't changed by logical argument. Ms. Rivers was an adult, and legally she had the right to do as she chose—unless we could get a judge to rule her incompetent. That process could be difficult and time-consuming, and might result in a major conflict with the patient that would be therapeutically harmful. The situation called for a chaplain to talk with her about her decision from a religious perspective. Soooo. . ..

"Hi, Ms. Rivers, it's Chaplain Maxwell back again. Can I come in?"

She nodded.

She was sitting partially upright in bed, lying back on a couple of pillows, the sheet pulled up over her chest. She looked tired but determined. I took a seat in the visitor's chair, after covering it with a spare plastic gown I had brought with me into the room.

Help! was the only prayer I could pray.

What came to me in response to that prayer was completely unexpected. I found myself saying: "Ms. Rivers, I was surprised to hear you don't trust God."

Her face hardened. "What you saying?"

Please, may I be doing the right thing.

"You say you're trusting in God to heal you, right?"

"Yes I am!"

"So how are you expecting God to heal you? Thunder and lightning? Jesus walking in through the window?"

"I don't know how he gonna' do it, but I'm trusting him."

"You know your Scripture; I can see that." I pointed at her Bible, well-thumbed and looking like a weird sort of porcupine, full of strips of torn paper serving as markers.

She nodded.

"So you know how Jesus works. He doesn't do thunder and lightning. He does little touches; that's all he needs. And he works through other people, the disciples, his followers. Scripture tells us that."

Her face didn't change.

Well, here goes.

"So Jesus works through other people, people like you and me, people like the doctors. And through human hands. That's his way. When Jesus sends the doctors with pills to heal you, why don't you trust him?"

Blessedly, in time and with more conversation, Ms. Rivers agreed that Jesus *was* sending the doctors to help her, and she agreed to take the pills. While she wasn't "cured," her viral load went way, way down.

An apocryphal story fits in here. Once there was a huge flood, and the waters started rising, threatening the residents of a village. A man who lived there ended up standing on his roof as the waters got higher and higher. A neighbor paddled by in a canoe and offered him a lift.

"No, thanks," said the man. "I'm waiting on God to rescue me."

Someone came by in a motorboat, but the man refused his help. The water kept rising.

Then a helicopter hovered right overhead, and the crew offered to lower a ladder to him. Once again he declined assistance, saying he trusted in God to save him.

At last the waters rose so high that he drowned. When he got to the entrance to heaven, St. Peter was standing there, and the man went right up to him.

"Why didn't you rescue me?" he asked. "I put my trust in God, and God never came."

"What do you mean?" St. Peter replied. "God sent you a canoe, a motorboat, and a helicopter!"

God and Me (2)

After my Maine experience of the Presence in silent prayer, I wondered like any good skeptic if it was a one-time happening. During the remaining days of our stay there, I attended a few more quiet-prayer gatherings. Each time was different, but Something drew me back again. (I'm writing about a total Mystery, and the capital letters are the best way I've figured out to indicate that.)

Our visit to Maine ended, and I found myself back in Washington, D.C. Where could I find people to pray with? Where could I find people to teach me more about this new form of prayer? Most of my friends were atheists, or not very observant Jews. I had never heard anyone in my local acquaintance even *mention* quiet prayer.

I decided to seek out a church. Since the church through which my "yes" to God had been answered was Episcopal, I started visiting local Episcopal churches. There were several near our home. I didn't know anyone in any of the churches I visited, and no one said anything about quiet prayer during the announcements that were made.[8]

8. There are many different kinds of prayer. The Episcopal *Book of Common Prayer* lists seven major kinds: adoration, praise, thanksgiving, penitence, oblation, intercession, and petition. Quiet prayer is a form of adoration. If you are interested, the others are defined in the 1979 edition on pages 856–7.

We lived near the Washington National Cathedral, and David and I loved to wander around its peaceful gardens. As a token of our gratitude, every year we sent the cathedral a small check toward the cost of upkeep. I mention this because our modest check got us a subscription to the institution's monthly magazine. And the month after we returned to the city, the magazine had a cover story on a little chapel where a small group practiced what they called contemplative prayer. From the article, it sounded a lot like what I had experienced in Maine.

I marched off to the cathedral the following day and to my joy discovered a small community of people, led by a priest on the staff, dedicated to silent prayer. I became personal friends with a few of them and felt a special kinship with them all.

Through this group, a whole new world opened to me. I began by attending teachings about contemplative prayer that were offered in the chapel on Saturday mornings. I studied books on the topic that were available in the chapel's little library. I talked with and learned from regulars at the gatherings, some of whom had practiced this form of prayer for many decades.

After all my years of seeking God, my prayer experience had shifted from unsatisfying attempts to richly fulfilling encounters. My hunger for more continued and strengthened.

For a while I combined a practice of silent, listening prayer with attending services built around formal, set, spoken prayers: Morning Prayer, Evening Prayer, and Compline (a set of prayers offered before bedtime), in addition to Holy Eucharist (Communion). I joined a local Episcopal church, headed by a priest I had met through a friend. After a while I found that attending the Sunday Eucharistic service and sometimes a simple Eucharist during the week satisfied my need for formal prayer, and silent prayer became the backbone of my spiritual practice.

I came to feel that simply praying a list of requests was not the right approach for me. I believe that God knows the thoughts of all human hearts, and knows all our needs. Believers are therefore called to listen for God's whispered suggestions of ways to help bring about the kingdom of heaven rather than to offer God advice as to how things should work out, no matter how well intentioned. I found that the Eucharist was an important part of my spiritual practice, and that the formal, set prayers of a church service were remarkably helpful to me in times of spiritual dryness—but seldom in others. I spent some private moments making my requests known to God.[9] The rest of the time I tried to listen.

9 Even though I believe God already knows them, I still feel the need to pray that

I learned about the Roman Catholic monk Father Thomas Keating of Snowmass, Colorado, and his teachings on a form of this prayer known as centering prayer. I learned about the Shalem Institute and its teachings on a variety of silent-prayer forms through brief workshops and long courses. I attended a few half-day and day-long workshops led by Shalem, and they helped deepen my practice. In time I took an eighteen-month course from Shalem on leading prayer groups which I found a wonderful experience.

Early in my practice I often felt an intense sense of communion with God, which is typical for people embarking on this spiritual path, and I was granted a few powerful experiences of mystical union. These experiences never announced themselves and never involved any effort on my part.

Other than my original and life-changing conversion experience, the one that stands out in my memory took place on an early summer day, also in Maine. David and I had arrived the day before to vacation at our farmhouse. We awoke to the silent beauty of the island and, as was my custom, I walked from the farmhouse to our little guest cottage to sit in silence. I remember walking across a field bursting with wildflowers, sunlight everywhere around me, the air full of the smell of the sea at the edge of the field, an osprey offering its insistent cry as it circled over the waters of the cove. I was overflowing with happiness at the glory of creation and at the prospect of spending leisurely time together with David.

When I got to the cottage I lit a candle and a stick of incense, sat facing the sea, closed my eyes, and gave myself up to the wordless joy. After a bit I was suddenly overtaken by an immense power. What happened was indescribable, but perhaps can be hinted at by a metaphor or two. Imagine yourself sitting quietly in a friend's back yard beside a small blue plastic "kiddie pool" and suddenly finding yourself on the crest of an enormous ocean wave. Or imagine walking peacefully down a country road and suddenly being whirled up into the sky by a tornado.

Somehow I was aware that I had been pulled into, taken over by, the prayer of God—that eternal love-prayer among God the Creator, Jesus Christ, and the Holy Spirit. It filled my entire mind and my entire body. There was nothing present. . .except for Everything, a love-current of unimaginable power coursing through my being.

And it was terrifying. I was totally overwhelmed; there was no more "me" except for a tiny sliver, and that sliver felt it was about to be obliterated. I had never heard of anything like this before and thought perhaps I was going mad. In my fear I clutched violently at that tiny sliver, which was all that

---

they be granted. Some spiritual teachers believe what we think of as our prayer is actually God praying in us. Praying for others helps keep their needs alive in our hearts and often prompts us to render assistance ourselves.

was familiar, and I pulled out of the immense love stream with an almost audible "pop!" The moment I did so I regretted what I had done, but I could not rejoin the stream.

I have never had an experience like that again.

Spiritual teachers advise not to try to hold on to unusual experiences like this one. If you do, they explain, your prayer shifts from offering yourself to the Mystery to your own desires for more experiences. After I began working as a chaplain, I heard many accounts from patients and families of unusual encounters and saw many unusual things first hand. I've learned that the Mystery comes in ways that are exquisitely custom tailored to each of us, ways that we can't control no matter how hard we try.

But we can intentionally open ourselves to the Mystery. Silent prayer is one of those ways. I was taught that it has a few key features. First, it is a search for communion with God. Second, it is a prayer of inner silence, attempting to be free of the intent to tell or ask God anything and instead to simply listen for what may be given in the silence. Third, the praying person gives themself as fully as possible to the present moment, just as it is.

Opening ourselves to the Mystery is called by many names, including but not limited to silent prayer, quiet prayer, meditation, and contemplative prayer. The variations, complexities, and implications of each of these approaches differ widely across religious and spiritual traditions.

There are many good sources about how to practice some version of this form of prayer, and this book is not one of them. If the topic interests you, you might want to consult one or two of the books on prayer listed in the Bibliography. And if it doesn't interest you, don't worry about that. As spiritual teachers say, "Pray as you can and not as you can't."

Vulnerability in the Hospital

Hospital patients are consigned to remarkable anonymity. They are nude under the same flimsy and inadequate gowns, in interchangeable rooms; women are generally too sick to bother with makeup, men are sometimes unshaven, and the hair of both sexes is often uncombed or given only a cursory combing by a staff member. If a patient has been seriously ill for a while, you can tell because their hair is long; roots show if they have dyed their hair in the past.

Patients almost always have a standard-issue hospital bed, with an inflatable plastic mattress, white sheets, a white pillow, and an open-weave cotton blanket. Because they are so ill, most of the time they are prone, or propped up on pillows, often covered so that all that is visible is their head, neck, and part of one arm—the arm with the IV in it. The comforts of home are gone.

Their physical stripping reflects their mental and spiritual stripping. When I first entered chaplaincy training, I was disoriented by the lack of social clues available in patients' rooms; but I quickly discovered that this lack helped me to focus on the patient's spirit. From a spiritual perspective a patient's social and economic situation is generally of little importance at the end of life.

Whether rich or poor, at the end we all have vital work we need to do if we are to have a sense of completion. We need to find closure in our human relationships, by speaking words of love, thanking, asking forgiveness, forgiving, and saying goodbye. We need to review our own lives, seeking their meaning, discerning the purpose of our existence on this earth. We need to consider our deepest hopes and fears about the nature of the universe, and confront whatever it is that we believe will happen after we are dead. Obviously this is a tall order, and many dying people do not have the time or strength to complete these tasks before their life ends. But it is important to try. (It helps if you've gotten a head start on this process before you are dying.)

However, many dying patients focus intensely on social and economic issues. When they have heirs who are dependent on them for survival, that intensity is easy to understand. Guardians are needed for children, people who are physically or mentally disabled, and the frail or elderly; savings need to be parceled out; family treasures need to be disposed of.

Sometimes patients will die completely destitute. Consider Ms. Pounders, who had three underage grandchildren living with her. Her daughter was on crack, and these were her daughter's children. The patient's elderly sister was doing the best she could to care for the children while Ms. Pounders was in the hospital, but now it was clear that Ms. Pounders would never be able to leave. She hadn't paid her rent for several months, because she had lost her job due to absences caused by her illness, and her landlord had just notified her that she was being evicted.

There she was, helpless in bed, her sister reporting considerable trouble with the children who missed their grandmother. Two of the grandchildren were acting out dramatically. Moreover, her apartment was about to be closed and her worldly goods put on the street, with nowhere for her grandchildren and sister to go.

Although Hoshi was able to arrange foster care for the children, the situation was clearly a disaster for the entire family. Somehow Ms. Pounders accepted this dreadful reality, looking it in the eye, so to speak, and not blinking. You could see how much suffering she had endured in her life by the uncomplaining way in which she bore the stream of bad news. Only her grinding jaws hinted at her pain.

As was often true in this work, there was nothing I could *do*. I could only *be*. I would sit by her bed for half an hour or so a day, often not saying anything, just holding her hand, sometimes praying silently, sometimes not even doing that.

What amazed me was that while Ms. Pounders was aware of the bad events falling on four people she loved deeply, she somehow managed to keep that knowledge from overwhelming her. She did what she could to convey her love to them, welcoming them warmly when they came to visit, dictating to Hoshi brief letters of encouragement and appreciation to be given to them after her death, promising them that she would continue to watch over them from heaven. But she also kept some part of herself free to do a life review, to talk about good and bad things in her life, and to pray. When she died in the hospital—blessedly, one night in her sleep—I had the sense that she had done the work she needed to do and expired at peace. In human terms, she died with nothing. In spiritual terms, she died complete.

On the other hand, some patients had so many material goods that they remained caught up with them until the end. For example, we had a patient named Mr. Jessup who was eighty-seven, a gay man without a partner of either sex, and with a niece whom he disliked but who was his only heir.

Born into a wealthy family, Mr. Jessup had spent his life filling his large apartment with a remarkable collection of native crafts from around the world, all of which he had purchased himself directly from the artisans. With the passage of time, many of his pieces had become extremely valuable. When Mr. Jessup was informed by his physicians that he only had a few weeks to live and would be moving to in-patient hospice, he spent his time with me talking about what he would do with his possessions. With a shared interest in art, Mr. Jessup and I had become friendly, and he sought my advice about how to dispose of his collection. He was clear that he did not want it sold, with the proceeds going to his unloved niece.

"She'll be getting enough," he said dismissively. "I wish you could see how beautiful these things are," he would say, and describe wonderfully divergent Inuit, Australian Aboriginal, and ancient Mesopotamian works that he clearly loved.

I was eager for him to be able to arrange his worldly affairs. Once he disposed of things precious to him he could go about the psychological and spiritual work we all should do at the end of our lives if we are granted the time to do so. He needed to be able to tell the people he loved that he loved them, to ask forgiveness and to offer it as appropriate, to say thank you, and to say goodbye—the five last actions we all need to take. Mr. Jessup, however, stayed caught up in his *things*. After a while I began to suspect that thinking about them was a way for him to avoid facing the reality of his impending death.

The physician Elisabeth Kübler-Ross published a pioneering and highly influential study at the end of the 1960s of how people go about adjusting—or not adjusting—to their approaching demise. Her *On Death and Dying*[10] describes five emotional stages most of us go through when death approaches. Medical staffers sometimes refer to the five stages by the acronym DABDA, which stands for Denial, Anger, Bargaining, Depression, and Acceptance. As Kübler-Ross explains, people don't go through the stages in a strictly linear fashion. That is, they may move through them more than once, sometimes skipping a stage, sometimes getting stuck in one.

I found the stages helpful in my work. They enabled me to assess how a patient was progressing, and identify for myself what was going on in a patient's consciousness. For example, lots of people would tell me that they had promised the God of their understanding that, if allowed to live, they would devote the rest of their lives to teaching others about their disease. They were often extremely passionate as they described what they would do. Knowing that this was the Bargaining stage made it easier for me to listen supportively without getting overly caught up in what the patient usually came to realize was a fantasy.

The biggest challenge, from my perspective as a chaplain, was to support patients as they tried to move from Depression to Acceptance. I learned that people who are poor, people who have suffered deeply, often find it much easier to acknowledge and accept their mortality. Rich people, people who have not experienced deep suffering, who are used to having things their way, are sometimes so astonished when told they are going to die that they have great trouble facing that reality. Denying the approach of death can take so much energy that the denier has difficulty focusing on anything else. Yet it is possible for people to live fully into their death, so that they fully complete their life.

When he first came into the hospital, Mr. Jessup—the patient with the art collection—had no visitors. After his terminal diagnosis three men began visiting him daily. One pronounced himself a nutritionist and brought little containers of mashed vegetables to counteract the "simply dreadful" hospital food. The food *was* pretty dreadful. But Mr. Jessup felt the mashed

10. Kübler-Ross, *On Death and Dying*.

vegetables were no improvement, and they piled up in the refrigerator reserved for patient use.

Although at first I was delighted for him, happy that old friends had rallied around, a few encounters made me and my palliative care colleagues realize that these were not simply friends. Apparently Mr. Jessup's collection was well known in the art world, and his distaste for his heir well known among his acquaintances. Lonely Mr. Jessup was pleased to have these sympathetic men spending time with him. Two were partners, and the third—the self-styled nutritionist—was also single, like Mr. Jessup. It was this third man who worried us. We feared he was doing what he could to ingratiate himself in the hope that he would benefit from the patient's death.

Because the team had no proof that these visitors were malevolent, we could only watch and wait. And as was often the case when a patient was close to death, Mr. Jessup left for a residential hospice before anything was resolved, with the three friends promising to keep visiting him there after he moved. I contacted the chaplain at the hospice, commending Mr. Jessup to her care and suggesting that she keep an eye on the friends. He died within a week, and I never learned what happened to his art collection, nor to his friends. But I fear he died with his end-of-life work undone.

In contrast, consider Mr. Berry, a thirty-three-year-old from Appalachia whose body was ravaged by advanced AIDS. His nurse asked me to visit him, saying he wouldn't eat and spent all his time crying. When I went in his room I found a frighteningly skinny man lying on his side in a fetal position, elbows touching his knees. His shoulders were shaking as he wept.

I introduced myself and asked if it was okay for me to come in. He looked up at me and nodded. No tears were flowing from his blood-shot eyes: He had wept himself dry. I stood beside his bed, not too close, so as not to crowd him, but not too far away, to show I cared about his situation.

Out of politeness, people generally pretend not to notice if someone is crying, but his sobs were why I was there. "Mr. Berry, can you tell me why you are crying?" I asked.

"I'm afraid I'm dying." There it was, in plain view, the elephant in the room.

"Why do you think so? What do the doctors say?"

"They don't say anything, but I can tell by the way they look at me. And they don't come to see me much anymore." *This is a smart man.* Physicians often back off when they think a patient is terminal and nothing more can be tried to save their life.

"What do you think?"

"I don't want to die and I'm scared."

"Mr. Berry, I'm really sorry." I stopped for a moment. Then, "I wonder, can I ask you something?"

"Yes." He sniffed a huge sniff.

"Just for a minute, suppose you were dying, just suppose. I don't know what the doctors think, and I certainly don't want you to die. But if you were, is there anything you'd want to do before you died?"

He sat bolt upright in his bed. The top sheet fell away and I saw every rib in his emaciated and blotchy chest. "See my sister!" he said loudly.

"See your sister," I repeated. "Where is she?"

He named a place I had never heard of. When I asked where it was, he said about fifty miles from the hospital. Then we had a strange conversation. Did she have access to a car? Yes. Did she know how to drive? Yes. Then could she drive to the hospital and see him? Well, no. She didn't know he was sick. Hadn't he let her know? Well, no, they haven't talked for a few years.

Then he told me of their childhood together, how she was his big sister, how she had tried to protect him when their father had beaten them, and how sometimes she had taken a beating in his place. He grew more and more animated as he talked of her and how good she had been to him.

I repeated the same series of questions about driving and letting her know and got the same answers.

This doesn't make sense. What's the problem here? The answer came to me, as it probably should have earlier: The problem was his having AIDS. *He's ashamed.*

"Mr. Berry, would you like me to call her and tell her where you are?"

"Yes!"

I went through the legal questions required for me to tell her where he was and give her information about how to contact him. Then: "When we reach her, which I hope we will, is there anything else you want us to tell her?"

Instantly he replied, like a seven-year-old child, complete with a little whine in his voice, "Don't be *maaad*!"

Of course. He hasn't contacted her for so long that he thinks she'll be mad at him. Perhaps she will be. . ..

We did reach the sister. She was upset to hear the news of his grave illness, and she appeared at Mr. Berry's bedside the following day. After she left I stopped by his room again. He was sitting up in bed, his face shining.

"How did it go with your sister? Was she mad?"

"It was wonderful. She's going to visit me every day!" And she did.

By the end of the week Mr. Berry was dead, but before he died, he had completed some extremely important end-of-life-work. His sister knew he still loved her, she had forgiven him for dropping out of her life for so long, and they had said good-bye.

My Lady with ALS

A nurse asked if I had time to "see my lady." I said of course I did. Nurses usually ask for a chaplain's visit only when the patient is in genuine distress, although occasionally they will when he or she is particularly demanding or troublesome. Even then almost always some emotional or spiritual problem underlies the patient's behavior. The chaplain's job is to find it.

In this case the problem was clear. The nurse said Ms. Bren had gotten a final diagnosis of ALS just yesterday and was understandably hysterical at the news. ALS, or amyotrophic lateral sclerosis, is sometimes called Lou Gehrig's disease. It is a dreadful disease of the nerve cells in the brain and spinal cord that control voluntary muscle movement. It is a painful way to die.

I went into her room and for about forty minutes listened to Ms. Bren literally howling in despair. She interspersed her howling with compellingly vivid reflections on what she had lost and was losing. She could not walk, even though she loved walking in the beauty of nature; could not feed herself, even though she was an excellent cook; could not wipe herself after using the toilet even though she prided herself on her cleanliness.

In addition, she was helpless at the exact time when she and her husband were retiring to spend time together in their "golden years." They had recently sold their house and made an offer on an RV, which they planned to drive around the country, staying in RV parks, going wherever the spirit took them, and staying as long as they felt like it. Now all these plans were never going to be fulfilled.

Moreover, her blunt-spoken physician had just told Ms. Bren that her condition was "only going to get worse." She was full of vivid imaginings as to what getting worse would be like—the increasing pain she would be in, and how she would die. She said she had stayed awake all the previous night worrying about how things were going to be for her. We were about the same age, and her story of her hopes and her losses moved me deeply.

All this time she held my hand as I leaned awkwardly over the high railing on the side of her bed, which I had to do since she couldn't lift her hand. After a while my arm and back began to cramp painfully, but I could hardly complain under the circumstances. I just murmured "Mmm" and kept on holding her hand as she mourned her situation. All I could do was listen.

Her nurse was sitting just outside the door, monitoring our exchange. I found myself wondering what the nurse was thinking about this seemingly endless agony and how I was doing absolutely nothing to stop it. At one point her roommate got out of her bed, walked around the flimsy curtain separating her from Ms. Bren, gave me a dirty look, and said to her, "Now don't get so upset, dear."

I told the roommate that I was truly sorry for the disturbance but that the patient and I were okay and firmly encouraged her to go back to her bed, which she did with reluctance. Although I had no idea how the situation would resolve itself, I was certain that Ms. Bren had to be allowed to mourn as long and as loudly as she needed.

At one point Ms. Bren said she couldn't stop crying. I said I was crying too, which I was, and then a second later, to my horror, a tear fell from my cheek onto her top sheet. Hospital staff are extremely sensitive to bodily fluids because they can carry disease. It was unacceptable for a chaplain to expose a patient to the chaplain's body fluids, especially a patient who was paralyzed and unable to protect herself. I quickly reached down to the sheet with a tissue to wipe the tear away.

She saw me do that and said, amazed, "You really *are* crying!" Instead of coming up with some sort of appropriate pastoral response, I replied to her in my embarrassment just as I would have to my own sister: "I *told* you I was crying!" To my astonished relief she gave a surprised giggle in response; the giggle grew into a laugh and finally into an enormous belly laugh, powerful, deep and full, which was completely infectious. We roared together, making at least as much noise as she had earlier when she was crying out in anguish.

Sharing almost hysterical laughter with another person is both joyous and intimate. Turning from howling agony to howling laughter seemed to calm Ms. Bren down. During the luminous silence that often follows a time of uncontrolled laughter, we looked deeply into one another's eyes. In that moment of shared being, for some reason it became clear to me that she had suffered as a child. With no preliminary conversation on that subject, I asked her if she had had a hard time as a child. Right away she said she had been abused by an uncle. Without a break she went on to say that she wasn't taking pain pills unless she really needed them; nor was she taking anti-anxiety pills, because she wasn't anxious. Not anxious? She had just been howling with anxiety.

Was there any way I could help her get in better touch with her own feelings? "Awfulizing"—a word I had been introduced to in chaplaincy training—came to mind. It seemed to me a bad time to introduce Ms. Bren to a strange word; but the word came to me strongly and I couldn't come up with an alternative, so I followed my inner prompt. "Ms. Bren, have you ever heard the word 'awfulizing?'"

She shook her head.

"It's a weird word, but on occasion it can be helpful. Sometimes people 'awfulize,' meaning we think of every possible thing that could go wrong. I know I do it—usually at three in the morning. I worry and fret and think of all kinds of terrible things that might happen. Nothing good comes out of it. I just get upset.

"Sounds to me as if last night you were engaged in what is called situational awfulizing. You were thinking about your illness and thinking of everything that could possibly go wrong."

"Yes!" she replied. "Just yesterday my doctor talked about that. But he called it 'situational anxiety.' That's exactly what I was doing." She nodded her head. "Awfulizing."

The fact that her physician and I had come up with the same word—"situational"—made me feel I was right to listen to my inner voice. It is said that God uses coincidences when God chooses to be anonymous. I try to pay close attention to coincidences.

So we had named what was going on inside her, which was a good start. But there was more that we might be able to do. Her nurse had mentioned that she would be discharged in a day or two. If we were to do anything more I needed to try now.

Since she had brought it up, I decided to see if she could connect her childhood abuse to her present mental state. "Ms. Bren, I find myself wondering if you are being just as mean to yourself as your uncle was to you when you were a child?"

She gaped at me.

Am I doing the right thing? Is this best for her? I don't know, but it may be helpful, so here goes.

"Are you really a cruel person?" I asked. She had told me earlier of all the generous and thoughtful things she used to do for her neighbors and her church family before she got ALS. Obviously she was far from being a cruel person, at least to others.

She was shocked at first by the question, as I knew she would be; it was a calculated risk. *Is she going to throw me out?*

"You say you're not anxious," I continued. "You say you're not in pain. You don't let the doctors and nurses help you with medicine that will reduce your suffering and make things easier for you. Isn't that pretty cruel? Don't you deserve to be helped just like everybody else?"

She blinked and looked at me closely. "Am I really doing that? Making myself suffer?"

"Are you?" I replied. "Is suffering what you deserve?"

She stuck her jaw out. "No, it isn't!"

Whew. Look at that jaw stick out. Yay.

We talked for a little more. As we did it came to me that I needed to make sure she remembered the reality of her cruelty to herself so she would be more willing to ask for and accept help. Since humor had broken through her wailing, and since her vulnerable little-girl self was so clearly in the room with us, I said at one point, "I really want you to hear my voice in your ear about being kind to yourself. Will you?" And I made a pretend scary face at her, held up my hands like claws, and growled, "Grrr!"

She laughed, but said she would remember. We parted with her laughing and telling me she loved me, and my telling her the same.

The next day I went back to see her. This time she was with her father and mother, who had driven up from Georgia to see her. I didn't know which parent's brother was the abusive uncle.

Ms. Bren was eloquent about how much I had helped her, which was generous and touching. We teased one another about how "You made me laugh"—"No, *you* made *me* laugh." She claimed that she had heard me, that she was being kinder to herself, had asked for pain pills, and had taken anti-anxiety pills. I praised her decision to do so.

I asked her about her sense of where God was in her illness. I was concerned that she might think God had chosen to give her ALS, but apparently that was not the case.

Her doctor came in and changed some bandages. She hollered during the process, and I encouraged her to do so. I had no idea why she was bandaged. Fortunately the pain didn't last long. After the doctor left, the four of us talked more and prayed together.

All the time we were together, her mother kept trying to get Ms. Bren to lift her hand from where it was lying on top of the bed sheet. Clearly she couldn't believe that her formerly healthy daughter was now incapable of making such a simple gesture. She urged her to put her hand to her mouth. "Pretend you're eating an apple," her mother said several times. "Just lift your hand." But Ms. Bren's hand remained at her side; she clearly couldn't lift it. Finally her mother stopped and sat silent, looking rather cross.

However, when it came time for me to go, Ms. Bren slowly raised her hand from the bed sheet to her mouth, gave me a huge smile, and blew me a kiss—twice. Her parents looked amazed, and I certainly was. I had no idea what to say, so I blew her a kiss back and left the room. She left the hospital the following day, and I never saw her again.

I have no idea why Ms. Bren suddenly lifted her hand. It is possible that she could have done so all the time, but had been intentionally disobeying her mother's request, perhaps as one small way of maintaining her autonomy. Having even a tiny sense of being in control is important to people anywhere, and especially to people who are in the hospital. But she had been unable—or unwilling—to do the lifting when we were together the day before. Perhaps the deep bonding we had experienced in her wailing and our laughter had somehow given her the momentary capacity to raise her arm; I have no understanding of the physical process that made it possible. Sometimes people do inexplicable and wonderful things. I do know that love certainly helps.

Deep Diving

Over the years I've spent about two hundred hours scuba diving. One of the many fascinating parts of the scuba experience is the increasing quiet you encounter as you go further below the ocean's surface. I used to love to swim down to one hundred feet and simply float, holding my breath for a moment to eliminate the loud noise of my breathing and enjoying the enormous silence of the depths.

For me, one of the most remarkable things about encounters in the chaplaincy was how deep they could go in a matter of moments, even with complete strangers. Time seemed to be unrelated to the institutional clock on the wall. Silences were flooded with unspoken communication. The profundity of these encounters often felt like soul-to-soul exchanges.

Several factors influenced these encounters. One was the medications the patient was receiving, some of which can sharply reduce the usual self-protective barriers people erect between themselves and strangers. Another was the particular experience the patient was having. Giving birth, suddenly learning you have a serious family problem, and, especially, being told you have only a short time to live, jolts most people out of their usual protective shell.

Another cause of these profound encounters relates particularly to chaplains and mental health professionals. One of the skills we are taught is called reflective listening. It is a special way of being with someone. You listen intently and single mindedly to what they are saying and reflect their words back to them in a way that shows them how closely you have heard them. This reflection often enables them to become aware of what's going on inside them. Only when we are aware of how we feel about something can we go to the next step, which can range from simply experiencing the emotion in the presence of a sympathetic other person to taking some sort of action.

This listening skill, when well developed, can be very powerful. Indeed, during chaplaincy training we were told not to use reflective listening in our ordinary social encounters. Doing so might result in friends and acquaintances revealing personal matters at a greater depth than they would wish.

Another skill encouraged in chaplaincy training is the ability to be fully present to the other person—truly "there"—whether that person is a patient, a family member, or a fellow staffer. Although this sounds simple, it's in fact remarkably difficult. To be fully present means that you're listening with your whole heart. Some spiritual teachers say you must put your mind in your heart. That sounds like a figure of speech, but I found it a helpful instruction.

Listening with that intensity has both negative and positive components. On the negative side, you must completely ignore the little voice that says, "I'm hungry," or, "Doesn't she see that she's making her situation worse by those choices?" The thoughts still come to you, but you just let them pass by.

On the positive side, you open your heart to the other person, listening with both your mind and your feelings. You use your body as a kind of tuning fork to vibrate to the tune the other is singing through their words and very being. If they're angry, you may find your jaw clenching. If they're sad, you may feel tears in your eyes.

Most people have never been listened to in this way, and find that the experience of being truly heard by another's open heart opens their own in response. We all have a need to tell our feelings, our story, and be heard. When we are face to face with our mortality, that need is intense.

When I was allowed to hear another's story, my heart opened as wide as wide.

One other force causes chaplain encounters to go deep. It is, I believe, the intervention of what Christians call the Holy Spirit. This force is not under the control of the chaplain, or of anyone, but in my experience it is always present. Before going on duty I always offered my inner being to the disposal of the Spirit, and time after time I would find myself saying or doing things that surprised me but that opened a deeper level of communication between me and the other person. Several stories in this book provide examples of this phenomenon.

The profoundly intimate nature of these encounters puts a strong ethical demand on the chaplain. You must be exquisitely careful not to advance your own beliefs and instead help patients access theirs. Proselytizing, whether for a religion, a philosophy, or a point of view, is strictly forbidden. And whatever information the patient shares is confidential, unless he or she gives permission to share it. (As I explained in my introduction to this book, since nearly all my patients are now dead, I cannot ask their permission to share their stories here. Consequently I have gone to great lengths to change names and identifying details. But the essential nature of our encounters is unchanged.)

Over time, as I used reflective listening, listened with an increasingly open heart, and relied on the Spirit's guidance, I found to my surprise that people reacted differently to me. They opened up faster and went deeper.

After I had been a chaplain for several years, a dear friend said to me, "Joan, you've changed. I don't think you even know it, but you're different." When I asked her what she meant, she couldn't explain, and I certainly was not aware of it; but that difference manifested itself in the increasing intimacy of my encounters. Upon reflection, I suspect that was a result of my more open heart, and to my increasing attention to the presence and action of the Spirit.

Elevator Chaplaincy

A woman in her forties was waiting for one of the hospital elevators. She was carrying a small vase filled with yellow flowers and was looking at the floor. A couple of feet away, a young medical resident from India gripped the lapels of his white coat and frowned. Behind them, a balding man held the hand of a little boy who fidgeted with a brown paper bag. "So which elevator do you think it will be?" I asked the woman, but included the others in my glance.

"Huh?" She looked up, surprised.

"Elevator one, elevator two, or elevator three? Which do you think will come first?" I gestured at the three possibilities.

"Well, I don't know."

"Three!" the little boy said.

"I'll take number two," said the resident. The group sorted itself by preference, and when elevator three arrived the little boy looked proud as he received the others' congratulations.

A couple of hours later I was called to the bedside of a newly admitted woman who was actively dying. The balding man and the little boy I had met at the elevators were there, as her family. The boy recognized me and smiled, and the man nodded. Because we had already connected, albeit at a superficial level, our re-encounter at this painful time was a little bit easier for the family.

I found that this sort of "coincidence," where in my professional service as a chaplain I met someone I had just chatted with casually at the elevator an hour earlier, happened at least once a week. The odds seemed to be against this, as the hospital had hundreds of patients plus at least as many staff, students, and visitors, and I only took the elevator a few times a day. Nonetheless, it happened so often that I made a point of trying to interact with people whenever I was waiting for one.

I learned in clinical pastoral education that people sometimes say significant things in elevators, and experience taught me the importance of trying to establish a connection with everyone I encountered there. That meant, of course, breaking the taboo of speaking in a crowded, silent car, where everyone was facing front, eyes downcast. To that end, I sought and shared elevator jokes: simple, easy-to-understand punch lines that can unite an entire car in a shared groan.

Here's an example:

Question: How does the butcher introduce his wife?

Answer: Meet Patty.[11]

One good groan and passengers started talking to me and to one another, and the mood lightened. Often a visitor or staffer would get off the car with me and raise a matter that had been troubling them.

Of course there were times when bets on when the elevator would arrive and silly jokes were totally inappropriate. Whenever I saw a waiting passenger standing alone and looking disconsolate I would stand next to them and gently ask how things were going. Almost always people appreciated the inquiry and frequently would take the opportunity to share some of what was on their heart. A similar inquiry of a staff member sometimes got the response, "Right now *I* need prayer," allowing me to comply on the spot[12].

The hospital elevator is a liminal space between the impersonal outside world and the intimate inside world of fear and pain and hope. It is where we grit our teeth for what lies ahead, where just for a moment we have taken off one self-protective mask and not yet donned the next. In short, the hospital elevator was and is a surprising and powerful place for chaplaincy.

11 Finding jokes that are short, clear, and inoffensive wasn't easy. A website that I found helpful is http://Jokesbykids.com. The *Parade* Sunday supplement magazine occasionally had something worth appropriating. ("Meet Patty" comes from that source.)

12. If you speak softly it is possible to pray privately with another person, even in public.

Exorcism

"I know I called earlier this morning, but she's awfully anxious. Do you have any estimate as to when you can come, so I can tell her?" On the line was a nurse from 8 East, calling about a patient named Ruby Nelson, who wanted a chaplain visit—urgently. The palliative list was long, and she wasn't on it, but two calls from a nurse indicated a problem that needed prompt attention.

"Do you know what she wants?"

"She didn't say, but she seems frightened. She keeps buzzing, asking when someone's going to come."

"I'll come right now," I said.

The nurse gave me the patient's chart. It showed that Ms. Nelson was thirty-four, diagnosed with full-blown AIDS and manic-depression. She was on her third hospitalization that year.

I found a woman sitting straight up in bed, eyes wide open, dark skinned, her hair in corn rows but with a blur of strands escaping the tiny braids, showing it had been some time since the braiding had been done. I introduced myself. "Come in!" she urged.

I took a chair near the head of the bed. "What can I do for you?"

"You do exorcisms?"

Oh oh, this is way out of my league. I don't do exorcisms. I'm not sure I believe in them—but since I don't do them, that doesn't matter.

"I'm sorry, I don't."

"Is there another chaplain in the hospital who does?"

"Not that I know of. What's going on that you need exorcised?"

"The Devil."

"The Devil? What do you mean?"

"The Devil, he haunting me." She fixed her gaze on me and seemed both serious and frightened.

"Oh, my, that must be scary."

"It is."

"How long has the Devil been haunting you?"

"A long time. But he gotten worse since I in the hospital. I want someone to make him go away." She wrapped her arms around her chest, hugging herself in fear.

Although I fully believe in the existence of evil, I don't believe in a specific evil creature called "the Devil." But this young woman's fear was somewhat infectious. *I know there's a lot more to the universe than my rational mind understands. She's scared.*

"I believe some Catholic priests do exorcisms. Do you belong to a church?"

"I'm Baptist."

"Do Baptists do exorcisms?"

"I'm Baptist, but I don't belong to no church."

"So you don't have a minister you could ask."

"No."

We sat in silence, pondering the situation. Caught up by her intensity and the novelty of the situation, my mind went into full fix-it mode. Could the Catholic priest assigned to the hospital help her? He was greatly overworked and committed to serving Catholics. Would he be able to take the time to help a manic-depressive Baptist?

Suddenly Ms. Nelson whirled and pointed to the blank wall behind her bed. "There he is! You see him?"

I turned and looked with some trepidation, but saw nothing but a blank wall. "Nope."

"He there—right there!" She pointed at the wall again.

"I don't see anything, Ms. Nelson," I repeated, trying to sound strong and comforting, but now feeling rather anxious myself.

"He coming for me! You gotta' make him stop!"

How the heck am I going to do that? Now she was squatting on top of the mattress at the foot of the bed, her face to the wall. *I don't want to encourage her delusion, but she thinks she's seeing something and she's scared. Maybe there is some evil there. . .? What can I do?*

The only possible answer came to me in a rush, and I was shocked by my having totally missed it before.

I turned to face the wall and made a slow, ceremonial sign of the cross. "In the name of our Lord and Savior Jesus Christ, I command you to leave this woman in peace. Depart from her and never return. Never." I felt silly (*what on earth am I doing?*); scared (*I'm just a human being, and if there* is *a Devil I won't be able to defeat him*); way out of my comfort zone; and deeply grateful to be able to turn to Jesus. Evoking his name gave me confidence that all would be well, no thanks to me. I made the sign of the cross a second time for good measure and offered a quick prayer of thanksgiving.

Then I turned to Ms. Nelson, who was now cross-legged on the bed. "Do you still see him?"

"He gone."

Whew.

"I don't think he's going to come back, but if he does you can say what I said. Just say, 'In the name of Jesus Christ, I command you to depart and never return.'"

She repeated the phrase a couple of times.

"You can count on Jesus," I added. *After all,* I *did.* But it sure took me a long time that day.

Ash Wednesday

Most religions have one or more special periods set aside each year in which to particularly encourage worshipers to seek a closer relationship with the Holy. In Christianity, there are two such periods: Advent (before Christmas) and Lent (before Easter).

The first time I practiced what is known as a "sacramental" ministry was my first Ash Wednesday as a serving hospital chaplain.[13] Many churches hold a special Ash Wednesday service, which includes having a clergy person use their thumb to mark each worshiper's forehead with ashes in the form of a cross. The ashes are the sacrament. As the cross is made the administrator says, "Remember, you are dust, and to dust you will return."

I have always been drawn to the Ash Wednesday ritual. I like the intentionality of Lent, when we are encouraged to examine our lives, repent our wrongdoing, increase or intensify our spiritual practices, and so claim our desire to grow closer to God. The starkness and physicality of the ashes seem a good way to make the beginning of the holy period concrete and the worship service is a good time to formally state our intentions to God.

I knew that many members of the hospital staff were Christian, as were many of the patients. And for hospital patients or hospital employees, the latter often working twelve-hour shifts, the ashes had to be brought from church to the people if the people were to be able to receive them. My goal was to take ashes around the entire hospital and make them available to anyone and everyone. I wanted to be sensitive to religious sensibilities, assuring at least myself that I was "making them available" rather than "offering them."

I'm not sure there is a difference between the two phrases, but to my way of thinking one exists. While the ritual is not known in all Christian denominations, I knew some Christians would want ashes. I also knew that most non-Christians would have no interest in the ritual, and some might even be offended if it were offered to them.

13. Ash Wednesday marks the first day of the forty-day season of Lent, which culminates in the memorial of Jesus' Passion (his crucifixion on what Christians call Good Friday) and Resurrection (Easter, when Christians believe the crucified Jesus returned from death).

I went room to room and said something like, "Hi, I'm Chaplain Maxwell, and today is the Christian holy day called Ash Wednesday, the start of Lent. I have ashes if you would like them." Then I smiled and added, "and not if you wouldn't!" I was careful to make the offer inclusive of everyone in the room—family, friends, and staff, as well as the patient. If they were not interested I tried to exit both quickly and pleasantly, making it clear that their disinterest was fine.

I gave considerable thought to the words I would use for the imposition (what you say when you apply the ashes to someone's forehead). I asked my priest if there was a way they could be phrased to offer a word of hope, since I knew that some of the recipients would be near death, and of course others would be friends and relatives of people who were dying. After some discussion we came up with: "Remember that God formed you out of the dust of the Earth, and unto God you shall return." Much less chilling than, "Remember, you are dust, and to dust you will return," and yet it is the same message.

In my chaplaincy training I had learned that many hospitalized people with Christian backgrounds seem to have a particularly urgent desire to receive ashes. People who say they haven't been to church for a long time, even some who ask what Ash Wednesday means, can be as eager for ashes as those who say they've never missed an Ash Wednesday until they found themselves in the hospital.

One possible explanation for this urgency is the fact that for believers ashes are a tangible outward expression of an inward hunger for God. The experience of being in the hospital and becoming more sharply aware of one's mortality can bring one's spiritual needs very much to the fore.

So that first year, using a little screw-topped container of ashes (blessed by my church), I made ashes available to patients with heart problems, patients with cancer, psychiatric patients and parents in the Neonatal Intensive Care Unit, mothers proudly nursing their newborns and fathers watching in awe . . . and to every staff person I encountered, from physicians to housekeepers. I went to parts of the hospital I had never visited before—the pharmacy, the morgue, the laboratory, the information technology department, the custodians' storeroom. Some patients were too weak to lift their heads from the pillow, but lots of them wanted ashes. A few staff members were so pleased to receive them that they did a little dance in the corridor.

All those foreheads. . .so many different colors, some unlined, some oily, some sweaty, some with acne scars, some powdered, some with age spots, all pressing forward toward the ashes. Everyone closed their eyes except for the ICU nurses. They remained wide eyed throughout, looking over my shoulder to their patients' glass-fronted rooms, constantly on the alert for signs of a patient in trouble.

Giving ashes in a hospital includes a special requirement: not to spread infection from one person to the next. Since applying ashes requires a naked thumb, in addition to ashes I also took a supply of sanitizing wipes plus a dry paper towel. When a patient requested ashes, I unscrewed the container, sanitized my thumb on the germicidal wipe, and dried the thumb on the towel. Only then did I place the thumb in the container.

It was at this point that the experience sometimes became extraordinary. Because in these circumstances (in a hospital room rather than in a church service) there is no set religious ritual before the actual imposition, I decided to say, "Let us take a moment to become aware of the presence of God, who is always present, but whom we so often forget." The patient and I then were silent for a moment, eyes closed, and their deep yearning for the Mystery that is God would often become so strong that there was an ache in the air.

Then I said, "Amen," and made a cross on the patient's forehead, using the words that my priest had originally suggested: "Remember that God made you from dust, and to God you will return." The patient would smile or weep or whisper "Thank you," and I would pray silently in my heart for them, say goodbye, and move on to the next room.

What was fascinating to me was the idolizing of the ashes. For most people who wanted them, it was as if the physical ashes themselves held something of God. One nurse, Marguerite, told me of another nurse, Rhonda, who had missed me when I made my ashes rounds. Rhonda asked to rub her forehead on Marguerite's forehead so some of the ashes would rub off on her, meaning Rhonda would also "have" ashes! Another patient, an ancient lady who'd had so many facelifts almost no face remained, just a flat front to her head with eyes pulled into slits, asked if the ashes would "last" until the next day when her daughter was due to visit.

A fifteen-year-old girl who was eight months pregnant heard the announcement that ashes would be available. She called her nurse and said she wanted some even though she'd never had them before. When I went to her room, she said she did not know the Lord's Prayer and asked me to write it out for her, which of course I did. She declined to pray it with me but said she would pray it on her own that night. Even on the psych ward one nurse and two patients wanted ashes. The patients seemed rather bucked up by them.

Then there was the dying matriarch of a Hispanic family. Several people were in the room with her. Everyone asked for and got ashes, and then we offered the prayers for a person near death. She was one handful of dust who was already on her way back to God.

There was also a lovely man whom I had been seeing for a few weeks and who had just taken a major turn for the worse. His whole face was that terrible grey people get when they are near death. His lips had no color at all. Hospital staff were trying to move him, while still alive, into hospice. They were giving him more morphine. His wife, literally bowed down by grief, wanted ashes for herself and for him. Another handful of dust on his way, he died later that afternoon.

I must have given ashes to over one hundred people in the hospital that day. They wanted a *thing*, a fleck of God; none of this talk stuff, a *thing*. My job was not to listen, which it usually was, but instead to lead and give in the name of God—and then to move on to the next room. I felt quite used, as in used by God.

When I reflected on the experience, it bothered me that I had had to be much more in charge than I was normally, other than at deathbed services. The ministerial role seemed to leave less room for me to respond to the patients' own individual struggles and situations.

But eventually it came to me that my response was egotistical. During the ashes ritual, each person came to the God of their understanding in their own fashion and directly. My job was to give them the ashes and get out of their way. You might say I was the hostess, ushering them to their table in the spiritual dining room and then returning to the welcome desk. God, the chef, did the feeding, not me. A humbling realization.

Praying, Out Loud

One of a hospital chaplain's key duties is to pray at the request of others, addressing all manner of desires, hopes, and fears. Out loud. In front of other people. In front of strangers.

When I first started chaplain training I found the prospect of praying in public terrifying. I knew that most people I would encounter in the hospital would want spoken prayers that helped to express their hopes and fears, and to ask the Mystery to help them out. My goal was to gather and lift to God the spoken and unspoken desires of their hearts, weaving them together in language that manifested awe, trust, and love, and reflected a theology that was true to them and to myself.

I worried that I would start to pray and end up standing open mouthed, not knowing what to say, blurt out something that was not appropriate for the patient's situation, speak awkwardly (when I did manage speech), or just sound like an ignorant chaplain-in-training, which is exactly what I was. Moreover, in my New England childhood I had learned that religion was not to be talked about in public and that any sign of public piety was hypocritical and shameful. In other words, praying out loud was Just. Not. Done.

My first teacher of how to pray as a chaplain was a lovely, elderly Episcopal laywoman who believed that formal, written-out, so-called set prayers were the way to pray on behalf of others. This approach is true to the Episcopal tradition, which has an extraordinary collection of glorious prayers in its worship book, *The Book of Common Prayer*. My teacher collected prayers, wrote them on index cards, and carried them in her pocket. When someone wanted prayer, she would pull out her stash, pick the prayer she felt most appropriate for the situation, and read it out loud from the card.

I had mixed feelings about her method. On the one hand, the prayers she read were beautiful, the words lovely and calming, the theology clear, all appropriate to the patient's situation. And she always seemed very much in charge, a true professional doing her job well, which I aspired to be. On the other hand, she *read* the prayers. She read them skillfully, but they were written words given voice and didn't feel like prayer to me.

As an obedient student I emulated my teacher, copying some of her prayers and adding others I ran across, well-crafted petitions that had been written by church authorities and applied to the typical concerns of the sick. I carried a pile of prayer index cards in my pocket. Although they made my jacket bulge unattractively, the bulge was a professional necessity.

I hated reading the prayers from a card, feeling like an actor who didn't know her part, and definitely not feeling that I was praying. I tried to memorize a few prayers, but found that surprisingly hard to do. I was even more afraid of starting to speak a memorized prayer, forgetting the words, and having to pull a card from my pocket to make it to the end of the prayer. Suppose I had forgotten to bring the card—what on earth would I do then? I certainly would not look as if I were in charge, nor would I be a professional doing a good job. Too big a risk to take when I was trying to be of service to people who were suffering.

These concerns, which showed how little I trusted God, almost paralyzed me.

Some Christian traditions, including the Catholic and Episcopal ones, have spiritual directors. These persons help others who are seeking a closer relationship with God. They do not provide the direction themselves, but pray for guidance and share what is given to them out of their prayer.

About a year before I began chaplain training I was blessed to make a connection with a wonderful spiritual director. When we met together, as we did every month or two, she would pray spontaneously for me and for our time together. We sat across from one another, closed our eyes, prayed in silence; and at some point she would start to speak, not reading from a card but instead, it seemed, speaking from the gracious heart of God. My experience with her became the gold standard of prayer for me, and I longed to be able to pray that way with and for patients.

But in my heart I believed that since I was a fallible person and a long-time agnostic I had no reason whatsoever to expect words to be given by the Spirit. So I clutched my cards.

One day I found myself with a weeping patient who had just been told she was going to die very soon. None of the set prayers in my bulging pocket seemed appropriate for her situation. I knew that *I* could do nothing whatever to help her, that the only place she could turn for solace was to God. The knowledge of my complete helplessness, combined with her dire situation, reduced me to silence.

Standing before the patient, my eyes closed and without any words to offer on her behalf, I was momentarily tempted to fill the silence by reciting the Lord's Prayer, which I had memorized as a child. But for some reason it felt wrong to do so. Finally, from somewhere deep inside me, words seemed to rise. I opened my mouth and let them come out. It was like freeing a bird from its cage: I opened the door and out flew the prayer. I didn't plan the words, or think about them, or even listen to them; I just let them come out like an exhalation of breath. I have no idea what I said. Nor do I know how long the prayer lasted.

I do know that when the words stopped coming, I stopped speaking and opened my eyes. To my amazement I saw that the patient had stopped crying and was herself praying silently.

When the visit ended, I went to the hospital chapel to give thanks for the grace of being permitted to serve my patient in that fashion.

Over the years I have come to know that words will be given to me if I just get out of the way. I stopped using the index cards. I stopped using the "forms" of the set prayers. I simply listened to the patients with an open heart. When they asked me to pray, I went to an inner state of prayer, opened my mouth, and prayer came out. Spoken prayer on behalf of patients became a time when I turned off my mind and let my heart speak. Sometimes the words were awkward, and sometimes there were silences. But I saw that those stumbles and silences were an inevitable part of genuine prayer.

Before I began I would have a general idea of what the patient wanted me to pray for. Frequently I said something like, "Can you tell me what you want the prayer to include?" and I'd be sure to include that request in the prayer. But I did not have any sort of an outline, or even a general plan.

Usually I could not even recall what I had said. . .because the prayer wasn't really originating from me.

Yet even today, when there are large numbers of people around me at a worship service or a memorial service, knowing that trying to remain in a state of prayer despite the noises and movements of the crowd will be challenging, I will sometimes prepare a prayer to speak. I don't know why I still think that it all relies on me.

I happened to meet an Episcopal priest named Debbie Little, who had been actively serving homeless people for many years. I went with her on her rounds to observe her ministry. Invariably she made a great effort to get the other person to lead the prayer. She explained that she always learned a lot from the other person's prayer, about them and about God.

While I was pondering this, I noticed something about myself. My own personal prayer life had changed, had gotten somewhat richer, and I wondered why that was. I hadn't changed any of my personal spiritual practices. After some reflection, it came to me that perhaps this was because I was spending a great deal of time praying out loud in the hospital. And these spoken prayers were usually built around patients' requests for healing for themselves and blessings for their loved ones.

Since my own private theology of prayer was not based on this, I was surprised that my practice would have affected my own spiritual life. Nonetheless, there was a positive difference. This seemed wrong to me: Why should I benefit in this way when I was trying to support suffering patients in *their* prayer lives?

So I decided to try Debbie's approach. At first I felt uncomfortable. The patients I was praying with were usually weak and feeling vulnerable, and they rarely agreed to lead the prayer without a little push from me. Early in this experiment, however, I had an experience that kept me on this path. I was seeing a homeless lady in her late forties, with full-blown AIDS, a lively faith, and innumerable family and personal problems. But somehow she had that spark of life that is a joy to see.

When she wanted to pray, I said to her, "Are you gonna' lead the prayer?"

She replied, "I can't. I don't know how to lead prayer. I know all these people at the shelter can lead prayer, but I can't."

Hearing her speak of a perceived barrier between herself and God distressed me. I knew I couldn't make her life better, but I was resolved to at least help her feel empowered to lead prayer. I said, "You know, it's really easy. You start by naming who you're praying to. Then you say what's in your heart. Sometimes you say, 'Thank you.' Then you say, 'Amen.'"

"What do you mean 'name?'"

"Well, do you call God 'God,' or 'heavenly Father,' or 'heavenly Mother,' or 'Allah,' or 'Holy One, or . . . "

"What do *you* call God?"

"It doesn't matter what I call God, it matters what *you* call God. When you pray in your heart, I mean?"

"'My heavenly Father.'"

"Great. You can start by saying, 'My heavenly Father.'"

She looked at me, openmouthed, then slowly whispered, "My heavenly Father." Then she looked at me again.

"What's in your heart? Just say what's in your heart."

And she began praying, first uncertainly, and then with greater and greater conviction, a beautiful prayer that was a pleasure to share. She ended the prayer by saying, "Thank you. Amen." Then she turned to me, eyes shining. "I did it!" she exulted.

"You sure did!" I agreed.

The next time I went to see her she was about to leave the hospital for hospice. We talked a little bit, and then the ambulance crew came for her. I took her hands and suggested prayer. "Who's gonna' lead?" I asked, hoping but uncertain.

"Me," she said resolutely, and again offered a heartfelt prayer. When we hugged goodbye I said, "Remember, now you can always lead prayer, wherever you are."

"I know," she said calmly, gathering up a plastic bag containing all her worldly possessions. She climbed on the gurney to go to hospice and die.

Ever since that encounter I became more and more convinced that encouraging the other person to lead the prayer was an important pastoral act. Occasionally there was a patient who happily claimed the leadership role, sometimes offering a formal prayer in a rote gabble but sometimes offering a glorious prayer. But most of the time I had to encourage them.

For example, once I was visiting a terrific great-grandmother in the ICU. She responded to my question, "Are you gonna' lead the prayer?" with a soft, "No, you."

I had observed that, although weak, she was functioning fairly well, so I said, "Tell you what. Why don't I pray first, and then you? Would that be okay with you?"

She nodded, a little reluctantly but a nod nonetheless, so I prayed. When my prayer ended, I stopped, leaned over the bed rail and put my ear about a foot from her mouth. There was a brief silence. Then she started to pray in a soft voice. It was a short, moving prayer. When she stopped, she leaned back and looked at me, a faint smile on her lips. "Thank you for praying with me," I said.

"You're welcome," she said, and we grinned at one another.

Facing an Amputation

She was in her early fifties, younger than my usual patients, swollen from weeks of IV infusions, greasy long hair badly in need of washing, with a loud, abrasive personality that inadequately concealed immense need. Tomorrow the doctors were going to amputate her right leg, after weeks of trying and failing to eliminate the infection eating away her bones. I was in my first phase of chaplaincy training, and she, in turn, was the living human document, my teacher.

Together, in silence, we regarded the substantial mound of her leg under the bed sheet. She looked at it with a strange combination of desire and disdain, which I later learned is not uncommon among patients facing amputations. The desire reflects the fact that it is part of the patient's very self that is going to be excised. The disdain reflects an interesting progression: The patient is beginning to accept that that part must be removed for the rest of the self to go on living.

Each amputation case is different, of course. Sometimes the patient is eager to get rid of the cancer or the gangrene or whatever it is that necessitates the procedure. Sometimes the patient is so attached to what the body part represents to them—maternity in the case of a prospective hysterectomy, freedom of easy movement in the case of a leg amputation—that the attachment overwhelms the comparatively abstract knowledge (often denied) that its removal is necessary for survival.

Over the course of this patient's hospitalization, we had talked a lot about her fierce commitment to saving her leg, her willingness to endure multiple operations, her fortitude under the onslaught of debilitating drugs. She had cried, yelled, sworn. Now she suddenly threw herself into my arms and wailed, "No one will want to love me anymore!"

I was astonished. Among the myriad of things I had never thought about was that this amputation was not only ending her easy mobility but also her sense of herself as a sexually desirable woman. Foolishly, because of her unappealing physical appearance and her difficult personality, I had never thought of her as a sexual being. I couldn't think of anything "helpful" to say, thank heaven; so I shut up, listened, and learned as she cried out about how her current "friend" would no longer want to make love with her.

It was a powerful experience for me, and it made me more aware of the diverse concerns of people facing amputations. I also learned that ritual could offer solace, including to patients who were not particularly "religious." Depending on the patient's wishes, I might offer a prayer that thanked the Creator for the many specific gifts the to-be-amputated part had given the patient. Even a diabetic's departing toe has been a gift (perhaps it once was a "little piggy [that] went to market," lovingly counted by the patient's mother). Thanking God and the part itself for its gifts could become like a little funeral, giving an opportunity for conscious mourning in the presence of God.

For some patients, a formal anointing of the departing part with holy oil, evocative of the anointing that can be given to a person near death, was a meaningful pre-amputation ritual. This can be combined with the prayer of thanksgiving mentioned above. A friend of mine with an active street ministry first suggested this approach to me. Initially I was rather skeptical, but I found that patients often responded eagerly to the offer of anointing, including patients from a wide variety of religious traditions, and some with no religious tradition at all. The tangible nature of the anointing was a big part of the appeal, I think, like the ashes I offered on Ash Wednesday, which many patients sought so eagerly.

I once had a young chaplain colleague tell me that she had been visiting a woman about to get a mastectomy. After a prayer of thanksgiving for the gifts of the breast, the patient had asked that the breast be anointed. My colleague said she hesitated, concerned about potential liability for sexual harassment, but decided that the request came from a deep place in the patient and complied; she carefully placed the oil on the appropriate side of the patient's chest just below the collar bone. After the surgery the patient told my friend that the anointing had provided her with real comfort and had helped her begin to accept the loss.

Sometimes Psalm 139, especially verses 13 and 14, could comfort a patient for whom Scripture was important:

> For it was you who formed my inward parts;
>   you knit me together in my mother's womb.
> I praise you, for I am fearfully and wonderfully made.
>   Wonderful are your works;
> that I know very well. (Ps 139:13–14)

The Crow

I was asked to see a one-hundred-and two-year-old woman nearly blind from macular degeneration and extremely hard of hearing. She had been living alone in an apartment with a home nurse coming in for four hours every day, a dangerous and frightening situation for such an aged and fragile person. Two days earlier she had fallen from her chair and broken her pelvis. She was brought to the hospital for stabilization and pain control before being sent to an assisted living facility. I had no idea about her mental status.

When I got in the room I said loudly, so she could hear me, "Ms. Dana, I'm Chaplain Maxwell, one of the hospital chaplains. Is this a good time for a visit?"

Slowly she raised her ancient head, which had been slumped forward on her chest. She opened her eyes, looked at me, opened her mouth wide, and said, extremely loudly, "CAAAW!" Her head fell back to her chest.

I thought perhaps she was teasing me, or testing me, so I said, "Ms. Dana, is there something I can do for you?"

Again she raised her head opened her eyes, looked at me, and croaked, "CAAAW!"

I had to bite my lip to keep my composure. The violent cawing sound coming from a tiny pale old lady was so incongruous it was nearly impossible not to laugh. But then I was seized by a thought. *Suppose she is "in there" mentally and this is the only way she can communicate? Perhaps her aged brain is so disoriented that she thinks she is speaking in a language I can understand. And I'm not replying to whatever it is that she's saying. What's that like to experience?*

All the humor drained out of the situation. My heart went out to her, totally isolated as she was in her collapsing body and by her inhuman voice, with nothing left to do but die. And how long would that take? I went to the side of the bed and gently slipped my hand under hers. She twisted her drooping head to look at me and once again uttered her cry, squeezing my hand as she did so. I was grateful for this little sign of connection and ashamed of my initial impulse to laugh. Then her head fell forward again, so her face was only an inch above the sheet covering her chest.

I stood by her bed, holding her thin, cool hand, unable to do anything else other than breathe. Her legs were uncovered, her calves like straight sticks. Pink heel pads (for protection against bedsores) cradled each foot, displaying deformed big toes that twisted nearly at right angles to the rest of her foot, crossing over the other toes, each of which had crumbling nails at their tips. *How can she still be alive? What is it like to be her?*

Ms. Dana slept quietly, only occasionally rousing herself to "CAAAW!"

Eventually a nurse came in to change her bed linen, and I was thankful to be able to leave. For the rest of the day I was shadowed by the memory of her dreadful state—deaf, blind, in a decaying body, unable to speak.

Ms. Dana's heartbreaking situation was not, alas, unique among my patients. Again and again I encountered suffering about which I could do nothing other than to bear witness and pray to the Mystery. Sometimes I felt jammed full of others' suffering. There were times when I desperately needed to be able to talk with a trusted person about what I had witnessed. This is a common problem among those of us working with people who are gravely ill.

I was lucky to have a spiritual director and a clergy friend who listened with compassion and understanding. They were safe because, as clergy, they were sworn professional confidence-keepers. Both had considerable experience working with dying persons. I don't know what I would have done without them.

Dead Bodies

The first dead body I touched was my mother's, warm and soft. But when it was clear she was dead, I was quickly taken away.

My brother's body was cremated before his memorial service, so I never saw it. When his widow scattered his ashes, I stood near her; the wind changed as she scattered and we both breathed in a few bits of him. Neither of us coughed.

The second dead body I touched was my father's, on a sheet-covered gurney in a funeral home. I touched his lips and was startled by how cold and hard they were.

All the other dead bodies I have touched were bodies of patients who had just died.

In chaplaincy training we were told to touch dead bodies as a way of encouraging families and friends to do the same. Many people have a superstitious fear of touching the dead, as if death can somehow be "caught" by touch. A body that has been dead for a while can indeed be dangerous as it starts to decompose; but the body of a newly dead person is safe to touch for a few hours if the deceased didn't have an infectious disease. Families and friends who are seeing someone they loved for the last time often benefit from touching their body. It is a way of absorbing that the person is really, truly dead, a way of saying goodbye, a way of expressing love when words have become completely useless.

When I first heard this wisdom about touching, I didn't pay much conscious attention to it. I was training in a community hospital, and people did not die there very often. When they did, a senior, experienced chaplain was invariably at the bedside, not a newbie like me. A few times I was invited by our training supervisor to join him and a family in a deathbed ritual after a patient had died; but the supervisor, not me, had been present for the death, and my duties at the ritual were simply to observe and serve as back-up support for the family.

The death of the first patient for whose family I served as primary, sole chaplain came as a surprise. I had completed my training and was walking down the corridor when a nurse came up to me and said, matter of factly, "Chaplain, they need you in 82. The patient just died." I nodded and tried to look matter of fact myself.

When I went into Room 82, an ancient-looking man with a gaunt, grey face was lying still in the bed. Even I could tell that he was dead. Two women in their fifties, standing by the side of the bed, looked at me with an eagerness that felt at the time rather odd but that I subsequently learned is relatively normal. When you are standing at the bedside of a person who has just died, your senses are on high alert, you are totally exhausted, and the arrival of a new person can be a welcome distraction.

I had never met this patient when he was alive, so I had no sense of personal loss. He was simply a dead person, and there were living persons grieving. It was easy to connect with the two women—who were, they explained, the man's daughters—offer my sympathy, and ask if they wanted a religious service at the bedside. They did not want a formal service, but asked me to pray at the bedside.

As I prayed, remembering my training I consciously placed my hand on the thin cotton sheet covering his upright foot. I felt uncomfortable doing that, as if I were violating the man's privacy. After all, I had never met him when he was alive, yet now was touching him without asking anyone's permission. I recalled, however, my training supervisor's counsel that such an act would be a service to his family.

I glanced at the daughters to see if their faces expressed any objection to my touching their father; they did not. Because he had only just died, his foot felt cool through the sheet, but not cold. I tried to keep my touch as light as possible, more a blessing touch than a regular touch. I tried not to be distracted by the feeling of his bony dead toes under my hand. . .oh my, so much trying. I was glad to see that the daughters soon also touched their father during the prayer.

Soon the prayer was over. The daughters stayed, then the morgue attendant came for the body and they all left. And that was the end of my first experience of presiding over a deathbed scene.

Over time, as deathbeds became part of my regular work, I found that when I touched a patient's dead body—a foot, a shoulder, a hand—it often felt as if I were breaking whatever taboo was preventing the others at the bedside from touching the body. After I touched, they usually would touch. It was a little gift I could offer out of respect for people who were only beginning to absorb the fact that the person they loved, alive just moments ago, was now dead.

Most major religions encourage the devout to contemplate death and, in some cases, dead bodies. In present-day American society, death-denial is so strong that we often lose sight of our mortality and live as if our own lives will continue forever. The act of considering the inevitability of our own death can encourage us to live our lives more fully, more intentionally, more generously. As the eighteenth-century philosopher Samuel Johnson said, "Depend upon it, sir, when a man knows he is to be hanged in a fortnight, it concentrates his mind wonderfully."

A good friend, a physician in his eighties, once told me of the first time he saw a dead body. It was his first day in medical school, some sixty years earlier. He and his classmates (all male, of course), stood in a row against the wall in a classroom. A sheet-covered gurney dominated the middle of the room, and they could tell by the shape that there was a figure under the sheet. The professor walked over to the gurney and said, "Gentlemen, meet the enemy you will be fighting for the rest of your lives." He pulled off the sheet with a dramatic flourish, and there was the dead body.

The student next to my friend fell in a faint at the sight. "He became a gynecologist," my friend recalls.

Everyone's life is limited. If we wish to live as fully as possible, it is good to be fully awake to what is, right now: the present moment which will never return.

Being with a dead body can help focus the mind on our mortality and on the preciousness of what time we have. Some Buddhist practices encourage monks to sit with dead bodies, sometimes for several days. In many Christian monastic communities, the members sit in vigil with the body of a monastic brother or sister who has died. This vigil is both a sign of respect for the one who has died and a lesson for those who are still alive.

I was both inspired by these spiritual precedents and aware that I was one of relatively few modern-day Americans with many occasions on which to be with dead bodies outside of a war zone or a natural disaster site. I therefore tried to make use of these occasions for my own spiritual growth. From time to time, when the morgue attendant was delayed in coming to pick up a body, the patient's family would ask me if I would stay with the corpse until the attendant came to pick it up—while they went home to grieve, eat, and rest.

Naturally I obliged, and after our farewells I sat alone in the room with the newly deceased patient. The dead person's nurse, who had other, living patients to attend to, closed the door to the corridor. If there was a window from the room to the corridor, she pulled the curtain to respect the privacy of the deceased and to spare passers-by the sight of a corpse.

I never found the presence of a dead person frightening. I would take a chair and sit a few feet away from the body, at right angles to the head. I'd begin my vigil by closing my eyes and scanning the atmosphere in the room to see if I had a hint of the presence of the former patient. I never did.

Then, in silence, I would offer a simple blessing and a prayer for his or her wellbeing and peace. I do not believe in hell or purgatory. I do believe that a person who is no longer alive continues in some way, but I have no idea how. Or, rather, I have lots of ideas, but I don't know what is actually the case. Of course, no one else does, either.

After that, I opened my eyes and looked at the body. Usually the face and an uncovered arm would be visible. I would look from my hand to the patient's hand and back again, reminding myself that one day my hand, although warm and responsive at the time, would be as still and waxen as was the patient's. This was a sobering thought.

Sometimes I played with the skin on the back of my hand, pinching it between my fingers, imagining how the dead body's skin would feel by contrast. Of course, while I was alone with it, I never touched the body. There was no religious reason to do so, and touching it for my own curiosity would have been an inexcusable violation of the dignity and privacy of both the deceased and their family. Then, eyes closed and in silence, I would offer my spirit to the Mystery on behalf us both, trying to be open to anything that might be given.

Usually the man from the hospital morgue would show up while I was deep in silence, his arrival announced by the sharp rattle of the gurney in the outside corridor (I never saw a woman perform this task). When he arrived my duty was done and I was free to leave.

A few times I remained in the room while he performed his task. He would place his cargo in an opaque white bag made for this purpose, roll it onto the gurney, and drape both body and gurney with a large, thick, black rubber cover. Somehow the top surface of the cover remained flat, so there was no indication of what lay beneath it. When he pushed the loaded gurney back down the corridor toward the rear staff elevators, visitors would walk by without a glance. Only hospital personnel knew what was hidden beneath the black cover.

There is a saying: "The crack is how the light gets in." I wonder if perhaps my relative comfort in sitting quietly with dead bodies might stem from the fact that at such an early age I had experienced, although briefly, being with my mother's.

On the Vent

When I first started working as a chaplain-in-training, our supervisor forbade all of us trainees to go into the Intensive Care Unit. "That's a place where I don't want any of you to go until—unless—I give you specific permission. All the patients in there are in an extremely delicate condition, and the nurses don't need anyone in the way." I was eager to develop sufficient competency as a chaplain to be allowed to work in the ICU.

Occasionally I had to go into that unit to check on the post-surgical progress of one of the patients assigned to me. But when I did I was careful to talk only to the clerk at the nurses' station and stay well out of the way of everyone else. While waiting to talk with the clerk, I would turn my head to look through the glass walls that separated the intensive care rooms from the corridor. Patients had no privacy except for when they were actively being cared for, at which time a white curtain would be pulled across the inside of the glass wall.

Almost always patients were lying flat, seemingly asleep. I learned that many of them were in drugged states to prevent them from fighting with the tubes that often invaded nearly all their body orifices. Every patient had a thin tube (known as a "line") running into the back of their hand or the crook of their elbow—or sometimes going into their chest or neck. At the other end of the line was a bottle or a plastic bag hanging from an IV apparatus, a tall metal pole on four short legs, each leg ending in a wheel to allow the pole to be easily moved. Sometimes the pole had a stack of light tan boxes mounted on it, each one blinking and sometimes beeping. These boxes precisely governed, drop by drop, the delivery of whatever medications the patient was receiving through the line. When the line kinked or was blocked for some reason, the alarm on the box would beep loudly. Eventually a nurse would adjust the line and silence the alarm. The alarms sounded frequently, increasing the sense of tension that pervades all ICUs.

Those annoying beeps were also common on floors housing regular patients. The ICU's special noises were loud, steady alarms. They sounded when there was a problem with an artificial ventilator. A "vent" is a machine with a rhythmic bellows that forces air into a patient's lungs through a tube that either goes through their mouth and down their airway or is inserted directly into the airway via a tracheostomy: a hole cut in the front of the base of their neck. Patients on the vent were unable to breathe on their own; if they started to do so it was a sign that they were getting a little stronger. However, patient-directed breathing could upset both the patient and the machine, since the patient's natural rhythm often conflicted with the machine's. It took a special act of will for a non-comatose patient to trust the machine and not breathe on his/her own. Heavy sedation was often used to prevent patients from "fighting" the vent.

I myself have had a few major surgeries, so I know I have been "intubated" in the fashion I've described; thanks to sedation I have no recollection of the experience. But it was frightening to imagine what it would be like to wake up and find a tube in my throat and air rhythmically invading my body. Many ICU patients had that experience, and I hoped that perhaps I might be able to comfort them.

After I finished my first course in chaplaincy training, I was pleased to be allowed to go into the ICU, at first just occasionally and then as a matter of routine. Over time I learned more about the medical equipment commonly used in the unit. Most patients had catheters to divert their urine into containers. The containers were usually on the floor beside the bed, partly covered by a towel, and I sometimes took a quick side glance at the contents as I walked in the room. Urine with blood in it or a strange copper color signaled problems. Some patients (not many) had rectal tubes to divert their feces into other containers. Several had what were called "wound vacs," machines that drew excess bodily fluid from recent surgical incisions. Occasionally a patient was given dialysis at the bedside to clean their blood of impurities not removed by malfunctioning kidneys. Other strange machines sometimes whirred next to the bed.

For me as a chaplain, the most significant machine was the vent. Even if they were awake, patients on the vent couldn't talk (except for a few who had what was called a speaking trach, quite uncommon). That meant that the patients were often extremely frustrated, wanting to say something but unable to do so. I was particularly drawn to people in this situation, and spent a good deal of time exploring ways to help them express what they wished.

The first and most obvious way was to read their eyes, their faces, and the grimaces they made with their mouths around the invasive tube. When a patient on the vent was awake, I would lean over the bed rail, look into their eyes, and smile gently to show I was harmless. My first job was to ascertain whether my visit was welcome. Often I was a total stranger, and ICU patients were helpless in the hands of total strangers. I would introduce myself slowly and clearly over the whoosh of the vent. Doing this was like jumping into a lake. Would the water be warm or cold, deep or shallow? I needed to react appropriately, however the patient chose to respond.

Usually, but not always, I was welcomed by a small nod. Occasionally a patient would give me an awkward smile around the breathing tube despite the discomfort of doing so. Sometimes they would start to cry. The drugs they were on often made them more vulnerable emotionally, but sometimes their tears expressed their pain, fear, and/or hunger for the sacred. Trying to discern the nuances was both difficult and fascinating.

In each visit with a patient on a vent, I was alert to three issues. The first and most immediate was whether the patient was in pain, physical or spiritual. To my surprise, many patients who managed to communicate reported no physical pain. But occasionally something about a patient's expression would suggest to me that they *were* in pain, and when I asked if that were the case, I'd receive an affirmative nod or grimace, and I would pass that information along to their nurse.

The second issue was whether the patient wanted me to pray for them. I had a horror of praying for patients who didn't. For an atheist, or for a person whose religious tradition taught that only prayer from a co-religionist would be acceptable, having prayer thrust upon them when they were completely helpless could be a strong spiritual violation.

Some people are so convinced of the importance and power of prayer that they believe praying for anyone is an act they are called by God to perform. Indeed, occasionally a visitor (usually a man) who was a believer would go from the room of the person he was visiting to other rooms nearby and start praying, usually loudly, for the patient there. Fortunately, uninvited visits by outsiders, however good the intention, were forbidden in the hospital. Such visits violated the patient's privacy, risked the spread of infection, and could upset the patient emotionally or physically. I would quickly escort the "believer" out, explaining the hospital rules as I did and thus avoiding a confrontation or a theological discussion.

In my ICU visits, some patients made it immediately clear that prayer was what they wanted. In such cases I needed to find out their religious tradition, if any, and what they'd like the prayer to include. I could usually figure out religious preference by naming the major traditions until they nodded or blinked: Christian (the majority)? Jewish? Muslim? But learning their prayer request was sometimes difficult. They couldn't speak, and often had great difficulty writing. Since I found it hard to read someone's lips, especially when they were pursed around a tube, I had to be utterly focused on the patient.

I received a helpful lesson when I was first learning about contemplative prayer. It went like this. "Have you ever seen a frog on a lily pad? The frog is completely still, so still that often you don't even see it sitting there. Yet it is fully alert to everything that is happening around it. And when a little bug passes by: zap! Out goes that long frog tongue, and the frog grabs the bug. The stillness, and the focus, are what enable it to catch the bug. That stillness and that focus are what you are invited to practice in contemplative prayer."

That same stillness and focus were necessary if I was to learn the patient's wishes. I would bend toward them, remain immobile, and train all my senses on them. The voices, beeps, whooshes, cart rattles, and other ICU sounds, lights, and smells would fade into the background. I would open my spiritual heart to try to receive the patient's desires, and at the same time try to listen for any hint from the Mystery as to what was called for in that situation.

As you might expect, patients who could speak most commonly requested healing. But often patients wanted prayer not for themselves but for their families and other loved ones; sometimes, for all people who were sick. A few times they wanted me to pray that they would die very soon.

The last request I mentioned was the only difficult one. The medical system valued life, as did I, and my job was to support patients in the context of that system. But I knew that on occasion, instead of sustaining life the medical system prolonged the dying process. What I didn't know were the circumstances of that particular patient.

And even if I had known them, I was not the Lord of Life. I lifted the patient's prayer to the Mystery, saying something like, "Loving God, you know the prayer of your beloved Lenny. He yearns to be home with you. We know that in your infinite mercy you hear his prayer. When it is your holy will, we ask that you bring him into the peace of your loving arms."

If you're a careful reader, you've noticed that this is something of a weasel prayer. I didn't pray for Lenny to die right then, because I couldn't do so in a clear conscience. But I knew that at some point the patient would die, as will we all, and because I do believe that God is loving and merciful, I believe that death leads us into peace. I prayed according to Lenny's request as fully as my conscience would allow.

I believe that God hears all prayers, spoken or unspoken, put into words or simply felt as a yearning or an aching. I also believed that whenever I prayed, God already knew both my prayer and the prayer of the person who had asked me to pray. In a sense you could almost say I didn't believe my prayers mattered to God. Rather odd, that, since I spent much of my time praying spontaneous prayers aloud, with a full and sincere heart, at the request of others.

But I did recognize that my spoken and unspoken prayers mattered to the people who asked for them. Through the work of the Spirit I sometimes expressed in spoken prayer the hopes of their hearts. This often resulted in a response that, although common, is rarely mentioned because it is both disconcerting and a constant temptation to the ego. Through what psychologists call projection, some people associated their personal spiritual feelings and experiences in our shared prayer with me as well as with the Mystery.

They would weep, or thank me, or refer to the prayer the next time we met, or even kiss my hand.

I knew that I was only a conduit, and all I offered was my helplessness. Because a time of crisis is generally not a teachable moment, I often had to accept their warm responses not just politely but with evident gratitude, while at the same time keeping my inward awareness that what was really going on was the work of the Mystery.

In addition to trying to discern patients' wishes with respect to pain control and prayer, I sometimes found that patients had something else they were desperate to communicate. The nurse would say she had tried to figure it out, but was not able to do so. Of course the nurse was handicapped in this respect: She usually had two or more gravely ill people to care for and so was frequently interrupted, or even had to abandon the process of trying to understand what was on the patient's mind. If the patient seemed seriously upset, and if my workload for the day permitted, I tried to help.

I found that if you are slow, patient, and creative, people on vents sometimes can communicate even when everyone thinks they cannot. The 2007 movie *The Diving Bell and the Butterfly* shows something of how slow and patient you have to be, but it doesn't begin to show just *how* slow and patient. I began by trying to see if the patient could give me a clue as to the general area of their concern. This would help me later as I tried to guess the specific words the patient was trying to express. I would begin by slowly naming topics and ask the patient to indicate if one was related to what was on their mind. This could be done by means of eye blinks, hand squeezes, or scrawls on a pad.

But this is not as easy as it may sound. Consider eye blinks. "Please blink once if 'yes,' twice if 'no,' okay? Please give me a 'yes' so I know what your 'yes' looks like." The patient would blink; and then blink again. *Is that second blink a "no"? Or did he get something in his eye? Or was it supposed to be a second yes? Or is he too loopy to do this little exercise?*

I learned I could use what's called a letter board if I wished. The letter board is a chart giving all the letters of the alphabet in type so large they can be more easily read by a person on drugs and without glasses. I learned that if you try working with letters, spelling things out one letter at a time, a key thing is to go *slowly* to make sure you have a letter "right" before moving on to the next one. Everything gets messed up if you go ahead to Letter #2 in a word when Letter #1 is not right. You therefore must confirm what you're doing, and write it down so both you and the patient can see and remember it.

What the patient was trying to communicate, if we were finally able to decipher it, usually involved the absence of a family member. "Bob?" might refer to a son, not at the bedside and sorely missed. Sometimes the person referred to might be long dead, but the patient in his drugged state had forgotten. Sometimes I wondered if Bob might be present in some way that the patient was unable to express. However, I did not get into conversations with gravely ill patients on the vent about how figures might sometimes appear from "the other side." Communications with patients on the vent were far too constrained, and their mental states were usually far too constrained as well.

The most difficult of all these interactions were those about wishing to discontinue care. That differed markedly from expressing a wish to die. Discontinuing care was ordering an end to life-sustaining procedures so that death would result. From time to time it seemed that a patient was *trying* to express the desire to cease treatment. But this life-and-death decision could not and should not be taken lightly. The patient had to express clear instructions to stop treatment and a physician had to determine that the patient was competent to make such a decision.

If the patient had executed appropriate Do Not Resuscitate/Do Not Intubate (DNR/DNI) instructions or had Physician Orders Regarding Life Sustaining Treatment (POLST) forms, things were pretty straightforward. Once the physicians came to believe that nothing more could be done to cure or delay the fatal disease involved, then, in accordance with wishes previously expressed in writing, the patient could be taken off the vent. If they could breathe on their own, they would continue to receive care. If they could not, they would die in relative comfort, with any pain or hunger for air typically addressed by doses of opiates.

In the absence of written instructions from the patient, the patient would be kept on the vent much longer—and sometimes be transferred to a "vent facility," where they could continue to live, perhaps for years. For some people, life in any form is more important than anything else, and they preferred life in a vent facility if the alternative was death.

One patient on the vent in the ICU, a gentle-faced man in his sixties with fingers gnarled by arthritis, made it clear every time I entered his room that he had something on his mind. The nurses and I guessed that he wanted to stop treatment, but we had no proof. We asked for consults from the hospital's speech pathologists to try to help him, but to no avail. I visited him several times, sometimes with another chaplain present to serve as a witness if he were to be able to make his wishes known. His face contorted with pain as he struggled to express what he wanted to communicate. Nothing worked.

After a long time in the ICU, he was discharged to a vent facility. Even now, I hate to think of this man's situation. I have no way of knowing what he was trying to convey during my wrenching visits to his bedside.

There's one final exchange that often occurred with patients: laughter. I often laughed with patients, very much including patients in the ICU and occasionally even patients who were dying.[14] I enjoy the funny side of things, even of dreadful things, and there is a special warmth or bond in shared laughter. Laughter gives the patient a brief break from a time of otherwise-unending pain and fear. This small bit of distance can provide a bit more strength and courage to endure what must be endured. If you can laugh, you can go on a little longer and with a lighter heart.

"Not Me"

He was tall, young, handsome, magnetic, a nurse. Most nurses are female, and most women enjoy the presence of a handsome young man. So whenever Chet was in the back office where the nurses assigned to the cancer floor logged in and out, several females were usually in the vicinity while he held court. I enjoy handsome young men myself, and it was a pleasure to see this smiling, smooth-skinned man after a day spent with sagging and suffering bodies.

Chet and I didn't have much of a relationship, just smiles as we passed in the hall. But I felt warmly toward him, and after I had been on staff for a while, he stopped by as I was charting a call. "Figuring EPIC out?" he asked, referring to the computer program we used to enter our visits into patients' charts.

"It's not a piece of cake, but I'm getting somewhere, I think."

"That's good." He perched on top of the desk, clearly ready to chat.

"Heard any good stories lately?" I asked, to give him a place to start.

"Have you heard the one about the oncologist?"

I shook my head.

"Seems there was this oncologist who went down to the morgue and knocked on the door. When the attendant opened it, the oncologist said, 'I'm here to see Ms. Jones.'

"'Well, you know she's dead,' said the attendant.

"'Yeah, I know, but I've just got this one more drug I want to try on her,' the oncologist replied."

14. If a patient was intubated, however, I would try hard to avoid laughter as the breathing tube would make laughing physically uncomfortable for them. Fortunately smiles and winks were okay.

Chet and I laughed at this dig at those cancer docs who give chemo after all hope is lost.

"There's more," Chet said. "The attendant took him into the morgue and led him to the drawer labeled 'Ms. Jones.' He pulled out the drawer, but when they looked they saw it was empty. In the center of the empty drawer was a yellow Post-It note: 'Gone to dialysis.'"

We both roared with laughter. When you spend your days with dying people in the maw of the healthcare system, sometimes a cynical joke is all you've got to sustain you.

"You know what the first thing I think is whenever I go into a patient's room?" he asked.

I figured he was going to give me a pointer from the perspective of an experienced nurse, and I was eager to hear. "Tell me," I encouraged.

"I'm glad it's not me in that bed," he replied. He smiled, but his eyes were somber. He pushed himself off the desk. "Gotta' go." He headed for the door.

Of course I was glad I wasn't the person in the bed too, even though I had never consciously thought about that before. At that point in my life I had been the person in the bed for three different surgeries, and all three times had involved pain and fear. Moreover, I knew that during my life I was likely to be the person in the bed again, perhaps many more times. But when I went into a patient's room that thought never crossed my mind. . .until I heard their story. Then I often felt huge compassion for the person, and frequently was amazed by their courage and ability to endure what seemed to me to be unendurable.

At the weekly palliative staff meeting one Thursday, a new resident presented a case involving a seventy-eight-year-old patient with metastatic cancer, currently in remission, who had lived with a colostomy for nearly a year and had just had a feeding tube inserted. The resident said the patient was upset by the feeding tube.

Dr. Hill, the senior geriatrician, said, "Of course he's upset, but remember, people can get used to just about anything. After three months he'll have adjusted to the tube, and he'll be okay with it. Just give him time and support him."

Although I had great respect for Dr. Hill, a brilliant woman, I wondered if what she said was true. I decided to field-test her opinion; if she was correct, it might help me to deal with severely disabled patients. Up to that point, whenever I was with a partly or fully paralyzed person I found myself caught up in the fact of their paralysis. Perhaps that wasn't the most important thing from their point of view. And their point of view was what mattered.

The day after the team meeting I paid my first visit to another handsome young man, this one a patient named Steve Scofield, age twenty-nine. He was in for spinal surgery, which was not expected to be life threatening. But what made him special from the perspective of testing Dr. Hill's theory was that he was a quadriplegic.

My assignment with Steve was simply to see how he was feeling prior to the surgery. As a chaplain's missions go, this was an important one. Once in a great while a patient would tell you they expected to die on the table. If that was how they truly felt deep down, the surgery was almost always postponed.

After introducing myself and checking to be sure that it was a convenient time for us to talk, I searched for the right place to sit. This is much harder when visiting quadriplegics than non-paralyzed people, because in some cases, like Steve's, the person cannot even move their head. Steve could move only his eyes and facial muscles, so I needed to find where his gaze was pointed and sit there. I ended up perched on top of the heating unit under the window—a pleasantly informal place to sit, but one that seemed to accent the difference between my mobile body and Steve's paralyzed one.

We chatted a bit how he felt about the surgery—he wasn't looking forward to it but didn't seem unduly concerned—and the conversation shifted to the history of his paralysis. "I skied right into a tree," Steve said.

"Ow! You must have been going kind of fast," I hazarded.

"Yeah, pretty fast. I hit the ground hard and broke my neck."

"Sounds terrifying."

"Yeah, it was pretty scary. I was on an advanced trail, and no one came my way for quite a while. But finally a guy saw me and called in the Ski Patrol."

"And in one minute you went from being an athlete to . . ." I couldn't bear to finish the sentence I wished I hadn't started.

". . .a quad," he said briskly. "That was two years ago."

How awful. Young, handsome, smart, articulate, and trapped in a bed for the rest of his life.

"I find myself wondering what it's like to be you now. Do you feel like talking about it?"

"There's not much to say. It's not great, but it's okay. I can surf the `net with a mouth stick, read, listen to music, watch TV and DVDs; and my friends come visit. Plus they're doing incredible things with quads and stimulation. I believe in a few years I'll be able to walk again. That's why PT [physical therapy] is keeping me flexible every day."

I tested Dr. Hill's theory with several other patients who had major physical disabilities, and generally she seemed to be right. People with new disabilities were usually distraught. But those who had lived with them for a while had somehow adjusted. They might have problems related to their disabilities—more frequent UTIs (urinary tract infections), say—but often the disability itself was dealt with as another given of their lives.

Some, like Steve, were sustained by hope for an eventual cure. Others felt that their misfortune had been bestowed on them so they could use it in some way to help others. As one elderly lady told me, "I'm showing my grandbabies what you can take if you have to." And some simply accepted their disabilities as the price of their continued existence: "I'm still alive," several people said.

What this meant for me was another lesson in the importance of not assuming *anything* when meeting with a patient, or anyone else, for that matter—a lesson that I still haven't fully learned. The old saying, that to "assume" is to make an ass out of you and me (ass-u-me), is certainly true.

3. Loving

Ms. Doka with Shining Eyes

Her eyes got me: surprisingly bright, not the unfocussed dullness you usually see in the ICU. But what grabbed me even more than the brightness was the intensity. Most patients on the ventilating machine are sedated to keep them from pulling out the invasive breathing tube grating on their windpipe. I had presumed she was sedated too, but her eyes told me she was not. They shone at me, seeking a connection, probing like a searchlight in a black night.

We looked at one another for a moment, the ventilator hissing as it forced air in her lungs, five pumps clicking as they dispensed medications drop by drop into her IV line. Her chart showed that she had developed a massive infection following colon surgery. In her early seventies, she had grey hair, a large, white body distended from being pumped with fluids, and cracked lips forced open by the breathing tube.

As I looked at her I reflected once again that being on the vent is like a form of crucifixion. Not only was this woman totally helpless in the bed, with its side railings surrounding her like prison bars, but her most essential personal act—breathing—was no longer under her control.

I was careful not to let the mutual gaze go on for long before speaking. People in the ICU are constantly being "done to," acted on, often without any warning or explanation, and that's not why I was there. "Ms. Doka," I said, smiling enough to show I was friendly but not so broadly as to seem insensitive to her plight, "I'm Joan, one of the hospital chaplains. I'm just stopping by to see how you are doing. Is that okay?"

She kept her eyes on mine. "I know you can't speak right now. I just want you to know that I am thinking about you and wishing you everything good." We continued our wordless exchange, her eyes steady and shining into mine. I saw within her a powerful determination to survive, like a rhinoceros hulking inexorably across a field. That's not a pretty image, but survival in the ICU takes a big dose of toughness. I tried to reflect the same sort of strength back to her. She'd need all that and more if she was to get out of there.

After another moment I said, "Ms. Doka, it's time for me to hit the road. Before I go, would you like me to pray for you?" I paused, scanning her face for nonverbal clues. Patients in the ICU, especially those on the vent, frequently have slow response times. One of my strengths as a chaplain is the ability to wait and observe. When believers are asked if they want prayer, a tender softening often shows itself, particularly around their eyes. But this woman's face was unchanged.

"Ms. Doka," I said, "I can't tell if you'd like me to pray, so I'm not going to. Please forgive me if I'm wrong in understanding your wishes. I wish you a good day. I'll stick my head in again tomorrow. Take care."

For the following eight days our encounters remained the same: glowing eyes, a sense of deep, wordless connection, no hint as to her beliefs and so no spoken prayer from me. The chart listed her as "nondenominational," a designation that was often inaccurate.

On the ninth day a new patient was in Ms. Doka's bed. The unit clerk reported that Ms. Doka had been successfully extubated, meaning she could breathe on her own, and had just been moved to the general medicine floor. When I went to her new room she said, her voice hoarse from the breathing tube, "I remember you!" and we talked briefly. When asked about her religious preference, she said she was from a Jewish family but waved her hand dismissively, saying "I don't believe in any of that God stuff." *Oh my, am I glad I didn't pray for her at her ICU bedside.* However, she asked me to keep visiting her. *Interesting.*

Her medical course was long and difficult, but she never complained. She wanted to talk with me about the ultimate questions of life—meaning, purpose, suffering, love—the kinds of things college students talk about until dawn and which fascinate me to this day. I was careful to listen, letting her talk things out, confining myself to empathic responses and occasional questions for clarification. As she considered the human condition in our times together, particularly as she mused on the role of the mind in connection with suffering, how if one accepted suffering as an inevitable part of life rather than fought it, suffering lessened, it came to me that she had a Buddhist perspective.

She was intrigued when I remarked on how Buddhist she seemed, but denied any contact with Buddhism or, indeed, any formal religious or philosophical system. Her courage in her suffering, her intelligence, and the intensity with which she wrestled with philosophical matters won my heart.

After a few visits something strange started happening to me. Each time I went into her room I felt a stronger and stronger desire to pray for her, not just on my own but out loud, in her presence. I had a physical sensation of something inside me, inside my chest, a kind of aching or throbbing, something pushing hard to get out. This was unusual. When I was with patients I prayed for and with them if they wished and, if they didn't, *I* didn't. My commitment was to supporting them in whatever spiritual path they had chosen.

It is considered unethical for a hospital chaplain to try to convert a patient to the chaplain's point of view. By virtue of their illness, patients are vulnerable; and by virtue of her health and professional position, the chaplain is in a position of power, making for an unequal exchange.

In my opinion, however, there's a second, even more powerful reason for this injunction not to proselytize. Often during an illness, patients have powerful spiritual experiences. These experiences differ widely, and often seem custom tailored to the individual, as is reported in this book. I believe, therefore, that a chaplain's duty is to be careful not to get in the way of the Mystery, but to be available if wanted to support the patient if they have a spiritual experience. It can help to have a friendly witness who understands something of what is going on between you and the great Mystery we call God.

But in Ms. Doka's case the physical sensation got so insistent that for the first and last time in my chaplaincy, I felt forced to raise the issue: "I wonder if I could ask you something?"

She nodded.

"You certainly don't have to say yes. I wonder if you'd permit me to pray out loud for you? I'd be short, and you could just listen." I added, shamelessly appealing to her intellectual curiosity, "It might even be interesting,"

She shrugged and said, "Sure, if you want."

"You really don't mind? I definitely don't want to pray if you don't want me to."

"No, it's okay."

I felt guilty, but the prayer spilled out. "Holy One, here is your beloved daughter, one of your chosen people, a beautiful soul. . .Give her your blessing. . .Continue to watch over her in her suffering. . .When it is your holy will, help her become aware of your loving presence. . .Amen."

I opened my eyes and saw her looking at me with mild curiosity, the way one might look at a strange bird sitting in a tree. "How was that for you?" I asked.

Another shrug. I thanked her for letting me pray and changed the subject, grateful that the insistent pressure in my chest had subsided.

The next day, when I went to Ms. Doka's room, the door was open and she was flat on her back, unconscious. Her hovering nurse was worried: "She's not doing well at all."

She remained unconscious for two days. But on the third day, Ms. Doka was awake, sitting up, eyes open, and when I stood in her doorway beckoned me imperiously to enter. "I've been waiting for you," she said impatiently, gesturing to the chair by her bed.

"Tell me," I invited.

"I was really sick, you know."

Really sick as in nearly died. I nodded. "Yes, you were."

She looked down at her hands. "I'm ashamed."

What could she possibly be ashamed about? I waited in silence for her to continue.

"I didn't have anywhere else to turn," she said in a rush, lifting her eyes to mine. "So I prayed." A pause.

"And?" I prompted.

"And God answered," she said, her eyes filling with tears.

We sat and wept silently together for several minutes, tears rolling down our cheeks as we looked into one another's eyes.

Then I asked, "Where is God now?"

She placed her hand gently on her chest. "Here," she said, smiling the special inward smile of a woman who knows she is loved.

We sat a little longer in silence. Then I said, "I should leave. You need to rest." She nodded. "Before I go, would you like to pray together?"

"No."

I raised my eyebrows.

"Too personal," she said firmly. Then she smiled and added, pointing to the hall outside her room. "But you can pray for me on your own out there if you want."

"I will," I replied, and I did.

She was in the hospital another ten days. Each time I saw her I asked, "Where's God?" and she would put her hand on the center of her chest and smile.

Then the infection roared back and she died.

It has been said: "God does not cause suffering or punish people with it, but God is present and known more intimately in the midst of suffering."[15] Of all my patients, Ms. Doka was the clearest example I ever saw of the reality of God's presence in suffering.

Many theologians and many books try to "make sense" of suffering and its relationship to God. This is not a book of theology, but because I had to live with suffering every day, I think I should say a word or two about my personal beliefs on this terribly difficult subject. First, I do not "understand" the connection between suffering and God and cannot make sense of it. Second, I have personally experienced feeling deserted by God in the midst of suffering. I can strongly relate to Jesus' despairing cry on the cross (Matt 27:46), "My God, my God, why have you forsaken me?" I find it comforting that in his time of greatest need he too felt deserted. If Jesus did, then I and

15. Katharine Jefferts Schori, then-Presiding Bishop of the Episcopal Church, speaking in South Orange, NJ, January 17, 2010.

the rest of us who sometimes feel abandoned by the great Mystery are in the best of all possible company.

The ten-dollar word used in seminaries and elsewhere to talk about God and suffering is *theodicy.* The origin of the word comes from Greek words for "deity" and "justice." How can a just God permit so much suffering in the world? Put another way, if God is all knowing, all powerful, and all loving, how can there be suffering?

If you dig deeply into this question, you may find you have to say that one of those three key characteristics must be incorrect. That is, either God doesn't know about suffering, or God is not able to prevent all suffering, or God doesn't love us who suffer. There are variations, of course. One key variation suggests that perhaps in the end suffering is good, not bad, and that God is always with us in our suffering and is even suffering alongside of us.

You can choose to throw up your hands and ignore the question, or call it a mystery (which it is); but sooner or later life will probably shove it into your face.

My own answer is imperfect and tentative, but it's all I have. You might think of it as a "field theology," somewhat like what's called a field dressing used to bandage wounds as well as possible in the middle of a battle. I believe that whatever is going on, God is with us in our suffering. That doesn't fix the suffering or stop it, but it does give us a companion whose compassionate presence somehow helps us to endure what we are given.

Patients on occasion quote the saying, "God never gives you more than you can bear." They find solace in that belief. I don't. First, I don't believe God is in the business of meting out suffering to each of us. Second, I have seen levels of suffering that are more than the sufferer can bear.

But experiences like Ms. Doka's and those of many others, including some that are reported in this book, have convinced me that while I have no answers in this area, something *is* going on between God and those who suffer. I believe there *is* a Light in the darkness. Of course we each must decide that for ourselves.

"Useless Old Woman"

Patients who were in two-bedded rooms were identified by their room number plus the letters "A" or "B." Letter A meant the bed nearest the door. An easy way to remember was A = "At the door" and B = "By the window." The small size of the two-bedded rooms, sometimes jammed with medical equipment, meant that even though a curtain could be drawn between the two beds, real privacy was impossible.

Whenever I went to visit a B patient, I had to walk across the A patient's territory to get there. I always stopped and spoke to the person in the A bed, saying I had come in to visit their roommate. Often the A person then asked for a chaplain visit as well. In such a case I always agreed, feeling that the Spirit might be tugging at my sleeve.

One afternoon when I walked into a double-bedded room to visit the B patient, I saw that her white-haired roommate was fully dressed and sitting on the edge of the A bed, her hands gripping the side of the mattress, her eyes on the floor.

"Hi, I'm a chaplain, just coming to visit your roommate. Looks like you're getting out of this joint."

She nodded, unsmiling. *Oops.*

Some people are scared leaving the hospital, not sure how they'll manage at home or wherever they're going. Sometimes they have good reasons to be scared, reasons they haven't shared with the discharge team; I always probed when people being discharged looked glum.

"How do you feel about leaving the hospital, ma'am? Looks like maybe you don't feel too great about it."

"I'm going home, but I can't do nothing anymore."

"You mean you can't do things around the house?"

"I've been taking care of my 'grands' for my daughter for four years now, but they say I gotta' stay in bed. I can't cook, can't take care of the little ones no more. They gonna' have to take care of me. I'm just a useless old woman, no good to anyone."

Her words twisted my heart with sorrow. Feeling useless was a common complaint among elderly patients, especially women. No matter what they had done for others in their active lives, when they lost their ability to be of service they were often stricken emotionally as well as physically. Many people who lose a sense of purpose in their lives feel their lives no longer have any meaning. *What a waste.* Fortunately, we had been taught in chaplain training a way to try to reframe the situation.

"Ma'am, I don't know you, but I can tell just by looking at you that you're the kind of person who likes to help others. I bet you've done a lot of that."

She nodded, a faint smile coming to her face. "I have, yes. Raised my children, help at my church, keep an eye out for the little ones in my building." She sat up a little straighter and looked me in the eye. "I like doing for others."

"It feels really good, doesn't it?" I asked.

Another nod, but the smile was replaced by a frown of sorrow. I could tell she was thinking of what she had lost.

"Ma'am, I hope you won't mind if I say so, but I think you might have been given an important way to serve others now."

She looked at me, doubtful, pursing her lips.

"You know how good it is to help others. Now is your chance to help others learn that. Remember all the people you helped? How they let you help them? How some of them, not all, but some, told you what a big help you were?"

"I do," she replied.

"Now, if you are willing, you can let others do for you, just like you used to do for others. You can accept their help graciously and tell them how much their help means to you. It's hard to do that, it takes courage and strength, particularly for someone used to helping like you, but I bet you can do it."

She was still, considering.

"And if you do, you'll be teaching them one of the most important things in life. You remember how when Jesus sent the disciples out to spread the good news he told them to accept hospitality from the people? Don't carry a second pair of sandals, he said"

"I remember, no sandals, no cloak."

"Do you think Jesus might be telling you the same thing?"

"I don't know."

"Me, either, but I hope maybe you'll pray over it. He just might be speaking to you."

We said goodbye and I went on to see her roommate.

I have no idea what happened after that with the lady in A bed. But I do know that ageism is alive and well in our society, among the old as well as the young. There's a big secret that few young people know: Old people have just as powerful emotions as do the young. They too yearn for love, they too yearn to be understood, they too yearn to be respected. Because I was in my sixties during most of my chaplaincy service, I was older than most of the staff and therefore much closer in age to most of my patients. Sometimes when I greeted elderly patients, I felt as if we shared an unspoken current of mutual understanding about being older.

The English writer Diana Cooper wrote:

"Age wins and one must learn to grow old. . .alive to blinding flashes of mortality, unarmed, totally vulnerable. . .[But], before the end, what light may shine?"[16]

16. Cooper, *Autobiography*, 734.

Hold the Phone

On many occasions the hospital had Ethiopian patients who shared a few key characteristics. They spoke no English, they were admitted through the Emergency Department, and they had dire and complex medical problems that had developed over time rather than striking suddenly—some sort of advanced cancer, for example, as compared with an auto accident. All were residents of Ethiopia; all said they discovered they were ill while on vacation visiting a relative in the United States. This last claim was almost always not credible, because on arrival at the hospital their grave conditions were obviously longstanding. None of these patients had any kind of health insurance, none was eligible for any kind of government assistance, none had any assets in the United States. But because they had come to the emergency department with a life-threatening condition, the hospital was required to admit and treat them regardless of their inability to pay.

The supposed relative, an English-speaking US resident of Ethiopian ancestry—sometimes a man, sometimes a woman; sometimes identified as a sibling, sometimes as a cousin—accompanied the patient through the lengthy admission procedure, then showed up for long periods during visiting hours. In all cases there was clearly no emotional connection between the relatives and their charges. The "relative" remained impassive and detached no matter what physical issues arose with the patient or what dire medical news was delivered. To staff who dealt daily with angry, despairing, and bewildered families, all emotionally entangled with the patient at hand, this lack of connection among these special Ethiopians was immediately obvious.

We supposed that somehow members of the Ethiopian community had figured out this clever way to game the system. We speculated that the assisting "relative" might be paid for his services, either in money or in a reciprocal exchange of favors; perhaps, for example, gaining support for other, real family members back in Ethiopia.

The patients were stoic and polite, and sometimes had an air of distinction. Some seemed to me, although I can't say why, to be heads of families. I often wondered if they were in America of their own volition or if they had come at the urging of relatives. I hated to think what it was like for them to be in the hospital. Knowing they were gravely ill, they had left their country for what was perhaps the first and maybe the last time, leaving behind family, friends, and a familiar world; boarded an airplane, probably alone, to go to a strange place whose language and customs were unknown to them; and put themselves into the hands of strangers.

Although the palliative care team would occasionally speculate on these matters, we never brought them up with the patients or the people claiming to be their relatives. The patients had been officially admitted into the hospital system, and it was our job to give them the best possible care.

Financial issues, major factors in our daily work, were always sources of conflict in the hospital between healthcare workers on the one hand and the administration and insurance companies on the other. Those of us involved in direct patient care took what might be viewed as the easy way out, picturing ourselves as the good guys saving lives battling against the bad guys wanting to reduce patient care in the name of saving money. Both sides felt they were just doing their jobs.

The issue of the Ethiopians offered a challenging moral dilemma. On the one hand, every bed given to and every dollar spent on Ethiopian citizens who had come to the United States to take advantage of the system—if indeed that was the case—presumably took those limited resources away from poor Americans. On the other hand, there in the bed was a suffering human being, and our jobs and our personal commitments were to do all we could to relieve suffering.

Providing spiritual care to these special patients was daunting. Consider the situation with a sixty-seven-year-old Ethiopian man, Mr. Bogale Nega, Ethiopian Orthodox, who was having a horrible hospital stay. He had come in for treatment of a brain tumor and a cascade of negative events followed, keeping him in the hospital for a month. One evening he asked his nurse, who happened to be Ethiopian (as was typical of such patients, the only language Mr. Nega spoke was Amharic) if he "should go on."

When she reported this indication of spiritual despair, I went to see him, but his "son" was there and the Ethiopian nurse was not. Although the son translated who I was, I couldn't provide chaplain services for two reasons. First, if the visitor really was his son this might make it impossible for the patient to speak frankly. People are often unwilling to express needs or fears in front of their close relatives. This is one of the reasons why chaplains, who are not emotionally involved with the patient and listen non-judgmentally and confidentially, can be helpful.

Second, the son might not translate correctly. Researchers have found that amateur translators should not be used by healthcare workers because they sometimes make mistakes translating complex medical concepts; *and* they sometimes change the patient's words to suit their own ends, whether to save face, preserve family secrets, or for some other reason. Moreover, amateurs sometimes do not explain important cultural differences, but professional translators will do so, and learning about relevant differences can sometimes be an essential part of a successful exchange of information.

In view of his son's presence, I asked Mr. Nega if he would like a chaplain visit at another time, and through his son he said he would. When I asked him if he would like to pray before I left, he said yes again, and we began to pray. He repeated the words that I said, as best he could, even though I was speaking in English. I wondered if Mr. Nega was trying to show respect to me, or if he thought the words I used had some sort of magical power. Whatever the reason, the patient was essentially gabbling what was meaningless from his perspective. I asked the son if he would translate my prayer and he said he would. Then I asked him to explain that Mr. Nega could say the words his son said, speaking in a language he understood. We did this, briefly, and I told Mr. Nega I would return the next day.

Clearly I had to find a way to speak to Mr. Nega in a manner he could comprehend but without the son present. I couldn't find an available Amharic speaker on staff. However, the hospital had just inaugurated a new phone translation service. To use the service with a patient, you needed a speaker phone. The following day I went to Mr. Nega's room carrying the only available speaker phone. I stood by his bed, gestured to myself, said, "English," then gestured to him, said, "Amharic," then to the phone and said, "English/Amharic." I wasn't sure he understood. But he nodded, so I went to work.

I swapped the speaker phone with the ordinary patient's handset at Mr. Nega's bedside, called the company, went through the identification procedure, got a translator in a few minutes, and we were away. But I quickly discovered that Mr. Nega was too weak to hold a phone, *and* the receiver on the speakerphone's handset didn't work. The only microphone we could use was on the base of the heavy instrument itself. I put the instrument on "speaker," and moved it back and forth between my mouth and Mr. Nega's mouth so we could speak into the microphone. The phone weighed several pounds, his bed was high with a raised bedrail, and he was on the far side, so I had to strain to reach.

The real strain, however, was how to talk with someone who was Ethiopian Orthodox, alone in the country ("son" wasn't there), sick, tired, and in pain. He was African and I'm Caucasian, and the conversation wasn't going to be about easy topics.

So I began by asking the translator, a woman, if she knew what a "chaplain" was, and she said she did. I asked her to explain who I was to Mr. Nega. I wanted to inspire her to do her best, so I added that he was sick and alone, a patient in a hospital, and she seemed sympathetic to his plight. Then, with her translation help, I began by asking him if a visit was okay, and he said yes.

At last I could ask him spiritual assessment questions. Did he think God was with him right now? Yes, he did. Did he remember asking if he should "go on"? Yes, he did. Did he have that same question today? No, he didn't.

When a once-suicidal patient denies they are still considering suicide, one has a hard time telling if that is really true. In some cases they are lying, perhaps as a way of keeping the hospital system from preventing them from taking action.

Patients who are known by the hospital staff to be considering suicide are sometimes "put on watch." That is, if they are in the general medical/surgical part of the hospital people are assigned to watch them day and night, one-to-one. Potential suicides whose physical condition is stable are often involuntarily committed to the locked psychiatric unit and monitored there.

Nevertheless, patients who are truly committed to killing themselves are difficult to stop. I had heard of a man, not a patient, who jumped off a high bridge in a suicide attempt. People who jumped from that bridge almost always died; but he landed in the water next to a boat, and the people on the boat rescued him. Although he suffered numerous broken bones, after a hospital stay of some months, he recovered sufficiently to be discharged. The first night he was home, he killed himself with a massive overdose of pills.

Because of the enormous cultural differences between us and because I am not a psychiatrist, I was not able to assess the seriousness of Mr. Nega's possible intent to kill himself. Someone from psych was scheduled to see him later that day. My job was to assess him from a spiritual perspective.

But Mr. Nega changed the conversation, saying he was very hungry. He was too weak to eat, felt his strength was ebbing away due to lack of food, and wanted to have a feeding tube installed in his body so he would receive sufficient nutrition. He asked me to speak to his doctor about that. I was encouraged that he expressed concern about getting adequate nutrition, since stopping eating is an effective way to commit suicide. I agreed to speak to his doctor as soon as we finished our time together.

Some time ago an Ethiopian nurse had told me that it was all right for me to hold a male Ethiopian's hand, explaining that Ethiopians are tactile people and that the gender difference between us wasn't a problem. When Mr. Nega spoke of his bodily hunger, I offered him my hand and he kept it in his for the rest of the visit—making the phone business even more challenging because I had only one free hand to use. I struggled not to be distracted by the increasing pain in my arm as I moved the heavy phone back and forth, trying hard not to drop it on the fragile patient or on myself.

Then we prayed. Doing so was awkward in the extreme, with me saying something like "Holy God" in English, the translator saying what I hoped was "Holy God" in Amharic, and the patient repeating her words in Amharic; and on we went. I tried to be both internally prayerful (hard when I was passing the cumbersome phone back and forth) and sensitive to his needs, which were more complicated than the usual ones. Finally we finished praying and I left.

His then-current nurse (not an Ethiopian) had been listening outside and asked me how it went. I told her I thought it went well, although I didn't know his real situation with respect to suicide, and brought up his desire for food. She agreed that improving his nutritional status might improve his mental outlook as well. The nurse had the good idea of asking for a nutrition consultation, since the doctor probably wouldn't order tube feeds without that. We got a consult arranged for the next day, and then went into Mr. Nega's room together to try to pantomime to him what was happening. I showed him my watch and made a circle around it to try to indicate he had to wait until the morning and that was the best we could do. At least he saw a team that cared about him.

I went home feeling that he probably wasn't suicidal but his situation was certainly bleak.

Although hospital authorities authorized tube feeds for Mr. Nega, he died anyway.

Mr. Nega's case is just one example of the many complicated and challenging cases where our best efforts felt like a single drop of water in a vast desert, a drop that was quickly burned off by the sun.

Bleeding Out

As soon as I walked in the Palliative office, Sarah, the team's senior nurse practitioner, said, "They just called us from ICU 8. A patient is dying." I grabbed my holy oil and *Ministry with the Sick*, and three of us went to the ICU.

There we found an African-American lady in her seventies with blood gushing from her mouth. I had heard staff speak of "bleeding out" a few times, usually mentioned with the kind of fear one associates with something like "nuclear waste," but had never witnessed it. As soon as I saw the patient I knew that this was someone bleeding out, and instantly I understood why the phrase provoked such distress.

A man and woman in their thirties were standing, with shocked expressions, by the bedside, and a couple of children—a slender girl in her early teens and a stocky boy of about eight—were in the doorway. Sarah grabbed a pair of gloves and moved immediately to the head of the bed, where a nurse wearing a plastic face shield was standing and looking shocked herself. The nurse stepped back, clearly grateful to be relieved of the responsibility of coping with the situation. Sarah pulled on the gloves, picked up the suction tube hanging on the wall behind the head of the bed, and put it in the patient's mouth. She moved the tube around and it began slurping up endless bright red blood.

With one hand Sarah manipulated the suction tube, with the other hand cradled the patient's head, and looked back and forth between the patient's mouth and the two adults at the bedside. "Don't worry, dear," she said to the patient. "You're safe. It's all okay." Then, to the adults, "I know it looks scary, but she can't feel a thing." Back to the patient: "Just let go into Jesus' arms." (Sarah knew from talking with her earlier that the patient had a strong Christian faith.) To the adults: "I'm just suctioning out the blood so she won't choke." To the patient: "It's all right, dear, everything is all right." It was an extraordinary display of presence and competence. Sarah's partner Alyssa and I stood immobile, stunned by the scene unfolding before us.

Meanwhile the clear, plastic container on the wall, hooked up to the suction tube, began to fill with crimson liquid. The blood got higher and higher and I wondered what would happen if it filled. But then my attention was caught by the little boy. He was bug eyed in the doorway.

I went up to him and gently put my hands on his shoulders. "Is she your grandma, sweetheart?" He nodded, tears in his eyes. I took him to a chair at the nurse's desk outside the patient's room and encouraged him to sit down. We were close enough to hear voices from the room but far enough away so he couldn't see what was happening. I started to talk with him and learned that he had three angels: his grandfather, his big brother, and his father. *So many deaths in his life already.* I said soon he would have another angel, his grandmother. He agreed.

His name was Troy. I got Troy some juice, and he pulled out from somewhere in his parka two cellophane-wrapped packages of what looked like deep-fried pork rinds. "I didn't have lunch today," he said defensively. This was the last thing I thought he should be eating; but given what was going on in the room behind us, this was not a teachable moment. I gave him a paper towel as a plate and stood beside him, my hand touching his shoulder, looking into the patient's room from time to time, hearing Sarah's sharp but calm voice, watching the blood level get higher in the quart-sized container on the wall. *How can that patient still be alive? How can Sarah do this and keep it together?* I gave Troy a tissue when he wept in between crunching on the pork rinds. Alyssa was standing at the foot of the bed, both hands on the footboard, leaning forward, mouth slightly open. Later, after it was all over, Alyssa said she didn't think she would ever be able to handle a bleeding-out situation the way Sarah did that day.

Eventually the heart monitor flat-lined, and Sarah said to the family, "She passed."

We said to the family, as we always did, "Let us clean her up and then you can come in and say your goodbyes." I took Troy and the rest of the family to the family room just outside the ICU, a small, windowless, dimly-lit chamber with ill-assorted furniture taking up too much space, where so many families are given bad news and so many grieving people wait to see their loved ones for the last time.

I often wondered why the room was allowed to be so unpleasant. Did the architect decide there was no point in trying to make it pleasant, because if the news the family got was good, they'd forget about anything else, and if the news was bad, it would blot out anything attractive? Maybe it was a re-purposed storage room. Perhaps simply a space for which no one was specifically responsible. The people who did notice its ugliness, like those of us on the palliative care team, had no budget to improve it.

Then I rejoined Sarah and Alyssa, and we cleaned up the body, removing tubes, wiping away the blood, smoothing the dead woman's hair. Sarah always rubbed lotion on the face, arms, and hands of the deceased, so that they would be soft and sweet-smelling when family members came to bestow goodbye kisses. I helped move the body back and forth so we could get her into a clean gown and change the bed linen. There was lots of blood and body waste, but eventually we got rid of everything stained, and the patient looked like a dead body, not like a war casualty. We knew the family would remember this last sight of their loved one for the rest of their lives. It was important for the sight to be as peaceful and contained as possible.

Cleaning up dead bodies is not part of a chaplain's job description, but I was glad to be able to help. It was a way to show respect for the dead woman and her family, and for Sarah, who had done such a superb job. It was also a way for the three of us to decompress a little from the experience.

Then I brought the family back in to say their goodbyes. After a bit I asked them if they wanted to have a bedside service. They did. I made copies for everyone from *Ministry with the Sick* and we read the service together. It is beautiful and compact (which is important when a life has just ended), with powerful prayers, including my favorite, "Depart, O Christian soul." It goes like this:

> Depart, O Christian soul, out of this world;
> In the name of God the Father Almighty who created you;

In the name of Jesus Christ who redeemed you;
In the name of the Holy Spirit who sanctifies you.
May your rest be this day in peace, and your dwelling place in the Paradise of God.[17]

When the service was over the little boy asked, "When's the funeral?"

His mother replied, "There's not going to be a funeral. She didn't want a funeral. She's leaving her body to the medical school at the university." *What a generous thing to do. But having no funeral service is tough on the survivors.* People who leave instructions in their wills forbidding any kind of memorial service forget they are denying their families an important source of possible comfort.

The mother continued, "This was her funeral." She looked at me and I nodded. So too, after a pause, did the little boy.

When the morgue attendant came for the body, the four family members left, carrying their copies of the bedside service we had done together as well as a plastic bag holding the patient's few possessions.

I often wondered what people did with their copies of the service. Did they save them as a memento of an important life experience, like the people who save the program from a moving artistic performance or a stirring athletic victory? Give them to family members who had not been present, perhaps as a way of showing how the time of death had been ritualized? Keep them by their bedside for a while and perhaps even pray them again? Or just throw them away? Of course different people must have made different decisions, including some that I've never imagined. But I always wondered.

Mr. Rupert's Blessing

One day in the hospital I was blessed by God.

Sarah had asked me to make a special effort to go see a Mr. Rupert, who was about to be discharged to hospice. She didn't say why, but she did mention that he liked Psalm 23: "The Lord is my shepherd, I shall not want. . .." I found a thin, elderly African-American man lying on his right side in a fetal position, with a tall and lovely woman and a tall and handsome young man (daughter and grandson, I guessed) standing to his left. Since the patient had his eyes closed and might be asleep, I spoke softly to the daughter. "Hello, I'm Chaplain Maxwell."

"They told us you would come," she said.

17. Episcopal Church, *Ministry with the Sick*, 100.

"I understand Mr. Rupert likes Psalm 23, so I just stopped by to see if perhaps he would like to say it to me or have me say it to him."

"Why don't you ask him?" she said, a tad sharply.

"I will," I replied, feeling somehow chastened, and went to the bedside.

"Mr. Rupert?" I said. He opened his eyes. "I'm Chaplain Maxwell, one of the hospital chaplains. I understand you like Psalm 23. I wonder if you'd like to say it to me, or if you'd like me to say it to you, or if you'd just like to lie here quietly." He looked at me for a moment and gestured with his left hand—lovely, long, thin, dark fingers—indicating I should say the psalm. I did so, slowly, looking into his eyes, while he conducted me, making graceful gestures with his left hand for each line before I said it. It was a kind of dance that we did together, he gestured, then I spoke, then he gestured, and so on.

When we finished, the daughter spoke. "He also likes Psalm 141."

I looked at him. "I don't own that one," I said. "I don't mean I own Psalm 23, I certainly don't. But it is written on my heart, and that's not true of Psalm 141. Do you have a copy?"

"Not here," the daughter said.

I looked at Mr. Rupert again and told him, "I can get a copy in just a couple of minutes if you'd like. Would you like me to?"

He made another hand gesture that I couldn't understand.

"Whatever you want," I said.

He pointed to the door, indicating that I should go get a copy. I quickly went to the Palliative office, grabbed a *Book of Common Prayer*, and was back in his room in a flash. "I have a copy, Mr. Rupert," I said, and opened it to Psalm 141. "Would you like me to read the psalm?" He made a firm gesture with his left hand—yes. I read the psalm slowly and carefully, smiling when I found a couple of lines quoted in the Episcopal liturgy for Evening Prayer.

> O Lord, I call to you; come to me quickly;
> Hear my voice when I cry to you.
> Let my prayer be set forth in your sight as incense,
> The lifting up of my hands as the evening sacrifice.[18]
> (Ps 141:1–2)

Again he "conducted" me, gesturing before the start of each line. I enjoyed our mutual love of the words and the communion of our spirits. Despite my consciousness of his serious illness, I can only describe reading

18. Episcopal Church, *Book of Common Prayer*, 797.

with him as a joyous experience; the liquidity and beauty of his gestures seemed to show that he shared my love for the words.

When it was over we looked at one another for a moment in silence. "Would you like to pray?" I asked. He nodded, closed his eyes, and I bent over him and closed mine. I didn't go through my usual pattern of asking who was to lead or what he would like the prayer to include. I assumed I would lead, since he had said nothing during the visit, and trusted that what was wanted in the prayer would be given to me.

Before I could say a word, however, a deep and powerful voice filled the room, asking a blessing on me. I was so startled I opened my eyes, looking for the person who was speaking—*could it be that someone has just come into the room? Could it be the voice of God*? But when I looked I saw that the voice was coming from the patient, the man who had not said a word until now. The blessing went on in the same strong, clear, and beautiful voice for nearly a minute. It was affirming and at the same time challenging, asking God to continue the good work God had already done in me, to increase my faith, and to bring me closer to God.

I'm fortunate to have been blessed by several dying people, but never like this, never. It was as if Mr. Rupert had somehow seen into the depths of my soul. It was a blessing that I would never have dreamed of praying for myself.

When he stopped, I stood up straight, tears in my eyes. I got a Kleenex out of my pocket and wiped my eyes. As I did so I saw that the daughter and the grandson had tears as well.

Suddenly I heard a faint but harsh whisper. "Bless me!" he said.

I felt completely inadequate to bless this remarkable man, but at the same time I realized that was of course exactly what I must do, and that I should have done it without being asked. I closed my eyes again and prayed a blessing on him unlike one that I had ever prayed before. I can't remember exactly what was said, but I recall thanking God for showing God's self through this man, who was clearly God's dearly beloved son. When the blessing ended, both the woman and the young man were weeping, and the patient was lying on his side again, eyes closed, a smile on his face.

I couldn't speak. I looked into the daughter's eyes, crossed my hands over my chest, bowed to her, bowed to the grandson, and then bowed to the patient, whose eyes were still closed, and left the room. In the hall I had to lean against the wall to steady myself. Then I headed back to the office to recover.

What had happened in that room? How could Mr. Rupert's vigorous voice suddenly arise so powerfully out of his dying body? And where did that extraordinary blessing come from, a blessing that was so beautiful and so intimate? I've thought about it many times. Clearly he was a man beloved of the Mystery. And when he conducted my reading of his two favorite psalms, I believe our shared experience tapped into the depths of his spiritual heart, which spilled over with years and years of love. For that moment, it was a love stronger than death, and that glows in my memory today.

The Singing Bowl

Every Thursday from 1:00 until 2:00 pm, the palliative care team had "rounds" in one of the staff meeting rooms on the cancer floor.[19] The practice of rounds, a long-standing medical tradition, allows a team to review the caseload, discuss problems, and get advice on possible new approaches, all in an exchange of information across disciplines. The core palliative team always attended, and others joined us when possible. These included the two splendid physicians who worked most closely with us, a dietician, a physical therapist, and often medical residents, medical fellows, or medical students who were interested in learning something about palliative care.

We reviewed every case that anyone present wanted to discuss, a practice that sometimes led to complex discussions of options. I couldn't evaluate the various drugs and surgeries being considered, but I loved witnessing how the various specialties exchanged information and how they debated with one another on what would be best for the patient. I also learned when big events were coming up for specific patients so I could support them as the events occurred.

At the end Hoshi would pass around a list of every former palliative patient whose death she had learned about since the previous meeting. As we each looked at the list, someone would say something like, "Oh, Mr. Miguel, I didn't know he had died," and that would be that. The list could be remarkably long, occasionally as many as twenty names.

19. In the movies—and in hospitals— "rounds" consist of a medical team walking from room to room, discussing each patient visited. However, rounds can also, as I describe here, consist of a medical team sitting in a conference room discussing patients. The weekly rounds allowed more in-depth discussion than was possible in hospital corridors. I found them highly educational.

It troubled me that staff had no way to mourn all these losses, and no way to center ourselves in the middle of the endless stream of death and dying in which we lived. A few weeks after I joined the team, I asked Sarah (by virtue of her experience and personality our de facto core team leader) if we might experiment with a little ritual to see if it would help us with all the losses. She suggested that I come up with one for the next meeting, and I said I'd try.

What to do? I had never seen a ritual that attempted to do what I thought we needed. It would have to be short, because it would be taking precious time away from case discussion. It would have to be absolutely free of any particular religion, because the meeting participants adhered to a variety of religions or none. Yet what we did had to be meaningful to the entire group, because we all needed solace.

After considerable thought and prayer, John Donne's beautiful phrase "Ask not for whom the bell tolls" came to me. It comes from his poem "No Man is an Island," which includes these lines:

> Any man's death diminishes me,
> Because I am involved in mankind,
> And therefore never send to know for whom the bell tolls;
> It tolls for thee.

In the poem Donne refers to the practice in his time called tolling: When someone died a church bell was rung once for each year the person had lived. Farmers working in the fields and villagers working in their cottages, counting the rings, usually knew by the number whose life had just ended. If they didn't know anyone who deserved, say, forty-seven rings of the bell, they sent someone to the church to find out. The practice may seem quaint today, but to Donne it was not. He believed that we are all intertwined in one another's lives, so that any person's death affects us all.

To me the poem touches on the reality we in palliative care were confronting. We were surrounded by our patients' deaths, each of which affected us in different ways. In turn those deaths were a constant reminder that one day each of us on the team would also die. Struggling to keep death's inevitability from overwhelming us, we joked as a defensive measure about our own deaths, sometimes debating which fatal illness we would prefer: a massive stroke that sadly would keep us from saying our goodbyes? liver failure that was relatively quick and resulted in a pain-sparing coma? a surgical error that would finish us off while under general anesthesia?

But mountains of mourning piled up as death after death occurred, both in the hospital and outside of it, and we rarely acknowledged them. When a patient died in the hospital, if the family wished a death-bed service, the team would attend—if its members weren't obligated to attend to other patients. Usually they had to be somewhere else.

I decided I could read Donne's poem, short, clear, and powerful, to the team at the next meeting. But how to develop a ritual that would work for our circumstances? We didn't have a church bell we could ring for our patients, and that would in any case be "religious" and potentially offensive to some. Was there a non-religious bell? I thought of the kind of little hand bell used by the head of the household in some upper-crust families to call a servant to clear the dining table, but that would be quite inappropriate.

Then I remembered this: For centuries Tibetan people and others have used what is called a singing bowl to assist them in their meditation. Genuine singing bowls are made of a special formula of twelve different metals and cast into a particular shape. When struck with a soft mallet, these bowls vibrate and make a lovely sound that lasts a long time. The virtue of the sound for someone who is meditating is that if you focus your attention, the sound will persist until it slowly, imperceptibly, declines. As it does so, the space once occupied by the sound is filled by silence. When the bowl is no longer ringing, if you have been paying close attention to its sound, you will then find yourself paying close attention to silence, and silence is a great aid to meditation.

Although Tibetan Buddhism is certainly a religion, meditation has taken on a life of its own, spreading far beyond Tibet, and inexpensive copies of singing bowls can be easily found. While these copies are trifling when compared to the real thing, they do make a pleasant sound, and in current Western society they are not viewed as religious. In fact, I had one of the little copies. I had bought it in Colorado, when I was on a religious retreat there with Thomas Keating, a leading teacher of a form of contemplative prayer known as Centering Prayer.

So before the next palliative rounds, I brought in my little bowl and asked Hoshi for the list of deaths. At the end of that week's palliative meeting, I read the Donne poem, explained about tolling, and asked Dr. Garthwaite, our senior geriatrician, if she would read the names and dates of the deaths on the list. I asked her to read them slowly, and said I would ring the bowl once after each name. Before that I would ring it three times so we could settle ourselves, and at the end would also ring it three times, so we could collect ourselves and go on about our work. I invited everyone to listen in silence and in the silence to do whatever they wanted to do, whether it was to pray or remember the person or simply to breathe.

I wasn't sure what would happen. For one thing, I worried that the professed atheists would feel a need to make a noise to reflect their point of view. But that was foolish of me. The weight of all the deaths was too great. A silence fell over the room, two people put their heads down on the table, and the rest closed their eyes. I rang the bowl three times, and Dr. Garthwaite and I exchanged names and death dates with the sounding of the bowl until the list was finished. I rang the bowl three final times, everyone sat up, looking just for a moment like the vulnerable human beings we all are. Then they shook themselves and again assumed their professional *personas*. And that was it.

We continued the ritual from then on. Sometimes I would bring in a poem to start us off; sometimes we would simply begin. Each week I assigned the task of reading the list to someone else so that everyone got to participate. The ritual only took a few moments. There was no mention of God, no spoken prayer. But as we continued it year after year the air would get thick with the prayers and emotions of our hearts.

Under the Pillow

I was asked to see a Mr. Miguel, a Liberian, who had a horrible, terminal case of throat cancer. When I asked if I could offer him any support he didn't answer and seemed in pain.

I was about to seek his nurse when his wife came into the room. She was a tired-looking woman with two big creases of worry between her eyebrows. I explained a bit about chaplain services and asked her if I could be of any support to either of them. She had never heard of chaplains and looked puzzled.

I asked if her husband had a faith tradition, and she said, "Yes, he is Bahá'i, we both are Bahá'i."

I said I had seen the Bahá'i Golden Temple in Haifa, Israel, a few years earlier, and told her what an impressive sight I had found it. I admitted I had not climbed the thousand steps to visit the temple itself. This bought me a little time with her, but not much. She said she'd discuss things with her husband and let me know. Later that day I saw her in the hall. "We're fine," she said, which I knew was a polite way of saying, "We're not interested."

When I went into the hospital the next afternoon, I thought of Mr. Miguel. Since his medical situation was critical and he himself had not told me he was not interested in a chaplain visit, I wanted to give him another opportunity. In my office files I had a copy of something called *A Chaplain's Companion*, a book of prayers from most major faith traditions. The

Companion included a brief description of the Bahá'i beliefs and four Bahá'i prayers.[20] I took it with me and went to see Mr. Miguel. I confess I was relieved his wife wasn't there as professionally I was treading on thin ice by going back to see him after her expressed lack of interest in what I was offering. I re-introduced myself to Mr. Miguel, said I had some Bahá'i prayers with me, and wondered if he would like to pray one of them with me.

He looked at me in surprise. "Bahá'i prayers?"

"Your wife told me you are Bahá'i. Is that correct, sir?" I asked.

"Yes, I am Bahá'i.."

"So I'm wondering if you might like to pray one of these prayers together?"

"Yes, I would indeed," he said, quite formally.

I reviewed the four prayers with him, and he chose the prayer for healing.

"Let us remember that we are always in the presence of God," I said, and closed my eyes and was silent for a moment. Then I prayed the Bahá'i healing prayer, which is a lovely text, reciting it sincerely for this suffering man.

He had closed his eyes, and when I stopped praying he opened them and looked at me. "I love that prayer," he said.

"I certainly can see why," I replied. For some reason I added, "Did I say it too fast or too slow?"

"No, you prayed it just right. I was surprised," he said.

I asked if he would like another prayer. He suggested one of the others, and I prayed that. When I finished it was clear that we were done praying.

"Do you have a card?" he asked.

I said I didn't have one with me, but I could get one for him and would be happy to do so. I asked him why he wanted it.

"I want to send it to our local temple and tell them that there is a chaplain who is not Bahá'i but who prays Bahá'i prayers," he replied.

It came to me to add that, if he would like, I could also Xerox copies of the prayers in enlarged type so they would be easy to read. Then, if he wished, he could put them under his pillow and they would be there whether he was awake or asleep. That way he could think of them as being prayed for him all the time. Some patients have a great need for something tangible to represent their faith, and I thought this might be true of Mr. Miguel.

"And I can give them [the enlarged copies] to my wife to pray," he said, and I agreed that that would be a fine idea. "You would really do that for me?" he asked, and I assured him that it would be my pleasure.

20. Joseph, *A Chaplain's Companion*, 101–105.

I did the Xeroxing, found a clear plastic bag to house the printed prayers (hospital beds sometimes get wet), got one of my cards, and returned to his room. I put the card on his night table and asked if he would like the plastic bag of prayers on the table as well or under his pillow.

"Under the pillow."

His nurse was there, and she told me that they were about to take him downstairs for insertion of a G tube, a stomach-feeding device used when patients were no longer able to take food by mouth. If I would leave the prayers on the night table, she would see that they were put under his pillow when he returned. Many nurses, such as this one, were deeply sensitive to the importance patients sometimes put on religious items.

I thanked her and said to the patient, "Mr. Miguel, I have never had the opportunity to pray with a Bahá'i before. That was special for me, and I thank you for praying with me. It was a blessing."

He replied, "It was a blessing for me. I have never prayed Bahá'i prayers with a non-Bahá'i before." He looked up at me and smiled. "You are welcome in my room any time."

I said I was honored, which I was. A dying man had given me just about the only thing he had left to give.

His wife's original negative response, and Mr. Miguel's surprise and pleasure at our later exchange, made me suspect that perhaps they had experienced considerable religious discrimination. I wondered if some of that discrimination had been in the hospital. Some of the staff were fundamentalist Christians holding strong convictions that the only way to God was through Jesus Christ. Although all staff were instructed not to judge others by their religious beliefs, nor to proselytize, a few of them did so when no one else was around.

After I went home that night, remembering Mr. Miguel's warm response to the prayers I had brought him, I searched the Internet to see what other Bahá'i healing prayers could be found. There were several. One was five pages long. Sensing that he might be of the more-is-better school of thought, and suspecting that a long prayer would give his wife something to "do" to support her husband in his near-death condition, I made a copy of it and put it in another plastic bag.

When I went back to see Mr. Miguel, his wife was with him. Both welcomed me warmly—he had told her of our visit—and she was glad to have the long healing prayer to pray over him. The following day he left to go into hospice care at home.

At the next palliative-care staff meeting, the list of those who had died that week included his name.

"I Know that Prayer!"

She had liver failure and was comatose in the ICU. A redhead in her mid-forties, she had muscular arms that showed she had been in good physical shape before her illness. Every time I saw her in the ICU she had at least two family members sitting with her. The air in her room vibrated with their energy. That was unusual among families of a patient who was in the ICU for more than a day or so; most soon drooped like a flower deprived of water.

The harsh lights, the complex, many-dialed, intimidating machines, and the unrelenting beeping of alarms normally left people slumped in rumpled clothes, with big circles under their eyes. But this family (the Cuniffs, Catholics from the close-in suburbs) was a close-knit one, and the patient, Jackie Cuniff, was an important member of the clan. Jackie was the oldest member of her generation and unmarried; most of the visitors were her siblings, usually there with their spouses.

As it happened, just before I started seeing Jackie, I had heard someone say a prayer that began like this: "O Holy One, close the doors of our minds, and open the gates of our hearts, that we may be truly aware of your presence with us." There was something about closing the doors of our minds and opening the gates of our hearts that I found appealing. Inviting people to join in this inner action seemed particularly appropriate in the hospital, where hearts were often flooded with pain and fear. Bringing that pain and fear to God could provide deep solace, even if no other solace was available.

So each time I visited Jackie, when the family asked me to offer a prayer over Jackie's comatose body, I would begin my offering with that "open. . .close" sentence, and the family would join in prayers for Jackie's recovery. By the sixth day I privately doubted that Jackie had much of a chance, but each day the family kept coming and the prayers and the energy continued. On the seventh day an older man occupied what had been Jackie's bed, and the unit secretary told me she had been extubated and moved to the general medical floor.

I was delighted by this happy development and went at once to her new room. When I got there, five family members sat in chairs surrounding the bed, and at the center, holding court, redheaded Jackie leaned against a pile of pillows. A couple of the relatives greeted me with "Hey, Chaplain!" and Jackie looked up at me questioningly.

"Ms. Cuniff," I said, "I'm Joan Maxwell, the chaplain, and I've been visiting you in the ICU for the past week. Your family and I have been praying for you every day."

Jackie nodded politely.

"I guess since you were sleeping you don't remember any of that."

She lifted her hands. "Nope, I don't remember you, sorry."

"That doesn't matter. What matters is you're sitting up and talking. That's fabulous. How do you feel?"

Jackie explained that her throat hurt—inevitable since she had been intubated—and she was tired, but, considering everything, she felt pretty good. I knew that after her ICU stay she was indeed tired and I needed to cut my visit short. "Time for me to hit the road," I said, and turned to the visitors. "Perhaps some of you might want to give your sister some space so she can catch up on her sleep. Being in the ICU is exhausting."

Three of the visitors began gathering up their things. "But we want to pray," one of them said. "We've been asking God for help, we should thank God. Will you lead us?"

"I'd be happy to. Is that okay with you?" I asked Jackie.

"Sure," she said, and bowed her head along with the others.

So I began in my usual fashion: "*O Holy One, close the doors of our minds, and open the gates of our hearts*. . . ."

Jackie jerked her head upright and looked at me. "I know that prayer!" she croaked.

"What?" I asked.

"I know that prayer! Doors, gates, I know that prayer!"

"But how could you? You've been in a coma, and you said you didn't know me."

"That's right. But I know that prayer!"

Prayer was forgotten as the family joined in the excited discussion. Somehow, although Jackie had no conscious recollection of having been in the ICU until she was extubated that morning, she remembered hearing my opening to our daily prayers.

Jackie's stunning remembrance is a fine demonstration of what some call a "spiritual heart." I know of no physiological explanation for what she recalled, since she had been so profoundly comatose that she was unable to breathe on her own. I believe that the answer was her spiritual heart. Although a spiritual heart has never been identified physically, I am convinced that it resides in everyone; and in Jackie, it had remained attentive.

Again and again during my work, I saw examples of such hearts. One was a mother from El Salvador who stood every day for hours and hours at the foot of her twenty-eight-year-old son's bed, praying passionately for his restoration to health. The victim of a violent robbery, he remained comatose in the ICU for what seemed like an interminable period with no apparent change. I was convinced he would not survive.

Yet he did, and left the hospital for home. While I know he received excellent care, I believe it was his devoted mother's prayers that encouraged his spiritual heart and enabled him to endure.

Encounters of this kind motivated me to advise visitors to speak to their loved ones as if they could be heard and understood, no matter how ill or near to death they were at the time. I believe the spiritual heart is attentive at least until the last breath has been taken.

Expletive Undeleted

A week ago Mr. Wilkinson's right foot had been amputated because of diabetes. After being in the ICU for a few days, he was back on the general floor. His hospital treatment had been difficult, and the team was concerned about him both medically and psychologically. A relatively young man—mid-forties—Mr. Wilkinson ran a small fence-building business in a rural area and had never been hospitalized before. He was single, with little family support. His two employees had visited, but only once, and the pain, enforced dependency, and strange surroundings were wearing this dedicated outdoorsman way, way down.

I visited him frequently, and I was sitting with him when the medical resident came in with Mr. Wilkinson's nurse. The resident wanted to take out his patient's central line (a long, thin, flexible tube threaded through a patient's vein until it reaches a large vein near the heart) and replace it with a peripheral line (the smaller, more commonly used tube typically put in a vein on the back of a hand or in the crook of an arm). But Mr. Wilkinson refused, his eyes filling with tears. "I've just had enough," he said. I had never seen his spirits this low.

Gently, the resident explained the infection-control advantages to him of a short peripheral line as compared to the long central line and he gave consent to the procedure. But I could see his body was rigid with tension. After the resident left, I looked at Mr. Wilkinson's tattooed arms and saw no easily visible blood vessels, meaning that he would be what is known as a "hard stick"—bad for the patient as well as for the staff person doing the sticking. I asked his nurse to see if she could find the floor nurse who was the best at finding almost invisible blood vessels. She agreed, and I stayed with Mr. Wilkinson until nurse Nina arrived.

I had worked with Nina before, and she gave me a quick smile while she prepped Mr. Wilkinson. When she tapped the back of his right hand to wake up the blood vessels he grimaced in pain. Taking his other hand in mine, I said, "I'm going to stay right here with you," and chatted about neutral topics until Nina said she was ready for the stick. His left hand gripped mine. She thrust the needle in, his face contorted, Nina tensed, worked the needle around, and withdrew it. "I'm sorry," she told him, "I'm going to have to try another spot." Mr. Wilkinson rolled his eyes.

"The next time," I said, "if you want to yell, you go ahead and yell. And if you've got something you want to yell, go ahead and yell it. I'll yell it with you."

"Oh, no, I couldn't do that."

"Why not?"

"I've got too much respect for the office of chaplain."

I smiled. "Mr. Wilkinson, I've heard just about everything, and I've said just about everything too. I'm a sinner like everybody else. You go ahead and yell whatever you want." He looked doubtful.

Nina had prepped his forearm, and she was ready. When she stuck him, he grimaced. "Go ahead, Mr. Wilkinson!" I urged.

He took a deep breath and yelled, "Shi-i-it!"

I yelled right along with him, "Shi-i-it!" Our joined voices echoed out into the hallway.

The three of us burst into laughter, Mr. Wilkinson dropped my hand as he roared, and just at that moment a glorious spurt of bright red blood burst from his other forearm into the syringe. We continued laughing as Nina finished off the line and taped it down.

Chaplains and psychologists know that "mirroring" is a powerful psychological tool. In mirroring, you reflect back to the patient what they have said to you, and your doing this makes the patient feel you have aligned yourself with them. In this case, I had no idea what Mr. Wilkinson would say. He had made it clear that his words would not be appropriate for a worship service. But I believed he knew what was best for him in this moment, and it was my job to support him.

Seemed to me God was in that "Shi-i-it!"

Psalm 88

Sometimes families are confronted with situations that seem truly unbearable. One such family belonged to a patient named Ben Part, who was in the ICU on a vent. Ben, in his forties, had had a massive stroke. Sometimes he opened his eyes, sometimes he seemed to track when you talked to him; but he couldn't speak or make any gestures so we had no way to tell what was going on inside him. Tests showed that one side of his brain was totally and permanently dead; the doctors said the other side might possibly recover a little in time.

The family loved him. Mother and long-time step-father, sister, and girlfriend (a new relationship, so she was quite the outsider in the family deliberations) were all there. They were from West Virginia, Presbyterian, conservative, devout. The docs told them that there was a chance Ben might recover some functions beyond his brain. He would never be what he had been: a party-loving, part-time cellist who chatted with everyone he met and couldn't sit still for a moment. But in time he might be able to speak a word or two, be "awake," feed himself, or at least eat food if fed.

But then Ben had another stroke, and it was clear that there was no hope for him to recover his mental faculties.

After he spent three weeks as a stroke victim in the ICU, the family finally decided he should be extubated. This meant that he would be taken off the mechanical breathing machine, and if he couldn't breathe on his own, he would be allowed to die naturally. When I went to his room, he had been extubated, was still breathing, and his family was all around the bed. They were tired, mad at God, wanting Ben to live, but if he was going to die wanting him to get on with it.

It sometimes takes a long time to die, especially for a relatively young, healthy man. Ben got cold in his extremities and then he got hot again. We kept feeling his hands and feet.

One by one, various family members stood by him and told him they loved him; some added that it was okay for him to go. Some people believe that a dying person hangs on almost beyond all endurance because they fear the suffering their death will inflict on those loved ones they leave behind. When I heard people saying, "It's okay for you to go," I sometimes wondered if they were really saying, "Hurry up and die so this will be over." Having said all your goodbyes, standing around an ICU waiting for someone you love to die can be agonizing.

Ben's mother sagged against the wall, her face grey. I was concerned that she would run out of strength before her son died and wanted to encourage her to pace herself. I leaned against the wall beside her and asked, "Remember when you were giving birth, and you asked them how dilated you were and they gave you some horrible little number and you couldn't believe it after all that time?"

She smiled ruefully and said she remembered.

"Dying's sometimes like that. It takes a long time, and it's as hard."

The mother agreed to sit in a chair for a while.

Ben's sister was particularly articulate about how her faith had been shattered, because her brother was dying "too young." She confided that she was worried about saying out loud how mad she was: She "knew" she didn't have a right to talk to God in any way other than a very respectful one. I prayed about this idea internally for a while and finally did something I've never done before. After telling the family it was a difficult psalm and receiving their permission to do so, I read Psalm 88 to them around the bedside. Although this seemed a risky thing to do, it also felt right.

Psalm 88 is the only one in the Psalter that expresses anger and despair without a ray of hope. I have never heard it used in worship, and in seminary they cautioned us to be keenly aware of how negative it is. On a few occasions, when things were feeling bleak for me, I have read it to myself. Feeling companioned in my anger was not a comfort, but it was somehow a help to cry out with the psalmist to God.

I read it to them with feeling. Here's how the psalm goes:

> Psalm 88—*A Complaint to God*
> O Lord, God of my salvation,
> when, at night, I cry out in your presence,
> let my prayer come before you;
> incline your ear to my cry.
>
> For my soul is full of troubles,
> and my life draws near to Sheol.
> I am counted among those who go down to the Pit;
> I am like those who have no help,
> like those forsaken among the dead,
> like the slain that lie in the grave,
> like those whom you remember no more,
> for they are cut off from your hand.
> You have put me in the depths of the Pit,
> in the regions dark and deep.
> Your wrath lies heavy upon me,
> and you overwhelm me with all your waves.
>
> You have caused my companions to shun me;
> you have made me a thing of horror to them.
> I am shut in so that I cannot escape;
> my eye grows dim through sorrow.
> Every day I call on you, O Lord;
> I spread out my hands to you.
> Do you work wonders for the dead?
> Do the shades rise up to praise you?
> Is your steadfast love declared in the grave,
> or your faithfulness in Abaddon?
> Are your wonders known in the darkness,

or your saving help in the land of forgetfulness?

But I, O Lord, cry out to you;
  in the morning my prayer comes before you.
O Lord, why do you cast me off?
  Why do you hide your face from me?
Wretched and close to death from my youth up,
  I suffer your terrors; I am desperate.
Your wrath has swept over me;
  your dread assaults destroy me.
They surround me like a flood all day long;
  from all sides they close in on me.
You have caused friend and neighbor to shun me;
  my companions are in darkness. (Ps 88:1–18)

When I finished, there was a brief silence in the room, Then the sister said, "Boy, he was really mad at God, wasn't he?"

We all agreed that he certainly was.

I asked the sister how she felt about the fact that this anger was considered holy enough to be included in the Bible. She said she was "really surprised." We talked about the implications of this sanctioned anger for her own angry feelings and explored the possibility that she could express them to God in prayer.

Of course nothing got "fixed," but my hope was that after her brother died (which he did later that evening) she might be able to turn back to God in the course of her grief. When you're angry at God, expressing that anger is telling God your truth, which God always welcomes, so it can lead to a deeper relationship. The Hebrew and Christian Bibles have many stories of people who railed at God—including Moses in the wilderness and Jesus on the cross—and whom God accepted and loved.

As is almost invariably true in hospital chaplaincy, I have no idea what happened to Ben's sister or anyone else in the family. But I remember her anger, and her mother's grey face.

This was one of those times when the question "How can you do what you do?" seemed to have a special bite to it.

Silent Night

I was making my rounds, and when I walked into ICU 8, the nurse said, "Thank heaven you're here, they're just about to extubate Ms. Ferris." This was Latoya Ferris, a twenty-nine-year-old African-American woman who had been suffering from metastatic breast cancer for five years and had been lingering in the ICU for two weeks. I walked a few more steps to the door of her room and saw a room literally jammed with people. The nurse followed me, and just outside the room asked, "Do you know the mother?"

"No, I just know the patient. Which is the mother?"

She led me through the crowd and introduced me to a distressingly young, wet-eyed woman—in her later forties, I would guess. When I identified myself as the chaplain she embraced me. "I'm so sorry," I said. So banal, but it's the only thing I say to strangers at a deathbed. I'm there to support them, so I need to show that I recognize and honor their suffering. After that I must wait and see from words or body language what might be wanted.

People were all around us, a few talking quietly, a couple at the bedside holding the patient's hands, a few weeping. They were mostly in their twenties themselves, looking frightened and agitated at the same time. My guess was that most of them had not been at a deathbed before.

"Would you like a service?" I asked the mother, and showed her the relevant service from the Episcopal book. It's called "A Service for the Discontinuation of Life Sustaining Treatment," a dreadful title for a mother to read in connection with a daughter, but it was what was needed. She looked at it briefly, unable to focus.

"Yes I would," she said, and then, gesturing at the crowded room. "But ask them, too."

Of course they were all total strangers to me, and clearly they were feeling extremely stressed. I went to the foot of the bed, put my hand on one of the patient's bed-clothes-covered feet, and prayed a quick silent prayer for her. I knew Latoya would be dead soon, and I wanted to touch her gently and pray for her while she was still alive.

"Excuse me," I said, and everyone stopped talking and looked at me. "Would you like to do a service together?" I gestured to the mother. I didn't even know her name, because her daughter was using her married name, but by then it was too late to do anything about that. "She would like one if it's all right with you."

People nodded.

"It's a simple service," I said. "There are several prayers I will say, and then there is a litany we will say together. All you have to say is, 'Good Lord, hear us.' I'll tell you when to say it. All right?"

More nods.

"Then let us gather together in a big circle of love around the bed."

Everyone stood up and formed a circle, holding hands. I did a quick count of the people in the room and came up with twenty-five, a staggering number. I kept one hand on Latoya's foot and the other on the book and led the service. It is a tricky one to lead because there are lots of prayers to choose from, and you must decide which ones, how many, and so forth, very much on the fly, with one eye on the book, one eye on the patient, and your senses attuned to the emotional temperature of the room.

Early in the service, one young woman by the bedside began sobbing loudly. I stopped reading and went up to her and put my arm around her. I feared that if she continued her noisy grief it might become infectious. A chorus of sobs from a big crowd could be extremely upsetting for the other patients in the ICU. "I am so sorry," I said, looking into her eyes. "But we do need you to keep control of yourself. It makes it so much easier for the other patients here in this unit. If you can't, we'll have to ask you to step outside."

She nodded in understanding and said, "I'll be all right."

I looked at her for a few seconds to see if she could control herself, decided that she could, and returned to the foot of the bed and the service, my hand again on Latoya's foot. When I finished the prayers and the litany, I led everyone in the Lord's Prayer and at the end said a firm, "Amen."

People slowly returned to their earlier positions; several thanked me. Now what? Where was the physician? I worked my way through the crowd and out into the hall. Sarah and Alyssa were there. It turned out that they had called the physician, and she had said, "I'll come when I can."

"I don't know how long we can keep it together in there," I said.

"What do you mean?" Sarah asked.

"There are an awful lot of people in the room, and the tension is rising, and several people are on the edge of falling out. We need to get going. Who is the doc?"

Sarah gave me her name, and explained that she was intubating someone on another floor. "So why do we need to wait? Can't someone else do it?" I asked.

No: She was the only doctor around who was known to the family. And she was close in age to the patient, so she *wanted* to be the physician directing the extubation. "That's all very nice," I said coldly. "But I don't want this to fall apart." Sarah gave me a look that made it clear there was no choice, and the three of us went back into the room, fanning out to give support to the people who were the most agitated.

I stood next to the mother. *What can we do with all these people to keep things calm while we're waiting for the physician?* I recalled being with an actively dying old lady a few years before, just me and the patient. I had sung Christmas carols to her. "Does Latoya like to sing?" I asked the mother.

"Yes, she loves music."

"I have an idea. Want to hear it?" I wanted to be careful not to push this suffering woman.

"All right." Her voice was flat; she was obviously near collapse.

"Are you a singing family?"

"We sing pretty well." *A bit of pride in her voice; a good sign.*

"How about us all singing a song together for her?"

"What kind of song?"

"You'll probably think this is crazy, but how about a Christmas carol? This is a kind of birth, you know."

"'Silent Night'?" she suggested.

"Oh yes, perfect." I raised my voice and said to everyone that we were going to sing 'Silent Night' together. A few people said, "Yes."

"Anybody know the words?" I asked. Silence.

I turned to the mother, who uttered the opening words: "Silent Night."

"Holy night," I responded, and we continued, speaking the words together:

All is calm, all is bright.
`round yon Virgin, mother and child.
Holy infant, so tender and mild.
Sleep in heavenly peace,
Sleep in heavenly peace. . .

The words took on great power and new meaning in the context of a deathbed.

"So who can start us off?" I asked, adding, "Not me. I'm a terrible singer."

"I can," a man said, and started us off on key. The singing was tentative, and I had to sing strongly, praying that I was somewhere near where I should be with respect to the melody. We got through it fairly well, and at the end several people looked satisfied.

Finally the physician, white coated, came calmly through the door. She went up to the mother, hugged her, and then moved to the bedside, saying nothing, and stood there looking serenely from person to person. People began coming to the bedside and saying goodbye to the patient.

What seemed like an eternity went by, but the doctor just stood there. At one point she looked at me and nodded. I wasn't sure if that was just a greeting me or if she wanted to speak to me, so I moved through the crowd to her side. "Do you want me to invite people to leave?" I asked quietly.

"Why?" she said sharply.

"I thought we were doing an extubation," I replied, certain that such a procedure should not be done in front of many grieving, non-medical people.

"They don't have to leave," she said, so I nodded and moved back into the crowd. *I've never seen an extubation done in front of a big crowd before.*

This doc certainly has presence. And what a wise decision—nothing secret, nothing left to the imagination.

Then I saw the nurse come into the room, a tall, dark-skinned, fit-looking Filipino man. He carried what seemed like many filled syringes in his hand, covered by a towel. I knew some of them contained morphine, and figured the others held sterile water to flush out the line through which he would inject it. He glided to the bedside, put the pile down on the bedside table, and, shielded by the towel, began injecting the contents of the syringes, one by one, into the patient's access port (a line leading to a vein, so injections can be given without piercing the skin again). When he finished, he tucked the syringes back into the towel and glided out.

More time passed. Suddenly, without any word or gesture that I could detect, Sarah was at one side of the bed and the physician was at the other. With quick movements, they turned off the monitors (so there would be no loud alarm buzzers) and unfastened the strap that held the tube in the patient's mouth. I couldn't see well, because I had shifted my position from the bed to behind the IV pole so relatives and friends could have easy access to Latoya. I didn't see when they pulled out the tube, but it was done easily and quietly.

The crowd moved closer. Sarah settled the patient, who was breathing unevenly, and the nurse came in with more morphine. Before he reached the bedside, Latoya lifted her head up and raised her arms toward the ceiling—as the dying so often do. The crowd moved uneasily, but she lay back down, the nurse gave her more morphine, and it was over, quietly.

After a moment Sarah said, "Now we need everyone to go down the hall so we can clean her up, and then Mom and Dad can have some alone time with her to say goodbye." We staffers knew the importance of ensuring that the family's last memories of this young woman would be of a figure lying peacefully in bed: no tubes, no medical apparatus, just a calm face, closed eyes, crisp white sheet pulled up across her chest, arms resting outside the sheet so she could be stroked and held.

It took a while to get everyone to leave the room. Finally we got them all out, cleaned up the body, removed as many medical devices as we could, and went to arrange with the family who would come back in and in what order.

The problem was, the patient's parents were estranged. I could see that Mom was near collapse, not only because of the death of her daughter but also because of the proximity of her ex-husband, who had brought with him to the hospital a woman who appeared to be unknown to the rest of the family. We decided to invite Dad to go in first, which he seemed to think was his right, and he brought his friend in with him. We left the room to give them privacy, although we peeked occasionally through a convenient hole in the curtain covering the window to the hall to make sure the couple didn't need anything. After a short time they stepped away from the bed and we could see that they were ready to leave, so I escorted them back to the crowded waiting room.

"It's just a corpse," Dad said to his lady friend as we walked down the corridor. I wondered if he was trying to comfort her or himself.

Mom was waiting down the hall, not in the waiting room, presumably to avoid Dad. I asked her if she wanted to be alone with her daughter, and she said she did. She stayed in the room a long time. Other family members followed in turn.

Finally it was time for us to arrange to remove the body. There isn't much time before a dead body becomes dangerous to living people, and the hospital needed the ICU room. The family wanted to see the body taken away; Sarah arranged for just Mom to do that on behalf of everyone else. But we got Mom out of the room while the morgue attendant came in and zipped the body up in the bag—not a last sight anyone would want to see—and then put it carefully in the remarkable cart used for dead bodies; it has as a cover a rectangular piece of black rubber so no one who is not familiar with hospital ways will know what's on board. Sarah and I stood on either side of Mom and supported her as the attendant walked out of the room past the three of us toward the staff elevator with the body of her daughter under the black cover.

The family stayed almost an hour after the body was taken away, talking and laughing loudly in the corridor outside the elevators, their gathering like a wake without food or alcohol. This sort of loud bonding was normal and healthy after such a painful experience, and I did what I could to get the group to keep the noise down so as not to disturb the other patients and trigger complaints. Finally it felt like time, and I invited them to leave. Mom had left quietly much earlier; Dad and the lady friend were almost the last to go. I confess that I had been feeling quite judgmental about Dad, but just as the elevator door closed I saw his face crumple, and I felt ashamed.

Witch Doctor

"Here comes the witch doctor."

The speaker was Dr. Pinella, one of the physicians specializing in intensive care. He was in his early thirties, unsmiling, with a thick bush of dark brown hair and a muscular body. He was standing behind the counter of the nurses' station in the ICU.

"That's me," I replied as I walked up to the counter. At least his calling me "witch doctor" let me know he was attentive to my role as a spiritual caregiver. *That kind of little needle from a physician is unusual. I wonder if he's a spiritual seeker.*

Dr. Pinella was leaning forward, resting his arms on the chest-high counter. I matched his position from the other side, hoping that perhaps my doing so would show I wasn't put off by his challenging remark and in fact would welcome more conversation. "How's it going?"

"The usual," he said, his eyes focused on mine, his face drooping slightly with fatigue.

I'd like to get to know him better, but there's never any time for that on the unit. At least we can talk about cases.

"Anybody special today?"

He glanced behind me, checking to see if anyone not on staff could overhear.

"813 could use a visit. We just extubated her and the family is there. She's not expected to survive."

Why don't they call Spiritual Care before *they do that?*

"Okay, thanks."

How I wish I could report that a rich friendship grew up between us and that over time Dr. Pinella opened to possibilities beyond the borders of his scientific world view. But I cannot. Dr. Pinella and many—but by no means all—of the other hospital doctors were atheists.[21] "Witch doctor" captured their opinion of spirituality and religion pretty well. Unlike many hospitals, City Hospital did not come out of a religious tradition, and Spiritual Care was a relatively new department. Palliative Care was even newer. The palliative care chaplain had to earn acceptance.

Over time more and more of the physicians who worked with the palliative care team found that chaplain services could help defuse emotionally charged situations, comfort patients and families who were struggling with dire prognoses and varieties of pain, and offer rituals that were often meaningful to families gathered around the beds of patients who had just died or were dying.

While it was nice to be increasingly accepted by the senior staff of the hospital, I was always aware that any credit due belonged to the Mystery, which many of them didn't believe in, and not to me. This awareness made me sensitive to the delicacy of my position. I needed to keep what I thought

21. According to a 2009 Pew Research Center report, 95 percent of all Americans profess faith in God or some other higher power, but only 51 percent of scientists do. Masci, "Scientists and Belief."

of as the ear of my heart cocked for the guidance of the Spirit. If I forgot to do that, I would not be of any use.

Occasionally I would forget this reality and try to help one of my colleagues get an important piece of information from a patient. One day, for example, as we were eating lunch in the crowded Palliative Care office, Hoshi mentioned a new patient, a Mr. Haskell, with advanced lung cancer and a moderate case of "chemo brain," meaning that he was somewhat confused following a long series of various anti-cancer chemotherapies. "His medical POA (power of attorney) is his brother," Hoshi said. "But the phone number he gave me for his brother doesn't work. I think he got it wrong. He's a little tired of seeing me. He's on your list, right, Joan?"

I nodded. "Haven't seen him yet. Gonna' try this afternoon."

"Can you see if you can get the right number?"

Happy to do something for Hoshi, I agreed to try.

I found Mr. Haskell awake and willing to have a chaplain visit. My usual practice in opening a conversation with a new patient was to listen for an inner prompting and go with that. But this time I couldn't hear any prompting. Instead, I heard my own voice saying, "Remember, try to get the brother's number." *Oh shut up,* I said to my voice, but that didn't work. For the first time in quite a while, I didn't know what to say.

Then I was reminded of my first CPE supervisor's early teaching when we chaplains-in-training asked him how to get the conversation going with a new patient: "Remember, they're in the hospital because something is wrong with their bodies. You can always start by asking them about their condition." This was sometimes called, in a nifty play on words, "an organ recital." The somewhat dismissive phrase reflected the fact that, as chaplains, we were concerned with the welfare of the patient's spirit, not their body. It took us trainees a while to learn how closely the two are connected.

"So, Mr. Haskell, what brings you to City Hospital?" I already knew the diagnosis, but patients need to tell you in their own way, and that way can tell you a good deal about them as well as their disease.

Mr. Haskell obliged with a detailed description of his lung cancer from when it was first discovered to the present day. I tried to listen for hints of spiritual or emotional difficulties, but all I heard was, "Remember, try to get the brother's number." *Shut up, shut up.* I prayed for help, but the voice continued.

Sometimes physical acts help lower one's inner noise. When I pray in silence, I close my eyes, open my hands as they rest on my thighs, and take a deep breath. When I was meeting with a patient or participating in a religious service, I had to keep my eyes open; and over time I had learned how to take a deep breath and open my hands while doing so. These intentional gestures were physical manifestations of my desire to seek the guidance of the Spirit. They helped center me on the Mystery rather than on myself or my concerns and enabled me to continue what I was doing in a more prayerful state.

But when I did them while listening to Mr. Haskell, I could feel myself losing my focus even more. No sense of the Mystery, no whole-hearted attention to this new patient, just, "Brother's number."

I knew I had lost it, so I waited until Mr. Haskell had come to a stopping point. Then, awkwardly, with no connection to what he had been telling me about the progress of his disease, I asked for his POA's telephone number, saying the one he had given Hoshi didn't work. As I did, I was keenly aware of how different our interaction was from my usual one with a patient. *I* was in charge, not the patient, not the Spirit. My usual prayerful acceptance of whatever was on the patient's mind and heart was completely missing. There was no sense of a silent shared communion.

Mr. Haskell, frowning, gave me the same number he had given Hoshi. Shortly thereafter I left. We never established a good relationship, and I knew why.

Subsequently, if my help was needed in trying to obtain a piece of information, as occasionally happened, I would treat the inquiry as a separate activity. I would never try to combine it with a "real" chaplain visit.

But there were occasions when I needed to be focused on a specific medical objective. One such time involved Ardine Flemming, a spirited African American woman in her late eighties. The absolute matriarch of an enormous family, she was suffering from metastatic breast cancer.

As soon as I walked in her room for my first visit I *knew* Ms. Flemming had a vital faith, which indeed she did, nurtured in the African Methodist Episcopal church. She loved to pray, loved to talk of Scripture, and most of all loved Jesus, in whom she had placed her trust since childhood. In our times together she won my heart. I was honored that she considered me a worthy recipient of confidences about family troubles and her life story, as well as some justified boasting about several of her "grands," as she referred to her grandchildren.

But in the weekly Palliative Care rounds I learned that things were not going at all well for her. The oncologist assigned to her case told the team that there were no more anti-cancer drugs to try. She was expected to die within the month. He had called a family meeting later that afternoon to break the news, and looked rather anxious at the prospect. Ms. Flemming had insisted that the meeting be held in her room, and that her eight children and their spouses or significant others were all to attend. Since she and I had a warm relationship, the oncologist made a point of asking me to come, and of course I agreed.

When we got to the large room, it was like walking into a lecture hall. Family members, all dressed as if for a formal occasion, were seated close together in side-by-side chairs lining the wall. A few without seats were standing quietly in the doorway. The room was as still as stone, but the molecules in the air seemed to be quivering. I took a position by the bed, and reached out to hold Ms. Flemming's hand.

The physician found a place to stand where most of the people could see him. Perhaps distracted by the large number of people present, he began a rather technical description of the chemotherapies that had been used, unsuccessfully, on the patient. Even though I had heard lots of medical discussions of chemotherapy, I never really understood them, and this lecture was even less comprehensible than usual. Everyone sat or stood completely still while the physician went on and on.

Finally he stopped. "Does anyone have any questions?" he asked.

No one moved.

He looked at me. "Chaplain, do you have anything to add?"

We both knew I had nothing to add about chemotherapy. He was looking for something different.

"Well, Doctor, I guess I'm a little confused. I don't understand medical talk very well."

"That's okay, Chaplain. What did you find confusing?" *Nice softball reply.*

Here it comes, the "d" word. So many doctors just can't bring themselves to use it, but patients must hear it. Wish I didn't have to say it.

"Doctor, are you telling us that Ms. Flemming is dying?"

His eyes opened wide and he took a tiny step backward.

"Well, yes, I'm afraid I am. Yes, she is dying."

The silence in the room became even deeper.

"And are you telling us that there's nothing more for her to benefit from by staying in the hospital?"

"That's correct."

"But I don't get it. You'd think it would be easier for her in the hospital."

"There is nothing more that we can do for her here."

He was talking to me, not to the patient. I turned to her.

"Ms. Flemming, I'm truly sorry about what we're saying here."

"You're nowhere near as sorry as I am," she said, taking her hand away from mine and tucking it under the bedcovers. I could hardly blame her for that response.

At least the ice was broken and considerable conversation followed. There were questions from Ms. Flemming and several of the other family members, especially her oldest daughter, Janine. Ms. Flemming's final decision: She would stay in the hospital until she died. Both the physician and I encouraged her to consider the alternative, of going home for her last days and being in familiar surroundings with her precious "grands," but she was determined to stay where she was.

Two days later she went into a coma, where she remained for over a week, with Janine by her bedside for many hours every day, until she died.

I'm not sure why Ms. Flemming made the decision she did. Many African-Americans believe that the healthcare system discriminates against them, so they need to aggressively seek maximum care—in this case by staying in the hospital. She may have felt that way. The horrible history of racism in the United States' health care system certainly gives rise to that belief.

One of the worst examples of such discrimination is the dreadful Tuskegee "experiment," which ran from 1932 to 1972. During that time, nearly four hundred African-American men with syphilis were observed by medical personnel of the Tuskegee Institute and the US Public Health Service as their disease ran through its course until they died. Shockingly, none of these medical observers made any attempt to cure the men, which would have been possible using penicillin.

I am glad to say that I never saw any medical discrimination against African-Americans in any of the hospitals where I worked, although I was aware of the possibility and stayed on the alert.

Another possibility is that Ms. Flemming might have feared that, outside the hospital setting, someone would divert the opiates given to her for pain control to their own use. Diversion occurred rarely within hospitals, where controls over opiate-based medications were extensive, but in the home setting a patient's medications were often in the day-to-day control of unsupervised family members. The number of opiates that were reported as having fallen into the toilet or otherwise lost was remarkable. This occurred from time to time among all racial groups.

Or, Ms. Flemming might have wanted to spare her family the trouble of caring for her in her last days, or thought they might not be able to care for her effectively. She might have felt she would have less pain in the hospital, especially in case of a medical crisis.

Acute-care hospitals do not want their beds occupied by patients who are no longer receiving acute care, but for some reason the administration allowed Ms. Flemming to stay. I wondered why, but didn't ask, since she wanted to stay and I didn't want to jeopardize her decision by drawing attention to the situation.

All I remember of her end is a small, darkened room with Ms. Flemming breathing gently in her coma and Janine beside her, reading the Bible to herself on a Kindle. Janine and I talked briefly, admiring Ms. Flemming's powerful will, and prayed together for a peaceful death, which was granted in due course.

No Family

Sarah, the head of palliative care, asked me to see a sixty-six-year-old woman named Klara Whiting, who had tongue cancer. According to Sarah, the patient's situation was the stuff of nightmares. Ms. Whiting had come in for surgery a few days earlier, and doctors had taken out her tongue and most of the inside of her mouth, rendering her incapable of speech—a ghastly scenario.

Because of the surgery she had a trach in her throat, which was how she breathed. She was in severe pain and was dying. Religion uncertain, both type and extent.

Because she was alone in the world, no family and no known friends, and could no longer care for herself, Ms. Whiting needed in-patient hospice care, meaning a nursing home where hospice staffers would come visit. The palliative team was finding it hard to find a spot for her because she was such a difficult patient and had no financial resources. Diagnosed as paranoid, Ms. Whiting had huge anger issues, was writing (in lieu of speaking) all kinds of swear words, and was giving everyone the finger.

Sarah said she needed a strong person as her chaplain who could take her anger. She sounded like someone who would push my envelope, just the kind of patient I liked. The more I was challenged, the less I could hold on to the illusion I was in charge, the more I had no choice but to trust in the Mystery.

As Sarah and I walked down the corridor toward Ms. Whiting's room, we encountered her nurse and learned that the patient had just had two huge bowel movements—a wonderful development as she was on morphine and had been severely stopped up. Sarah was fond of saying, "The hand that writes the order for opiates and doesn't write the order for motility agents is the hand that will have to disimpact." This is a fancy way of saying that painkillers stop people's bowels from moving, and if you can't loosen their bowels through medicine and enemas you'll have to remove the impacted stool by hand. Sarah always tried to arrange for the offending prescriber to do the unpleasant job of disimpaction. "Helps them remember the next time," she said.

With the fecal "passing," her nurse told us, Ms. Whiting's mood had greatly improved. Not surprising. In the hospital, much of patients' and nurses' time and energy are tied up with urine, bowels, and vomit, the earthy, smelly stuff we humans like to deny and ignore. I think we don't like them because they remind us how fragile we are. A bout of vomiting can reduce most people, very much including me, to feelings of helplessness and despair. A long run of constipation makes you feel heavy, stuffed, logy, your body being taken over more and more by a hostile visitor. Yet serious illness usually makes the smelly stuff unavoidable for people caring for the ill person.

When we went into the room, Sarah introduced me, then turned to some other topics with the patient while I watched. She was a tiny person with huge flaps of skin hanging off her upper arms, rather like bat wings, from so much weight loss. Totally bald from cancer treatments, her head looked just like a skull, no meat, only skin. And her skin everywhere was the whitest I had ever seen, not a hint of color, as if she had spent her whole life in a cave. I wondered when she had last seen the sun. Of all the deprivations hospitalization imposes, the loss of contact with sunlight and nature is for me among the most depressing.

Limited to communicating by written word, Ms. Whiting was running out of room on her paper and was writing all around the edges. I got her a few more sheets from the copier at the nurses' station. Perhaps ashamed that she had no teeth left, she kept her lips tightly shut as she wrote.

Eventually Sarah left, and I pulled a chair close beside the bed, trying to position myself so Ms. Whiting could see me easily. *This is going to be tough. Here's hoping those two bowel movements lifted her spirits sufficiently so we can form a bond. Maybe she can tell me what she wants.* "What can I do for you?" I asked.

She furrowed her brow, so I explained. "I can talk, I can read Scripture, I can pray, I can sit in silence, I can go away. You're in charge." It is always important to let the patient know that she is in charge as far as my services are concerned, both because she truly is, and because illness and hospitalization are inherently disempowering. Increasing a patient's sense of autonomy can cheer them up a lot.

She gestured in a way that I figured out meant she wanted to pray.

"Are you Christian or Jewish or Muslim or. . .?"

She made a cross with her fingers.

I said, "Are you seeking? Questioning?"

She wiggled her fingers: Not quite.

"Do you know God exists?"

A nod.

"Do you know that in your head, or do you know that in your heart?"

She pointed to her heart.

"Good. You were given some training as a child, yes?"

Yes.

"You're lucky, there are lots of people here in the hospital who don't know God." I had just come from one.

I needed to pray as she had requested even though I knew almost nothing about her. This is probably my favorite chaplain task. I had no idea what she wanted other than for me to speak to the God of her understanding and to put in words something of what was hidden in her heart. Although I obviously didn't know the secrets of her heart, I imagined that she must be feeling alone, abandoned, helpless, in despair. I didn't know anything about her concept of God other than that she identified herself as a Christian.

With a quick inward cry of "Help!" I closed my eyes, took a deep breath, shifted my mind into neutral, opened my heart, and let the prayer come out of my mouth. The prayer was to Jesus, about how when he was suffering on the cross he was silent a lot of the time (*never thought about that before, but he was there for six hours and according to Scripture he said very little*), so he knew everything about pain and silence, just as Ms. Whiting did.

I asked Jesus to help her. I asked for strength and healing and love and patience and all the myriad things we ask for in horrible times like these. When the prayer ended, I offered to anoint her with holy oil. She accepted the offer eagerly, so I anointed her, dipping my thumb in the oil and gently making a cross on her forehead and the back of each hand. The giving and receiving felt like Communion.

After the prayer and anointing were over, we talked a little bit, I speaking and she writing. First she wrote, "I have gone home 3 times, no problem. Now they want to give me a ball and chain."

I said, "Is the 'ball and chain' where they are sending you?"

A nod: Yes. Then she wrote on her pad, "I never had to plan to die before."

I said, "Is that what you want me to help you with?"

Yes.

"Well, Sarah can help you with the physical stuff, what's going to happen and all that. She's good. And there are people who can help you with the financial stuff. And if you want I can help you with the soul stuff." *I haven't died yet myself. But I'm willing to be here with you and trust that the Mystery will pull us through.* I said that if she wished I would be back tomorrow at 10:30. It's important to give people a specific time, and it's essential to be faithful to that appointment.

I suggested that she might want to write down on her paper the things she wanted us to talk about, and then we could do that tomorrow. She nodded that she would.

I said to Ms. Whiting, and meant it, "I really like you. I hope you like me."

She put out both her hands, grasped mine, and nodded.

Wonderful! I was thrilled that we had begun to make a connection. Her desperate situation appalled me, and I was happy to be able to be of service to her. Once again the Spirit had shown the way.

The next day I went back to see her. On the way, I passed by the hospital gift shop. It was having a sale, and seeing as Mrs. Whiting was bald, I bought her a little head covering, a simple turban. I chose a strong pink; I felt that expressed how she was—strong and angry. Definitely angry. She liked the turban. She put it on and pointed to the air conditioner vent in the ceiling, and when I "got it" that she had been cold, she nodded vigorously.

Then she showed me what she had been writing since I had seen her the day before: three sheets of paper covered on both sides in tiny writing. Her medical record had said she was paranoid, and indeed she had written lots of stuff about how two doctors were trying to poison her and other attacks that were being planned against her. I read it and made no comment beyond "Hmm."

I didn't feel capable of engaging with Ms. Whiting on this in a way that would be helpful to her. I was confident that no one was trying to poison her, but it might have seemed possible to her since she had undergone such disabling surgery. I didn't know the details of her condition before the surgery or what she had understood about what might be done before she gave consent. Now she was in severe pain, and on strong pain-relieving drugs which often left people confused.

Then she said, or rather wrote, "I have no family. You are all I have now." *Amazing, since we've just met, and yet it's true. A giant responsibility. I'm glad we connected, but I can't be the only family to this remarkable woman. I don't want to take her on until she dies—I can't take her on until she dies. But I sure will take her on while she's in the hospital.*

When I slipped back in later in the day, she had her hand over her face and looked the picture of despair. Her eyes were closed. I didn't bother her because she might be sleeping but stood in the doorway and prayed for her. She had written that she lived in DC public housing, fairly near the hospital. *She'll never go back there now. She's just rolling down the hill to die. Please may she do so not in the hospital but in some hospice, somewhere where it'll be gentler.*

On the third day I visited Ms. Whiting again because she was such a desperate case. She had shown me what I thought of as her real self, which was a terrified but brave and loving person. To everyone else, i.e., the hospital staff, who knew she had no family and no friends, she was abusive, angry, obscene, and a tad dangerous. She frequently lashed out at people with her ballpoint pen, a sharp instrument but one we couldn't take away because it was how she communicated.

I admired her anger in the midst of her despair. I wished I could help other staffers see how she was inside, but she kept that hidden. I was lucky she showed it to me. I kept wondering how God would make something good come out of her horrible situation.

There was one deeply touching moment. Ms. Whiting wrote out a blessing and gave it to me to read. I can't recall the whole thing. But I do remember one sentence. It said that my visits had reminded her of God's caring presence in her life, making me an angelic messenger from God. It was a beautiful blessing, especially considering the anguish out of which it flowed.

Fortunately I had been a chaplain long enough to know that *receiving* from someone in tragic circumstances can be one's greatest gift *to* them. I read the blessing slowly, out loud so she could hear her own words. I took them in as I read, and teared up. She saw that, and smiled to herself almost secretly, eyes lowered, mouth carefully closed but corners of her lips turned up, and it gave her some of her power back, at least for a moment. That delighted me.

The fourth day brought new difficulty: Ms. Whiting would not let anyone care for her trach. Trachs must be periodically cleaned; if they're not, the throat can become infected. The process calls for removing the little plastic insert in the patient's neck, cleaning the hole, putting in a new insert, and reattaching the breathing tube. Unpleasant for both patient and staff, but imperative to avoid infection.

When I came into Ms. Whiting's room, Fran, the head nurse, was trying to convince her to let them clean the trach, and she was refusing. Her neck was covered with bright red blood that looked awful, and the accompanying smell was even worse. Fran handled her well, was polite and at the same time insistent, but Ms. Whiting held firm—and nearly struck Fran with her pen, but Fran dodged. Fran warned her repeatedly that by not submitting, she was risking infection. I found myself wondering if Ms. Whiting was trying to get her life over with, even though the previous day I had asked her if she wanted to die, and she had replied that she did not.

Fran finally asked Ms. Whiting if she wanted the mess around for the doctors to see when they come on rounds so they would begin to understand something of the pain and suffering she was enduring.

She nodded, painful to do when there's a trach in your throat.

"I can understand why you might feel that way," Fran said gently, put her hand on Ms. Whiting's shoulder for a moment, and left.

I was mightily impressed that Fran empathized and didn't try to bully Ms. Whiting into doing what would have been best for her medically. This respect for the patient's autonomy was a far cry from the paternalism of the past. I stayed by the bed and managed not to let the sight of the blood bother me. The smell was more challenging, though, filling the room with a rusty, wet scent that invaded the nostrils.

Ms. Whiting also needed to be suctioned, that is, have a second tube inserted so a machine can suck out accumulated blood or mucus. But she had refused that procedure as well. Thus, as we "talked," she would occasionally cough and literally almost choke to death, a large balloon of bloody spit several inches in diameter slowly emerging from the bloody hole in her neck, but with incredible self-control she would not cough much, just enough to pop the balloon and get some blood and spit out of the tube, where it would pool on her chest, and then go back to regular breathing. Each time she did it I held my breath, watching her, praying that she would be able to manage. I had no way of helping her if she couldn't, other than running into the corridor and shouting "Help!"

As I watched her I reflected on how much pain the human body can endure when a powerful will is directing things. *What a strong woman she is. Completely helpless, can't say a word, and yet she has figured out a potent way to let the doctors know something about how much she is suffering. Smart lady. And determined. I can't imagine being that strong. But she* must *be strong, she has no choice.*

On the seventh day, the palliative care social worker somehow found a nursing home that would take Ms. Whiting and the staff told me she was being discharged. The home was in a bad part of town, and not a good facility, but it was all they could find for a destitute and difficult patient. *The system is terrible for the poor. It's not great for anyone, but it's* really *bad for poor people.*

I went to her room to say goodbye, glad she was getting out of the hospital and yet sorry our connection was coming to an end. I found her alone, ready to go, her pink turban on her head and a small pile of hospital items—soap, skin lotion, tissues—stored in a rectangular yellow plastic washbasin by her side. She gave me a piece of rolled paper, secretively, even though there was no one else in the room.

"What's this?" I unrolled it and read a man's name ("Mr. Tanis") and a local phone number.

She scrawled, "Tell him where they're taking me." She gave me a card from the nursing home, jabbing with her ballpoint pen at the name and phone number. Then she put her index finger to her mouth, her long yellowish nail curving in front of her thin lips, as if the information must remain a secret.

I couldn't imagine what she was trying to hide. No one I knew cared what happened to her. No one at all, other than me, and perhaps Sarah and Fran. I was glad she had someone she wanted to be called.

"I'll go do that right now," I said. She nodded approval, and I went out and found a phone in an empty waiting room. I dialed and, wonder of wonders, a man answered. "Mr. Tanis?"

Cautious. "Yes." He sounded like an older man, with a certain gravity and formality in his voice.

"Mr. Tanis, I'm Chaplain Maxwell at City Hospital. I'm calling you on behalf of a patient, Ms. Klara Whiting."

A little less cautious, curious: "Yes?"

"She asked me to call you and tell you they're taking her to a nursing home today. If you've got a pencil, I can give you the name and number." I gave him the information.

"I know that place. It's just a few blocks from here. What does she want?"

My antennae were on high alert. There was a certain warmth in his voice. *Come on, Mister, be a nice guy. You're all this lady's got.* "Well, Mr. Tanis, she's really very sick. And I think you're the only person in the world she can turn to." I paused, and he was silent. "Mr. Tanis, I don't know if you're a praying man, but if you are, you might think of this phone call as something of an invitation from God. It's a chance to help someone who's in great need." *God on the phone. Where did that come from? I hope I haven't offended him.*

Silence. "I think what she'd like is a visit, perhaps tomorrow. They're taking her there in a couple of hours. Frankly, sir, if you don't visit, no one is going to visit." *Please, give her a break.* Silence. "Mr. Tanis, I can imagine this might be a hard phone call for you to get. I know Ms. Whiting can sometimes be a little difficult."

"She sure can." He gave a little snort. I had to hope it was an affectionate snort.

"But right now she doesn't have anywhere else to turn. Just a visit could make a huge difference for her, Mr. Tanis." *And how: If the nursing home staff knows she's got an able-bodied person interested in her, they're less likely to take advantage.* I'd heard chilling stories of how people are mistreated in some of these places. Silence, still. "Mr. Tanis, you sound like a kind man. And Ms. Whiting needs a kind man. If you'll forgive a little moral blackmail—after all, I am a chaplain—I really hope you'll go see her tomorrow."

"Well . . . " Another pause. *Time for me to shut up. What will be will be.*

"Mr. Tanis, I know you'll make the decision that's right for you. Thank you so much for your time. You have a good day."

"You too." *Now his voice sounds warm. That's encouraging.*

I said goodbye and went back to see Ms. Whiting. She was already stretched out on a gurney and two uniformed ambulance people were poised to wheel her out of her room. But they were waiting for Fran, the head nurse, who came in carrying a small clear plastic bag containing Ms. Whiting's valuables. I was surprised to see Fran doing this menial task, and decided that she was as impressed by Ms. Whiting's raw will as I was. Ms. Whiting checked the contents of her bag carefully. They were all the possessions she had in the world—which turned out to be three twenty-dollar bills, a few coins, some newspaper clippings, and a thin necklace of tarnished silver chain.

After she decided the contents were complete Ms. Whiting pulled out one of the twenties and pushed it at me. I was astonished. "No, Ms. Whiting, no, thank you very much, but I can't take that. You keep it."

She scrawled on her piece of paper, "I won't need it where I'm going!" She probably wouldn't, but she might, and in any case I certainly couldn't accept money from a patient.

"Ms. Whiting, thank you, but I'm not allowed to accept money. I'm very touched that you wanted to give me something. I'll remember that, and I will remember our times together."

She scowled, but not for long. I leaned down and whispered in her ear that I had made the phone call. Then I tucked her plastic bag under her hands, hoping that no one would steal it from her. I told her I'd be praying for her, and watched as they rolled her out of the room and down the corridor. Fran and I looked at one another. Neither of us said a word. Then Fran said, "She'll be back."

But we never saw her again.

As I think back on Ms. Whiting's story, I am struck by her generosity to me from the depths of her poverty. She possessed virtually nothing, and she was voiceless, helpless, in great pain, and completely alone. Yet she gave me a beautiful blessing, a gift from her heart, and she tried to give me part of her tiny store of money. More importantly, we shared some deep soul-to-soul times together. I believe these offerings and that sharing were good for her, psychologically and spiritually.

So how did this come about?

When I first went to see Ms. Whiting, I was anxious because of what I'd been told about her: her anger, the dreadfulness of her situation. I wondered, as I often do, if I was up to the job. This wondering increased my abandonment of control into God's hands. I was absolutely in the moment all the time I was with her. Not knowing what would happen, I rested in that reality. I didn't even think about it, I just was: present, and empty.

I gave her some gifts, not as part of a conscious care plan but spontaneously. I offered anointing because it just seemed right. I brought her the pink turban because I passed by the gift shop and it happened to be on sale. I saw her more than I might normally see a patient because her tragic situation called out to me to attempt a deeper connection. I attribute these actions to the promptings of the Spirit. And she responded with a generosity that far exceeded mine.

From a public healthcare perspective one could argue that in Ms. Whiting's case chaplaincy services accomplished little. Her behavior with the rest of the staff became slightly less aggravating, but her death wasn't delayed by so much as a second. To the outside world she was a dying, poor, angry old woman when she came in the hospital and a dying, poor, angry old woman when she left.

Yet I am convinced that our exchanges restored some of her dignity as a human being and, I hope, increased her sense of connection to the God of her understanding. To me, the insistent dance of the Spirit on her behalf demonstrated once again God's compassion for people who are destitute, afraid, and alone.

Peace—Be Still

"Is Ms. Haines on your list?" Tammy asked. Tammy was an oncology nurse, and we had worked together on several cases.

I flipped through the cards for patients on the palliative care list. *The list is huge, so many people still to see. Please let her be on it, because I'm not going to turn Tammy down, and it's getting late.* "Yup. I haven't seen her yet. What's up?"

"She's really strange," Tammy replied. "She is so uncomfortable, and she keeps saying 'Help, help,' even though you're in the room with her."

"'Strange.' You mean demented?"

"Yes. I feel so sorry for her. She's only thirty-eight."

"Okay, I'll go see her now." Tammy gave me a smile as I turned toward Ms. Haines's room. Oddly, perhaps, I rather enjoy seeing demented people, so long as they're not dangerous. (We had one person with AIDS who tried to spit in staffers' eyes. That was scary. Everyone going near that patient had to wear a plastic face guard and be on the alert. This necessity made for challenging chaplain visits; definitely no praying with eyes closed.) Often considerable sanity resides beneath what appears to be "crazy," and I find it challenging and rewarding to tease that out.

Outside the door to her room, I stopped and said in my heart: *I am at peace, I am at peace. Hope we can bring some to her.*

Ms. Haines was so thin that the skin of her arms showed no muscles, just the outlines of her bones. She had removed her hospital gown and was only partly covered by a sheet. A blue adult diaper revealed a catheter taped to the inside of one thigh; a flattened breast rested on her chest. "I'm Joan Maxwell," I said by way of introduction. "One of the hospital chaplains. Is it okay if I come in?"

Ms. Haines tossed her head from side to side, not as a "no" but as a form of thrashing. *Well, looks like I can give it a try. Maybe that motion stems from pain.* I asked if she was hurting, and she thrashed some more, not responding. I gently pulled the sheet to cover more of her body. *At least I can give her a little dignity. Perhaps that will make her feel calmer.*

She looked at me for a minute, then she reached out toward me, long unkempt yellow nails curving from her fingertips. *Bet there are lot of nasty germs in those nails. But she is reaching, not clawing.* It seemed she wanted something to pull on rather than a hand to hold. I held my forearm so she could grab it, and she did, her grip weak. "Help," she said. "Help, help, help."

"I'm here," I said. "Tell me what you want."

"Help . . . help, help," she said again, more forcefully. *What can it be? If I look closely, perhaps I'll find it's something physical. Aha! Her right knee is wedged into the opening of one of the bed rails.*

"Your knee is caught," I said, and when she didn't respond I gently pulled her calf to free the knee from the metal opening. It came out, redness marking her dark skin where the knee had rubbed on the bed rail, but she put it back in the hole at once.

"It's caught," I repeated, but she ignored my remark and reached out her hands toward me again. *Guess that's not it. What's bothering her?* I'd *feel much better if I knew what the problem was, even if I couldn't do anything about it.* I gave her both arms this time, distressed by her distress and by my own inability to understand what was going on.

"Do you like hymns?" I asked. Her case record stated she was Christian. I have found that hymns, particularly Christmas carols, irrespective of the time of year, can sometimes give solace to demented persons. She nodded briefly, and I started singing "Silent Night" softly. Quickly she shook her head—*I'm singing off-key, she's not so demented*—and I stopped.

Then she began thrashing more of her body back and forth in the bed, not just her head but her whole upper torso. *Oh Lord, she's so upset and unhappy. How can I help her?*

"Would you like to pray?" I asked, but she shook her head. *All I'm doing is asking questions, but what else can I do? This is hard.*

"Do you want to turn in the bed?" I asked, and she seemed to indicate she did. I went to the other side of the bed and offered both my arms again. "Hold on to my arms if you want, and I'll help you."

She took my arms but had no strength to pull, and I knew that it wasn't safe for the patient for me to try to move her. "I can call your nurse," I said, hoping she'd agree—*I'm way over my head here*—but she shook her head (*darn!*), and continued to thrash back and forth. Then she gagged, I grabbed a basin and she vomited in it. *Yuk, do I hate holding the basin. Hope I don't whoops too. Ugh. The vomit is brown; not good stuff. Bet her intestines are blocked. Poor soul.* When she finished, Ms. Haines returned to thrashing and saying "Help, help, help."

We're getting nowhere. Am I upsetting her even more? That's not the plan. There was nothing I could "do." I could only be, as I well knew, but I wasn't doing an effective job of even that. Her condition so distressed me that a prayer emerged from my mouth without any conscious thought on my part. *What's happening? Prayer is happening . . .* Normally I would never pray when a patient has declined prayer, but this prayer had a life of its own. I had closed my eyes when it began. *Hey, she's silent. No "Help, help, help" and no thrashing. What's with her?* I opened my eyes and looked at Ms. Haines. She was still in the bed, her eyes wide open and fixed on me. *She declined prayer just a few minutes ago, and now look at her.*

Before coming to the hospital that day I had been working on a sermon based on Mark 4:35–41, where Jesus stills the storm in the Sea of Galilee by saying, "Peace. Be still." *When she rocked in the bed she looked just like a person rocking in a storm-tossed boat. And now she is still. Thank you, Lord.*

I allowed the prayer to continue, keeping my eyes on Ms. Haines as it did so, trying to return her gaze gently and acceptingly. For what seemed like a long time, but was probably just a minute or two, we looked at one another while the prayer continued entirely outside of my conscious control. Ms. Haines's eyes remained fixated on my face, her body immobile, her hands curved over her chest. *This is remarkable. What's happening? And what will happen when the prayer stops?*

Out of the corner of my eye I saw the resident enter the room. "Do you want me to come back?" she asked.

Oh dear heaven, no, don't leave. You've been Sent! You're a miracle and you don't even know it! "No, Ms. Haines needs you, and we are just finishing." I looked back at the patient. "You know Jesus is here with us? You felt his presence?" *I sure hope so.* She nodded. *Whew, she did!* I put my hand on the resident's shoulder. "And now Jesus has sent your doctor—*Yes indeed, has he ever*—and Jesus will work through *her* hands, and she will help you feel better.

"Thank you for praying with me," I concluded. *Why did it take me so long to get out of the way? Trust, trust, trust.* Ms. Haines turned her gaze to the resident, and I left.

I thought of the disciples in that rolling fishing boat two thousand years ago. When all their skill had proved inadequate to the challenge of the storm, they had turned to the Master; at his word, there was peace, and the waters were still.

"We Have a Situation"

Sometimes I got so caught up in a case that I had trouble seeing what was right in front of my eyes. Consider this one. . ..

"Chaplain, this is Pam on ICU4. Can you come now? We have a situation."

I'm a sucker for drama, no question about it. I like something new, something that stretches me. And although I didn't know Pam, I could tell from the urgency in her voice that something big was happening. ICU nurses pride themselves on their ability to stay calm no matter what. But Pam, although contained, didn't sound calm.

"I'll come right now. Anything I should know?"

"It's a patient's family. They're pretty upset." In the background, I could hear a woman's voice, shouting. *People don't shout in the ICU. I better get down there.*

"On my way," I said. I clicked off the trauma phone, and clattered down the inside stairs to ICU4. In an emergency, we never relied on the slow elevators. I passed the ICU4 family waiting room and saw that it was jammed with people talking intently to one another. There were more people than seats, so most of them were standing. *Should I go in and see what's up? No, Pam called, need to check with her first.* I clicked the passcode into the locked ICU door and pushed it open. A circle of staff members stood in the inner hall surrounding a large black woman in her forties. She was shouting and tears were running down her face. A nurse with "Pam" on her name tag nodded to me. "They're going to extubate him, and he's not expected to survive," she whispered. She moved to one side so I could join her in the circle.

"He's my *brother*," the woman shouted. "And I'm not gonna' let him die alone. *We're* not!" she added, waving her hand toward the door to the family waiting room. "The family is here and we need to be with him! He's not gonna' die alone."

As she yelled at the staff her voice got stronger and higher. She was about to totally lose it. *Why doesn't someone have their arm around her?* Usually nurses are splendid at calming patients down. *Perhaps they've all tried and it's time for a new face. Probably that's why they called me.*

I stepped up to the woman so we were face-to-face. "I'm Chaplain Maxwell," I said, speaking softly and looking into her eyes. "One of the hospital chaplains. Can you tell me your name?"

She looked at me for a moment. "LaShawn," she said. "LaShawn Randolph. That's my brother, Chuck Randolph, in there." She nodded her head at one of the ICU patient rooms. Through the glass windows I could see a black man lying flat on the bed and two police officers, also black, sitting on chairs by the window but turned so they could see him. Clearly he was a prisoner. "They say he's dying and we can't be with him. I can't let him die alone!"

I love the Bible passage where Jesus talks about the importance of visiting prisoners, giving drinks of water, and visiting the sick, and tells the disciples that whenever they help "the least of these," they are actually helping him. When he says this, he doesn't mean the disciples are helping Jesus serve others; he means that the person they are serving is Jesus himself. When I do those things, I have a strong sense of Jesus' presence in the other person, drawing me to try to respond to the best of my ability. When I learned that a sick prisoner was dying and his family was not allowed to be with him, my whole inner being went into Condition Red.

I put my hands on her shoulders. They were firm and strong. "LaShawn," I said, "I promise you your brother will not die alone. Let me find out what's going on. If I can change it, I will. If I can't, I give you my word I will stay with him for you." *David's not going to like it if I have to stay at the hospital all night! I'm not either. But this is just totally wrong.*

I kept my hands on her shoulders. "Is that okay?"

Why would she trust me, a strange white woman? If she's not religious, my being a chaplain won't mean anything. Please, God, let her be religious.

I had come on awfully strong, and she took a moment to reflect. The circle drew a little closer. Then she nodded. *Thank you, God.*

"Okay, here's what I need you to do. You go to the family room and tell the family what's happening. We need to get everyone calm while we see what we can do. And it needs to be quiet in here for the other patients. Lemme see what I can find out, and I'll come and let you know. Okay?"

She nodded and went into the family room. When the door closed behind her, the staff circle broke up immediately. I spotted Hoshi, my palliative care colleague. I knew she was superb with people in crises. "Hoshi, can we please work together on this?"

"Sure."

"Let's go talk to the cops," I said, and we walked together into Mr. Randolph's room. He was on a mechanical ventilator and his eyes were closed. Normally I greet a patient, whether or not he's conscious, before talking with anyone else in the patient's room. In this case, however, I wanted to get on good terms with the police officers as quickly as possible, so I nodded to Mr. Randolph and walked past him to the first officer. He was an older, thin man, curly grey hair close cut, sitting very straight in the chair. I stuck out my hand.

"Hi, I'm Chaplain Maxwell," I said. He shook my hand briefly, saying nothing, unsmiling, remaining seated. "And you are.. . .?"

"Sergeant Tompkins," he replied.

"Nice to meet you, Sergeant. This is Hoshi. She's one of the hospital social workers."

After they shook hands we went over to the other officer and repeated the process. He was Corporal Anders.

We pulled up chairs and sat down next to the officers. Obviously they had heard the noise in the hall outside, but the door had been closed so I didn't know just what they'd understood. It seemed best just to take it from the top.

"So, Sergeant," I began. "I guess you know the family's pretty upset."

He nodded, his face blank.

I continued, speaking softly in case the patient could hear. "I gather they're going to extubate him, and he isn't expected to survive. Can you tell me how come the family can't be with Mr. Randolph when that happens?"

"It's regulation," he replied. "A prisoner in the hospital can have a visitor only one hour out of every shift. The family has already been with him for an hour. They can't come back until the next shift."

"Hmm, I never knew that. Thanks. But in that case, why can't we wait until the next shift to extubate him?"

"The captain said it should be done by five today."

"But doesn't the family have any say?"

"Chaplain, he belongs to the state. His body. All of him. The family doesn't have any rights. The state decides." *Oh, dear Lord. So like Jesus. Totally in the hands of the system.*

"Even the time of his death?"

"That's right."

"Can't an exception be made for the family if someone's dying?"

"I can't make an exception. Headquarters has to give permission."

"Even if someone's dying?"

"That's the regulation." *No wiggle room here. We've got to do it by the book.*

"So how do we ask headquarters for permission?" I worked hard to keep my voice even and my posture open. But inside I was shocked that nobody was doing anything to help the family of a man at the brink of death, and I was angry at the uncaring police officers. *This dying man is just a thing, not a person. He's* owned. *No person should be owned when they're dying.*

"I gave Dr. Balbi the captain's name and phone number about twenty minutes ago. She said she'd call him." He spoke quietly, looking straight ahead.

Here I've been judging this man, and all the time the fault has been ours as much as the system's. So what's taking Dr. Balbi so doggone long?

"Thanks a lot, Sergeant, I guess we'll go check with Dr. Balbi."

Hoshi and I went to the ICU nurses' station, but no Dr. Balbi. "She couldn't reach the captain, and she got a call to come to ICU 2," the unit clerk told us.

Now what do we do? Back to the sergeant, I guess.

Hoshi and I trooped back into Mr. Randolph's room and told Sergeant Tompkins what had happened. "Is there anyone else we can call?"

"You could call the lieutenant," the sergeant said.

"But Dr. Balbi isn't on the Unit, and I'm not a doctor." *After all this talk about "regulation," I bet a chaplain won't have any clout with a lieutenant.* "Is there any chance you could make the call, Sergeant?"

He looked at me expressionlessly. *I judged him, he knows it, and now I'm asking for his help. I can be so quick to assume. Rats, rats, rats.*

"Please, Sergeant?" I begged.

Taking a notebook from his uniform pocket, Sergeant Tompkins stood up and went to the corded hospital phone hanging on the wall of the room.

He called the captain's office. The captain was gone for the day. He called the lieutenant's office. The lieutenant was in a meeting. He called someone whose name began with "Mr." but who was out sick. Time both crawled and raced by. I worked to keep a calm expression on my face and to refrain from twitching with impatience. Inwardly I prayed for Mr. Randolph to keep on living just a little longer and for Sergeant Tompkins to reach someone in authority.

Hoshi slipped out of the room to tell the family what was going on.

Finally, on his fifth call, Sergeant Tompkins reached someone. Briefly he reported the family's request to be able to stay with Mr. Randolph while he died. The person on the other end did a lot of talking. Sergeant Tompkins stood at attention as he listened. Occasionally he said, "Yes, sir," always respectfully.

The talking went on and on. There was no way to tell what the person on the other end of the line was saying, but I sensed that Sergeant Tompkins' calm and respectful behavior was carefully calibrated to call forth a favorable response. Hoshi came back from talking with the family and sat down next to me. As we listened and waited, I put my hands under my thighs and impatiently wiggled my fingers in a way that I hoped was invisible to the officers.

"Yes, sir," Sergeant Tompkins said. "I understand, sir. Thank you, sir." He hung up.

Hoshi and I rose to our feet, looking at him eagerly. The corporal stayed in his chair.

"They can come in," the Sergeant said, "but no more than three at a time. They can swap so all of them can say their goodbyes."

I was tempted to throw my arms around him but feared that might seem disrespectful.

"You did a fabulous job, Sergeant," I said. "Thank you."

"I understand," he said.

I looked at him questioningly.

"My mother," he said. "She died."

"I'm so sorry," I said.

"It was four years ago, but I'll never forget. We all got to say goodbye."

For an instant I had an image of a weeping family surrounding a dying woman, Sergeant Tompkins among them. *It is stunning how in the Mystery's economy, good can come out of someone's suffering.*

Hoshi and I shook hands with them both and went to tell the family. They all got to say goodbye.

Garden Communion

Sometimes a patient was too sick to take anything by mouth, yet wished to receive Holy Communion. The various Christian faiths deal with this situation in several ways. In my own Episcopal tradition, we are told to assure a patient "that all the benefits of Communion are received, even though the Sacrament is not received in the mouth."[22] This is called "spiritual Com-

22. Episcopal Church, *Ministry with the Sick*, 9.

munion." The practice makes sense theologically, but for a gravely ill person accustomed to ingesting the Host, words do not have the same impact as touch.

Some priests have expanded the spiritual Communion practice. Patients needing to receive "spiritually" are told that, if they wish, the consecrated wafer will be gently touched to their lips, then wrapped in linen (just as Jesus' body was wrapped in linen after he was taken down from the cross) and taken away to be returned to the earth. Patients seem to find this practice meaningful.

One Christmas I was privileged to offer the Sacrament to patients and their visitors in the ICUs. In three cases the patient received spiritually. One of those was a person on life support. The family was waiting for one more member of the clan to arrive before consenting to extubation. They asked that they and the patient be able to share Communion one last time.The cloth that held a Host for me, after it had been used for spiritual Communion, was a small, embroidered linen handkerchief that had belonged to my long-deceased grandmother. Unfolding the handkerchief by the bedside, seeing my grandmother's initials, and wrapping the cloth around the Host always touched my heart.

The second patient was a woman I had been following[23] for a couple of months. She had been in and out of the ICU several times. She had just been readmitted that morning, and from the deep furrows on her husband's face it was clear that things were not going well at all. They were grateful to be able to receive together for what we all knew was their last Christmas. A second wafer for the handkerchief.

The third patient was a wild-haired man who had recently been admitted from the street. He could speak just enough to say that he wanted to receive but couldn't eat. He was entirely alone, surrounded by monitors and IV poles. After he received spiritually he watched me wrap the Host in the handkerchief along with the two that were already there. "You are not alone," I said, and he nodded, both of us aware of the holy Presence the Hosts symbolized and of others in the unit who also were unable to receive in the normal fashion.

After completing my rounds I went home, the handkerchief and its cargo light in my pocket. It was raining and growing dark. I felt it was imperative for me to bury the Hosts before rejoining my family. Most (perhaps all) Christian traditions teach that consecrated bread and wine need to be

---

23. When a patient is assigned to a hospital staffer, the staffer is said to be following that person.

returned to the earth if they are not consumed. This practice reflects the theology that in addition to being fully divine Jesus Christ was also fully human, and therefore came from the earth.

Some Christians view the bread and wine as the actual body and blood of Christ, others as symbolic of Christ's body and blood, and still others, as reminders of both. In any case, they need either be ingested by Christ's followers or returned to the earth from which he and we all came.

For some reason I decided I needed to dig the hole in the earth with my fingers. I went to a garden bed near the base of an old oak tree near our house and knelt on the soggy mulch to dig. The tree's thick trunk reminded me of the base of the cross driven into the earth. The cold water seeped through my trousers to my knees. When I parted the mulch the earth opened easily to my hands. As I unfolded my grandmother's handkerchief and looked for one last time through the raindrops at the three wafers, I prayed for the patients for whom they had served as tangible reminders of God's loving presence in the midst of pain. When I let the wafers slip from the cloth into the brown earth, the rain and my own tears marked not only the sorrow of the present moment but also the hope for what is yet to come.

The Holy Koran

Following the terrorist attacks of 9/11, patients who were Muslim were often careful to conceal their religious affiliation. Given the anger Americans felt toward the attackers, and the fundamentalist Christian faith of many hospital personnel, this was probably wise. But it created some difficulty for me as a chaplain committed to an all-faith/no-faith ministry, and I didn't want to use religious terms or imagery that were not within a patient's faith tradition.

So when Mohid Amin, in his sixties and suffering from COPD (chronic obstructive pulmonary disease), appeared on my patient list, I was grateful that his religious preference was officially listed as Muslim. That saved me from needing to tiptoe around the subject. I knew that some Muslim males do not associate with women to whom they are not related, let alone non-Muslim women, but I decided it was all right for me to speak with him since he had female nurses and I was part of the hospital staff.

Entering his large, single-bedded room, I was careful to leave the door wide open and stand well away from his bed. He was sitting up against a couple of pillows, leaning slightly forward in the bed.

Mr. Amin acknowledged my self-introduction, and I asked, "Is there anything I can do for you? Would you like me to bring you a Koran, or do you have one here?"

He looked surprised. "I have the holy Koran here." He had a slight accent. "It is on the shelf behind you."

I turned and saw a large, well-bound, hardcover book, too far away from his bed for him to reach. Unthinkingly, without asking his permission, I took his Koran from the shelf and held it toward him. As I always did when touching a patient's holy book, I removed it gently and carefully and held it out with both hands.

"Do you know the holy Koran?" he asked.

"No, sir, I do not. I am Christian, and my holy book is the Bible. But I would like to learn about the Koran, the holy Koran. I have recently been on pilgrimage to Jerusalem and was fortunate enough to attend several lectures by a Muslim teacher, a Sufi."

Gesturing toward the book, he said, "I do not need it right now."

"Then I'll put it back." I returned the volume to the shelf slowly and reverently.

Mr. Amin was in the hospital for a long time, and I called on him every day I was on duty. He always smiled warmly when I appeared. When I think back on my negligence in touching his holy book without his permission, I am moved that he welcomed me at all. The reason he did so, I think, was that from the moment we met we started talking about our gratitude for the profound wisdom contained in our respective holy books. The fact that I love the Bible means that talking about it with someone makes me happy. I recognized the same love for the Koran in Mr. Amin.

It turned out that Mr. Amin was a teacher of the Koran, not just a reader, and my interest in the book (I am interested in the holy books of nearly all religious traditions) called forth the teacher in him. Each time we talked, he always said, "One day I will teach you about the holy Koran." I always thanked him and said I looked forward to that. Indeed, I would have welcomed the opportunity. However, each day he got a little weaker, and without saying it we both understood that he would never be able to teach me.

Nonetheless, his repeated offer and my repeated acceptance cemented our curious friendship. He was very alone, with no visitors that I ever saw. I hope that in our times together he was able to put his disease out of his mind, and instead remind himself of who he was and his deep love affair with the God of his understanding.

Many Mansions

Sarah asked me to see a Mr. Waterson, what hospital staff call a frequent flier—someone who is in and out of the hospital a lot. He was "in" at this point, with gravely advanced cancer. I had never seen him before, but he'd completely resisted the advances of people from Palliative Care; all he wanted, Mr. Waterson said, was to get fixed up and out of the hospital. As I'm sure has become clear to you, I particularly liked that kind of patient, because I enjoyed trying to soften their resistance.

I had only a moment to plan the visit. Mr. Waterson was in his early eighties, that's all I knew. I decided to take a very low profile, to come in, in effect, as a servant. My approach was always to be simple and to put myself at the patient's disposal; but this time I made a conscious decision to be almost *invisible* and see what happened.

Mr. Waterson was in the A bed in a double room at the end of the hall. He turned out to be thin, dark skinned, quiet, and unsmiling. I found him lying flat in bed with the TV off. I asked if there was anything I could do for him, making no suggestion of any kind.

"You could take this tray if you like," he said, pointing to his dinner tray.

"Of course," I said, "It's a pain to have those things around when you're finished with them." I took the tray out of the room and put it on a stray file cabinet in the hall. Food Service hated it when dirty trays were put in the hall. But right now, I told myself, it was a necessary part of my attempt to develop a relationship with a gravely ill patient. "Would you like some fresh water?" I offered. He looked at me with more interest than he had shown when I first came in the room.

"I'm all right," he said. We had made the start of a connection.

"Do you have a Bible?" I asked. "Were you able to bring your Bible with you?" I have no idea why I was sure he was a Christian and sure he was a Bible man.

"No," he said. "I didn't bring it with me." He looked sad.

"I can get you one if you would like."

He accepted readily; we discussed the version he would prefer—King James.

"And when you bring it I want you to read something to me."

"Of course, what would you like me to read?"

"You choose, whatever you want."

"All right."

Before going to get one I approached Mr. Waterson's roommate. From the other side of the curtain separating the two beds he had, of course, heard every word. I believed it was important to be respectful of roommates, whether or not they were on my list of palliative patients. I checked to see if he too would like a Bible. (He did, also the King James version.) The roommate, African American, too, looked to be in his early sixties.

I found two Bibles in the office, but only one was King James; the other was a contemporary version. When I brought them to the room I stood in such a way that both patients could see me and said, "Gentlemen, I've got good news and bad news. I've got two Bibles, but only one is King James. You'll have to work out between you which one of you gets which." I held the two Bibles out to Mr. Waterson since he was my "official" patient. "Which do you want?"

"I'll take that one," he said, pointing to the contemporary version.

"Are you sure, sir? That's the modern translation."

"I know, that's the one I want."

That meant the King James went to his roommate. *Way to go, friend.* "Fine, here it is."

I gave it to him and then went around the curtain to his roommate. "Mr. Moore," I said, "your kind roommate has given you the version you wanted. This is a King James version." Mr. Moore reached out for it quickly, and I went back around the curtain to Mr. Waterson.

"Mr. Waterson, you said you'd like me to read. Do you have a favorite passage?"

"You choose," he said again, and the way he said it made me aware that there was something more to the request than I understood.

"I like John," I said. "Do you like the Gospel of John, Mr. Waterson?" He looked at me silently, so I took that for consent. "I like Chapter 14," I went on, and began to read Jesus' consoling words from his Last Discourse to his disciples:

> Do not let your hearts be troubled.
> Believe in God, believe
> also in me. In my Father's house there
> are many dwelling places. If it were not
> so, would I have told you that I go to
> prepare a place for you? (John 14:1–2)

After a few verses I noticed that behind the curtain, Mr. Moore had turned off his TV, and I read a little louder so he could hear easily as well. I read the first fourteen verses of the chapter, losing myself in the words. Then I noticed that Mr. Waterson was totally still. I could feel his eyes fixed on me, so I stopped reading and looked at him to see if he had anything to say.

"I've been real quiet," he said. "That's because that passage you read was what I was praying on when you came in. 'In my Father's house there are many mansions.'"

We looked at one another, unsmiling, silent, not even nodding. I remembered how fixed he had been on my choosing the passage. *What a grace. He was testing me. Perhaps he was really testing God.* I thought again of my friend who says that when there are coincidences, it's just God preferring to be anonymous. *That usually seems a little pat to me, but perhaps not in this case.*

After we prayed together and he thanked me for the visit, I returned to his roommate. When Mr. Moore told me his story it sounded as if he too were dying. He had fallen ill suddenly in a McDonald's, and now the doctors were talking about trouble with his pancreas. "Have you heard of a 'pancreas?'" he asked. I nodded. If he had advanced pancreatic cancer, and that seemed to be what the doctors were suspecting, Mr. Moore didn't have much time left; that is a fast-moving form of cancer.

He and I prayed together as well. As I turned to leave Mr. Moore stopped me. "That's the first time anyone gave me a Bible," he said. "I'll cherish that all my life."

All his life won't be very long. I didn't know what to say in reply. All I could come up with was a rather banal, "Well, I'm glad you have one now, Mr. Moore."

"Me too," he said and I left.

Maria, Full of Grace

"My son keeps calling me and crying and asking me when I'm coming home. He misses me so much." Maria Torrez's gentle eyes filled with tears. "How to tell him I'll never come home again?"

It was true. She would never go home again. Maria was dying from metastatic ovarian cancer that had already paralyzed her from the waist down.[24] I had been called to her hospital room because she wanted a chaplain, and

24. Even though I usually called patients by their last names, she insisted that I call her Maria; but out of her sense of propriety, she refused to call me Joan. She called me "Shap-e-lin"—all short vowels—her version of Chaplain, and she pronounced the variation with such affection that I loved hearing her say it.

her concern for her son was why. She told me that he was nineteen, that he loved her deeply, and that it was time he knew she was dying.

As we talked it became clear that he was a healthy, devoted young man, and she was an adoring mother. Inwardly I prayed for guidance. What immediately came to me was a heartbreaking story from the life of Thomas Merton. Merton's mother developed stomach cancer when he was a young child, but his parents hid this fact from him in an attempt to keep him from becoming "morbid." When she was hospitalized, young Thomas was not allowed to visit her.

Finally, Merton writes in his autobiography, when he was six years old, "Father gave me a note to read. I was very surprised. It was for me personally, and it was in my mother's handwriting. . .Then I understood what was happening. . .My mother was informing me, by mail, that she was about to die, and would never see me again.. . .And a tremendous weight of sadness and depression settled on me. It was not the grief of a child, with pangs of sorrow and many tears. It had something of the heavy perplexity and gloom of adult grief.. . .I suppose one reason for this was that I had more or less had to arrive at the truth by induction."[25]

I was flooded with the knowledge that a third-party message of his mother's forthcoming death would be a terrible thing for Maria's teenage son to experience. I suggested, "Why don't you call him and ask him to visit you here in the hospital, just you and him?" I took a breath. "And then why don't you tell him what you just told me, that you won't be coming home ever again?"

Maria's eyes widened. "And when you tell him, he will cry, and you will cry, and you will hold him and cry together. Who better to tell him than his mama? Who better to hold him than his mama?"

I watched her closely to see if she felt up to the task, or if I should back off. She paused and then squared her shoulders. "Yes," she said. "Who better than his mama?"

Her son came the following evening, and the next day I visited to find out how things had gone. "I told him," she said, "and we cried together, just like you said."

"And was it okay?"

"It was hard, very hard, but it is okay."

When I think back on all the patients I have known, Maria is the one who shines the brightest in my memory. I met her in my second year of training, while I was still attending seminary. Our initial encounter was curious. When I walked into her room I saw a plump Hispanic woman in her

25. Merton, *The Seven*, 14.

late fifties in a wheelchair. But while most wheelchairs look like the name—an arm chair with wheels—this was more like a recliner with wheels, tilted at a forty-five-degree angle to the floor. She was lying rather than sitting on it, strapped in so she wouldn't slide off. When I said I had come in response to her request for a chaplain, she looked disconcerted.

Her surprise might have been because she was Catholic and so had expected a male priest. A priest did come daily to the hospital, but the demands on his time were extreme, and he focused on a sacramental ministry, meaning a service that, according to Catholic tradition, could only be provided by a Catholic priest or in some cases a specially trained Catholic layperson. Since there had been no specific request for one of the sacraments typically requested by sick Catholics (the Eucharist, the Sacrament of the Sick, Reconciliation of a Penitent), my intuition told me that she might not actually need a Catholic priest for whatever was on her mind.

"You asked for a chaplain," I said. "How can I be of service?"

"Now?" she said.

"No time like the present," I said. "But you need to decide if you think I can help you. Why don't I sit down here"—I gestured at the visitor's chair near her odd wheelchair— "and you can see if you feel comfortable with me. If not, I'll be happy to get you another chaplain. Would that be okay?"

She nodded. We looked at one another for a moment. She had a soft, round, light brown face with almond-shaped eyes. Her nurse had tucked her into her recliner-wheelchair in such a way that her crisply wrapped blanket made her look like an outsized papoose.

How to start the conversation? I noticed the furry brown head of a teddy bear peeking out from the blanket. "Oh," I said. "A teddy bear. I love teddy bears." Which is the truth. Terminally ill patients often have stuffed animals with them, usually given by a friend or family member offering an object of comfort. "Does he have a name?"

Turned out he did have a name—Eduardo—and was a gift from her daughter. The conversation flowed warmly from there. A few minutes later she asked my advice about how to tell her son she was dying, and things went as I described above.

Our shared experience of this painful truth-telling created a bond. Every afternoon when I came on Maria's floor, I stopped by her room, and with an expectant smile she asked me what I had learned that morning at seminary in my Scripture class. I loved the class and was delighted to have the opportunity to share some of its fruits with such an appreciative listener. I soon learned that she had never had an opportunity to engage in Bible study, and that the church she attended did not focus its sermons on the Scriptures. The nuggets I could pass on fascinated her.

Maria had not known, for example, that Jesus was persecuted because he was upsetting the established religious and social order. She was quick to grasp that the people out to "get" him were trying to protect their own powerful positions.

Over time more of her own story emerged. She and her husband had married in their teens. Fleeing the terrible poverty of their hometown, a mountain village in rural Mexico, they had somehow managed to walk alone together, with no guide, through the mountains and across the border into the United States. Now he worked as a dishwasher in a Korean restaurant.

In addition to her husband and son, Maria had a daughter who was shortly expecting her first child. I met Maria's husband, a short, compact, unsmiling man whom she invariably called "*Papi*" and who stared at her with wordless devotion; and her hugely pregnant daughter, whose long black hair glowed down her shoulders; both parents called her "*Mamacita*" ("Little Mother"). It quickly became clear to me that these parents loved one another deeply and derived the meaning of their lives from their beloved offspring, both those present and those anticipated.

It also became clear to me that there was something extremely special about Maria. She exuded love that could be felt from the moment you entered her room. She affirmed everyone's beauty and worth, sincerely and wholeheartedly. When you asked her how she was, she would reply, "I'm fine, how are *you*?"

I noticed that staff members assigned to the floor always dropped by her room just before going off duty. While there, they would do a few things to make her a little more comfortable, but their real purpose was to restore themselves for a moment in the warmth of her presence. I did the same.

Maria remained in the hospital for nearly two weeks, much longer than the usual stay. I never was told what treatments she was undergoing, but I knew they were all palliative and that there was no hope of a cure. She only complained once. She had been given too much pain medicine, which reduced her defenses, and when I came into the room she was weeping.

"*Shapelin*," she told me, "I'm paralyzed. I cannot walk!" Of course I had known this ever since I met her, but this was the first time I'd seen her openly grieve this dreadful loss. I could do nothing but hold her hand as she sobbed and occasionally murmur, "I'm so sorry, Maria, so sorry."

She had a great love for the Virgin of Guadalupe, and whenever I visited she liked us to say the "Hail Mary" together in her honor. One day it struck me that we were praying in English, but of course her second language (after her Indian dialect) was Spanish.

"Maria, I'm sorry that I don't speak Spanish. Would you like to teach me the Hail Mary in Spanish? Then we could pray it together *in* Spanish."

"Oh, *yessss*, I would like that very much." She paused, and I could see her searching for the words. To my surprise, and her sorrow, the words did not come. "I am so sorry, *Shapelin*, I cannot remember them."

The cancer had reached her brain. Naturally, I was horrified that what had begun as a kind impulse had turned into a source of pain for this remarkable woman. "It doesn't matter at all, Maria, don't worry about it, we can pray it in English. Let's do it now. Hail Mary. . ." We prayed, and I thought the incident was forgotten.

But a few afternoons later she said to me, her eyes shining, "*Shapelin*, I have a present for you."

I was astonished. How could this poor, paralyzed, dying woman have a present for me? "It's over there, on my table. Go see." She pointed to the table at the foot of her bed. Next to the plastic water pitcher and a couple of Styrofoam cups, I saw a brochure. It was the Rosary in Spanish!

"Maria, this is terrific! Thank you! But how did you get it?"

"I made my husband get it," she replied firmly, making it clear that no resistance would have been accepted.

Oh my goodness, that hard-working man, with his wife dying, went off to get a brochure for me. I was deeply moved. "This is great! I will keep it with me in my Bible bag. I'll use it with every Spanish-speaking patient I have, and think of you each time. Thank you so much, Maria." I gave her a big hug, and she grinned in delight.

"But," I added, "I don't know how to pronounce the words correctly. Will you teach me? Can we pray it together now?" And we did, the sacred words coming back to her in a rush: "*Dios te salve, Maria, Llena eres de gracia: El Señor es contigo.*"

The following afternoon, when I looked into her room, everything was different. Maria was lying flat on her back in the bed, her empty wheelchair recliner shoved in the corner. And beside the bed was a middle-aged Hispanic woman I had never seen before, wailing loudly. I raced to find her nurse.

"What's with Ms. Torrez?" I asked.

"She failed during the night. I don't think she has long."

"Does the family know?"

"They've been called. He works, I think he'll come later."

"Who's that with her?"

"I don't know—a neighbor, I think. She's been there for nearly an hour, just crying."

"Thanks. I'm not going to let her go out that way, that's for sure," I said, turning on my heel and striding back to Maria's room. The wailing neighbor was seated at right angles to the middle of Maria's bed, her back to the hall door. I went to the other side of the bed, where someone had placed a second chair. Nodding to the neighbor, I sat down, heavy hearted, took Maria's cool hand, and looked at her face, her closed eyes, aching at the absence of her special warmth.

If I had been less personally affected by Maria's condition, I would have tried to engage the neighbor directly. But my need to pray for Maria took overwhelming precedence. I decided to start praying, hoping that the sound of the prayer would help calm the weeping neighbor. "Hail Mary, full of grace," I began, and stopped. Thanks to Maria's gift of the day before, I had the Spanish version with me. If ever there was a good time to use it, this was it.

I pulled out the brochure and began again. "*Dios te salve, Maria, Llena eres de gracia: El Señor es contigo.*" I still had Maria's limp hand in mine. I focused on reading the words, trying to reproduce the pronunciation Maria had taught me the day before.

As the prayer continued, I noticed that the neighbor had stopped wailing. *Thank you, God. She doesn't need to die with that going on.* The third time I said "*Dios te salve,*" I heard a hoarse voice saying the words with me, saying them tenderly, with great love. *Hey, this neighbor's got a real faith. This is good.*

I looked up from the brochure at the neighbor to thank her. . .but the neighbor wasn't looking at me. Nor was she speaking. Her mouth was wide open and her eyes were bulging as she stared at the head of the bed.

I followed her gaze, and to my astonishment met Maria's smiling eyes. It was *her* voice I had been hearing, and as we looked at one another she continued to pray. We finished the prayer together, me stumbling with the Spanish, Maria speaking to her beloved Virgin of Guadalupe in confidence and love.

She died three days later. But before death came, she learned that her cherished *Mamacita* had safely given birth to a baby girl. She would be christened. . .Maria.

Ending

When I came upon my seventieth year, it turned out to be a good time to retire. I loved the work as passionately as ever, but I was getting a bit worn down, and my feet had increased a whole shoe size from walking all those hospital corridors!

I also felt that there might be another reason why I had been called to hospital chaplaincy and permitted to witness the benevolent, graced, and always-surprising actions of the great Mystery glowing forth in the lives of my dying patients. Perhaps the stories in this book are that reason. My hope is that reading them has inspired you to give some thought to your and your loved ones' inevitable deaths and has sparked some conversations among you as to your end-of-life wishes. My prayer is that as you contemplate the end of life, which will come for us all, you will do so with less fear and more hope.

May it be so.

Afterword

As you might expect, I believe that every acute-care hospital of any size should have—on staff—trained chaplains available to serve patients, especially those with life-threatening illnesses. I have tried to show some of the advantages chaplain services offer to patients and their families. A considerable body of research indicates that religious/spiritual faith and practice have a positive effect on humans' emotional and physical wellbeing.[26] Chaplains provide spiritual and emotional support to patients, as well as their families and friends, in extremely difficult situations. Chaplains also provide support to hospital staff.

A white paper prepared by five major chaplaincy organizations declares in part:

- Healthcare organizations are obligated to respond to spiritual needs, because patients have a right to such services . . .
- Fear and loneliness experienced during serious illness generate spiritual crises that require spiritual care . . .
- Spiritual care plays a significant role when cure is not possible and persons question the meaning of life . . .
- Chaplains not only help staff members cope, but empower them to recognize the meaning and value of their work in new ways . . .
- Spiritual care is important in healthcare organizations when allocation of limited resources leads to moral, ethical and spiritual concerns . . .[27]

Unfortunately, it's hard to design, operate, and fund spiritual-care services in acute-care hospitals. Many not-for-profit hospitals come out of a religious tradition, and in some cases they continue an established practice

26. VandeCreek and Burton, "Professional Chaplaincy," 81–97.

27. Ibid., 83–84.

of providing spiritual support. However, some of them have only limited services for patients who are not members of that hospital's religious tradition. Some hospitals use as chaplains people (both clergy and lay) who have not had significant training in providing spiritual care for sick people involved in the healthcare system. And many for-profit hospitals have *no* tradition of spiritual care.

All hospitals are constrained by their need to keep costs as low as possible. Administrators who are unaware of the benefits to the hospital of skilled spiritual care are therefore reluctant to invest time and funding in it.

Once administrators open the metaphorical box labeled "spiritual care" and try to make choices in view of limited funding, they encounter many difficulties, ranging from competition among various faith traditions to claims for space at the table by many forms of alternative medicine.

Another problem is the discomfort and sometimes disdain felt and expressed by quite a few medical practitioners for religious and spiritual matters. Many scientists believe that if something doesn't make scientific "sense," it doesn't exist. Since no one has been able to capture part or all of what some call "God," they believe God can't be real. And, perhaps since surveys indicate that many scientists in the biological and medical fields do not believe in God or in a "higher power,"[28] some hospital administrators are unwilling to allocate hospital funds for religious/spiritual support.

But people who have experienced grave illness, either themselves or in family members, learn that the human spirit cries out for support at such a time. People need and deserve spiritual encouragement and understanding that serves all people, whatever their beliefs; that is compassionate; and that is knowledgeable about and responsive to human needs at the end of life.

Therefore, all profits from the sale of this book will go to the Shalem Institute for Spiritual Formation in Washington, DC, which is committed to nurturing a contemplative approach that is so needed for the kind of spiritual support I just described.

28. Masci, "Scientists and Belief."

Appendices

The following two checklists stem from my hospital experiences as a chaplain. They have been field tested and improved by several personal friends who used them before undergoing in-patient surgeries and/or long hospital stays. I offer these ideas to you in the hope that, when you or someone you care about must go into the hospital, you will make use of them for a safer, more pleasant experience.

1. Surviving the Hospital

Here are a few tips to help you get back from the hospital in good shape.

Insist that everyone who comes into your room clean their hands. No exceptions. Hospitals are world-class germ factories, and hospital germs are potentially lethal. Healthcare workers are sometimes careless; this includes physicians. *No one* should be insulted or cross—or allowed to be so—if you say to them, "Have you washed your hands?" And if you see them doing so before you ask, reinforce their act with: "I saw you cleaned your hands, thanks."

Be totally nit-picky and tiresome about this: It could save your life. This applies to your own visitors as well. Why? Because they touch hospital surfaces, like elevator buttons and door handles, which are crawling with germs. If any children visit, make sure they *do not* play on the floor; floors are impossible to keep germ free except in very special circumstances. If you drop something unimportant on the floor, like a towel, for example, just forget about it. If you drop something valuable to you, get your next visitor to clean it with hospital-strength germicide before you let it anywhere near your bed. Your visitor should be able to get germicide from the nurse.

Check every dose of medication you are given. Staff giving medicine are busy people, sometimes not perfectly trained, and always human beings. That means mistakes can be made—and often *are* made—in the type and amount of medication given. Again, be totally nit-picky and tiresome about this; it could prove life saving. And resist the impulse to chat with the person giving out the pills while they are doing so—distracting them from their task is unwise.

When a caregiver hands you a little white cup with pills in it, ask them to identify each one. What is it? What is the dosage? What is the purpose? If they're not sure, or you're not sure about the answers, ask to speak to someone in higher authority. It is better to be a bit of a pain than to get the wrong medicine. *Two people who used this checklist have told me that this bit of advice saved their lives.*

If you don't feel right, speak up. Don't be a "nice" person. If you hurt more than you think you should or in the wrong place or more than you can tolerate, or if you have a noticeable physical symptom that you were not told to expect, let your nurse know, fast. Things can go wrong; that's why you're in the hospital. But if the staff doesn't hear from you that there's a problem, they may not discover it on their own.

If you ask for your nurse and she doesn't come promptly, ask again *if* it seems serious. Tell the person who answers your call why you're asking. Someone known as the unit clerk gets most of the buzzes requesting assistance, and occasionally the clerk can be overly protective of the nurses' time. If you don't feel you have gotten the help you need, ask to speak with a physician. An acute-care patient has the right to ask to do that for a medical concern, and the request must be honored. It may not be honored fast, but if you keep asking it will be eventually.

If you have a personnel problem as distinct from a medical one, you must go up the chain of command: nurse assistant, nurse, charge nurse (the person in charge of your unit or floor), director of nursing (the big boss). However, if your problem is not serious from a medical point of view, it may be best to wait your turn. Most nurses have too many patients to look after, and in an acute-care hospital, one of the other patients may be in serious trouble. If you complain loudly over a matter that's not truly urgent, you may find staff slower to respond if later you do need them urgently.

Don't let your pain get away from you. Pain medicine can make you feel "dopey," and you may wish to avoid that feeling as much as possible. Bear in mind, however, that it's much easier to keep pain at a manageable level than to bring it down from a high level. Some patients try to tough it out or cut back on pain meds on their own. Not smart: The staff will be working to help you cut back as soon as that's appropriate. Let them guide you.

Ask your physicians how you can reach them and colleagues who will be acting for them in their absence, 24/7. If you develop a serious problem in the hospital, you may need to reach your physician to get it put right. This is unusual, but it happens. Without the correct emergency-contact information, you could be in big trouble. Get the right info *before* you enter the hospital, and write it in your notebook (see below).

Ask your physician about ordering a bowel regimen along with pain-control medicines. Unfortunately, some doctors consistently forget to do this; unfortunate because opiates are powerful intestinal plugs and post-surgery is a particularly unpleasant time to be constipated. You will likely want a stool softener *and* probably a motility agent (which makes your intestines move to expel your feces). Presumably, your surgeon is highly experienced and should write these orders automatically; even so, better to be safe. These meds need to be in writing on your chart for the nurses to follow the regimen.

If you take non-surgery-related medicines, don't assume the hospital will have them for you. This gets complicated. You should not take anything in the hospital without your doctor's and the hospital's knowledge. Begin by telling the doc what you usually take. If it's okay for you to continue using that medicine, make sure the hospital has it on hand, or ask your doctor if you can bring your own. And be sure the physician writes in your chart that it *is* ok for you to take it. Nurses are not allowed to accept a patient's word for what the doc says. They must get that authorization in writing. This requirement is a valuable safety feature. Don't try to get around it.

Write things down. Always have a notebook and pencil by your side; tie the pencil to the notebook so it's there when you need it. Jot down any questions that occur to you during the day so when a doctor or a nurse comes bursting into your room, you'll have everything ready to ask them. Medical-team visits—typically sudden, brief, and *very* early in the morning—can drive everything out of your mind just when it needs to be clear and focused. Your little book will keep you on track.

Whenever a caregiver delivers instructions— "use the spirometer every sixty minutes," say—write it down. You may forget whether it's every sixty minutes or every six hours. Write down the names of every staff member who works with you. Because you'll be stressed and perhaps on pain medicine, you'll also be forgetful, and most staffers appreciate it when they are called by name. If you want to try to arrange a change, it's also a help to know, for example, that Jeannie is the respiratory therapist who was so nice and Andrea the one who had a bad attitude. In addition, before you go to the hospital, write in the front of the notebook, clearly and in large letters that you can read without glasses (since you may not always have them available), the phone numbers for family and close friends. Your cell phone may go missing, you may not have your glasses, and anesthetics and pain-control meds can make you forget even the most familiar things.

In case of emergency. What if you need help urgently, and you ring your call bell and yell and no one responds? (This happens, although rarely.) Pick up your room phone and ask the operator to get you the physician on duty. Every hospital is supposed to have at least one physician on duty 24/7. I hope you won't have to use this tip, but you should know it in case you need it.

2. Care Package for a Hospital Patient

This list is designed for someone going into the hospital for scheduled surgery. It can easily be adjusted for hospital patients in other circumstances, such as an illness that has required hospitalization or an emergency admission.

When you go in the hospital for surgery, you are stripped of possessions. That's a necessary part of the process. But here's a list of a few special things that can help you retain a sense of yourself in the middle of all the new experiences.

If you're going to be in the Intensive Care Unit following surgery, have a family member check with the staff before bringing in anything listed below. ICUs are extra careful about possible sources of infection, and hospital rules may prohibit some or all of these items in your ICU room.

Before admission, make up a little care package for yourself and give it to the person who will be coming to see you after the surgery is over and you're in your room. Don't try to have it with you when you go *into* surgery, because patient belongings sometimes get misplaced—or stolen. Here are a few suggestions. The first five, in my opinion, are important. The others are nice but not essential.

Photograph(s) and religious symbol(s): It is sweet to see something that is *yours* in your room, so a snap of someone you love and/or a symbol or image of a religious figure will help remind you of who you are/whose you are. Be sure not to bring anything that is unique or valuable—only a copy of a photo in an inexpensive frame, etc. Size matters; small is good.

Eye mask—some lights get left on day and night; roommate watches TV; the nurse comes in to check on you and flips on the big overhead light, and so on. If you don't have an eye mask, a slightly damp, folded face cloth over your eyes can help a little.

Ear plugs—hospitals are incredibly *noisy*. People yell, TVs roar, carts rattle, floor-polishing machines whine. Sleep is remarkably hard to come by. Ear plugs can help. Let your nurse know you're using them so she won't think you're deaf. And if you don't have plugs, take a square or two of toilet paper, chew it briefly until it is wet, and fit it into your ear. Solders do this in war zones, and it can be quite effective.

Eyeglasses. If you wear them, remember that you'll need to arrange for them to be brought to you after the surgery. Have a spare pair stored with a family member or trusted friend in case your first one gets lost.

Regarding reading glasses, as an extra backup step, tell family or friend the strength of drugstore spectacles that work for you. You won't be doing much reading when you're first in the hospital, but it's an enormous help to have glasses on hand.

Notebook and pen or pencil. See "Surviving the Hospital" for why these are needed.

Less essential but very nice to have:

Lavender oil or something similar to put on your pillow. The antimicrobial gels the caregivers use can have an unpleasant smell.

Cheap, brightly colored blankets. Patients often feel cold, even when the room is warm, and hospital blankets are remarkably flimsy. Bring a clean blanket or two. Make it a cheap one, so you can leave it—and its hospital germs and smells—behind when you check out. A brightly *colored* blanket will stand out, make staff a little more aware of you. This can be a help generally—and particularly when you really need assistance.

Cell phone. Hospital rooms usually have land-line phones, but often you have to stretch to reach them, which can be painful or impossible after surgery. It is easier to lie in bed just the way you want with your cell phone at your side. Other advantages: You can identify the caller, which you can't do on the room phone; you can usually take your cell with you if you're taken out of your room for a test or whatever; it is more convenient for people you want to hear from to call you directly rather than going through the hospital switchboard, especially if the operator doesn't know what room you're in or if you've been moved.

Of course, your cell might not work in the hospital; you'll have try it there to find out.

Portable music players. After you begin to recover from surgery, you might welcome the chance to listen to a little favorite music. It could help re-establish your own internal rhythms. It also could serve as a welcome sound screen between you and the hospital racket. If you have an Apple gadget or something similar, with earphones, get it prepared and fully charged, and give it to family or friend to bring in once you have come through the surgery and the anesthetic. The downside is that a valuable gadget may "walk," but something inexpensive is worth risking.

Reading material. It's highly unlikely you'll read anything demanding until your pain meds have been cut back. In fact, you probably won't feel up to any serious reading until you get back home. Consider bringing several light magazines—light in both weight and intellectual content. You'll have something you can flip through without any exertion. You probably won't want to do even that much for the first day or two.

(For women) A pretty bed jacket or shawl. Although this won't appeal for a while, once you're starting to recover it might be nice to have an attractive, morale-boosting garment to put over your shoulders. Because you'll probably have an IV for a while, you won't be able to put your arms through sleeves unless the staff can disconnect and reconnect the IV line, and they'll probably be too busy to do all that cheerfully.

Having something pretty will lift your spirits and send a positive signal to your caregivers. A man might want to bring a flannel shirt—again, in a bright color—to serve the same purpose.

Chewing gum and/or candy. Your mouth may crave something other than what the hospital provides. Mint gum, say, or a sucker ball might be a pleasant change. Don't take those or similar treats for the first few days after surgery or after tests requiring anesthesia: You'll be dropping off to sleep suddenly and might choke. And before starting, be sure to check with your nurse to make sure it's okay.

3. When Someone You Love Is Terminally Ill Resources and Tips for Caregivers

Nearly every one of us will sooner or later be the caregiver for a terminally ill person whom we love. If you're not doing that right now, remember where you've put this book, because this brief section contains knowledge you will someday almost surely need to have.

The first and most important thing to know is:

You can bear this.

Truly. It is hard, so hard, and scary, and painful, yet you will find the strength within yourself to endure what must be endured. What people can bear, when they must, is astonishing. You have more strength—emotional and spiritual strength—within you than you may realize. When you contemplate the death of someone who is very dear to you, know that it may be very hard, but you *can* bear it.

Know what your loved one wants at the end of life. Please be sure you or someone you know has a Healthcare Power of Attorney for your loved one. That's all but essential, because at the end of life, dying people are often unable to make their wishes known. Should they have assisted breathing—a ventilating machine? Heart compressions if their heart stops, knowing that this is very painful and ribs will likely be broken and that although the heartbeat can sometimes be restored, it will probably fail again soon?

I had a dear friend who did not have someone to speak for her when she needed it. (I couldn't do so; I was out of the country at the time.) She wound up having six "Code Blues" —heart compressions, electric shocks to the heart, breathing tube inserted—in the last ten hours of her life before she was finally allowed to complete the dying process. Many of her ribs were broken in the process. It was horrific. It never should have happened.

You need to have clear conversations with your loved one about their wishes for end-of-life procedures. Even then, you'll almost surely not cover what may actually occur, because so many different things can happen. But the more you know about their preferences, the more you can help manage things so they proceed as your loved one would wish.

Key questions to ask them are:

1. Do you want to be resuscitated if your heart stops?

2. Do you want aggressive treatments such as intubation (breathing tube) and mechanical ventilation (breathing machine)?
3. Do you want antibiotics?
4. If you can't eat on your own, do you want to be fed artificially either through a tube that goes into your stomach or a line that goes into a vein (intravenously)?

Sometimes it's easy to have these conversations, and sometimes people just won't go there—no matter how close you are to them. Just do what you can and take note of the responses.

There's a fine book by Atul Gawande, MD called *Being Mortal.* I think every adult over thirty should read it. It's difficult reading, not because it is hard to understand—it isn't—but because it makes us look at the painful realities of being mortal, aging, and dying. Hiding from these realities won't make them go away. And Dr. Gawande's book is wise, calm, and helpful. Read it!

Care for yourself. You, the caregiver, must take care of yourself. You are the most important resource your loved one has. If you get sick or are so wiped out you forget things, your loved one will suffer at least as much as you will. Eating right, exercising, taking care of your body and your spirit—doing all these things is vital for the welfare of the person you love.

Check out hospice. It is one of the best sources of help as life draws to a close. If your loved one is dying, consider hospice for support for that person *and* for you yourself. Good hospice services are sometimes superior to hospital services in certain areas: pain control; handling some of the seemingly mundane but potentially difficult physical aspects of dying; providing social, psychological, and spiritual support.

Understand that going on hospice care is not necessarily the end of the line. If a miracle occurs and your loved one is restored to better health, it is easy to discontinue hospice services. Gravely ill people on hospice can obtain services that can help when things are beyond their ability to control on their own. Alas, not all hospice services are equal. If more than one is available in your area, compare them.

Find ways to keep people informed. If someone you love is ill, keeping all the people they and you care about up to date on how they are doing can be immensely time consuming. Sending out group emails may seem efficient; but the replies to your messages will flood your inbox, and you may feel overwhelmed if you try to answer them individually. A better way to manage the flow of information is to use one of the free web-based services designed for this purpose.

As of this writing, two such services (one non-profit, one for-profit) you might want to check out are "Caring Bridge" (http://www.caringbridge.org/) and "Care Pages" (https://www.carepages.com/). Each provides easy-to-follow instructions on how to set up a web page in as little as five minutes. Once it's ready to go, you provide links to whomever you wish. Then you post updates whenever you like, and your friends respond as they choose, right on the web page. Their posts do not have to be personally answered; but you can read them yourself and read them to your loved one as well. Over time a community forms in support of you both.

Get help from others. You need *relief* when you're caregiving. Don't try to tough it out by attempting to take care of everything yourself. Accept help—ask for it! Some—or many—people honestly would like to help, even though in most cases you'll need to tell them how. Figure out what you need that someone else can do and let them do it. You can set up a website, or get a friend to manage the lists of needs and offers, and let people *do* something. Among the most obvious things others can do for you:

— bring you meals: Specify when you'd like them and how many people need to be fed. (You may have extra family members staying with you.) Let the givers know of any dietary restrictions;

— run errands: Pick up something at the drugstore; take clothes to the cleaners; shop for needed items;

— help with chores: Rake your yard, water your plants, run a few loads of laundry, or do some other home chore for you;

— sit with your loved one while you take a well-deserved break.

It can be extremely hard to *accept* help gracefully. But doing so is an important piece of personal growth for us all. Many of us like to think of ourselves as self-sufficient and independent. In fact, however, we are all connected, and the help you need today may be the help you give others—or have already given them—at another time. Moreover, if you keep turning down people's offers of assistance, they may eventually get discouraged. Then, when you truly need them, they won't be available.

Anticipate exhaustion. Even if the caregiving isn't that physically arduous, it will be emotionally draining. You'll need to be able to take a purpose-free walk, pay bills, go to the dentist, call a friend. Arrange for coverage so you can do these things. If you can afford it and can find a reliable person, have him or her come in from time to time so you have a pre-established period for your own appointments and leisure activities. If you can't, ask a friend or relative to plan and commit to a certain time—as a gift. It means a lot to know that you'll have, for example, Thursday from 2:30 to 5:00 covered. When Thursday comes, you might decide not to leave your home, but it will be good to know that you can.

As part of dealing with exhaustion, take care of your body and your emotions, which may be sore, respectively, from unusual physical effort, from seeing the deterioration in your loved one's health, and from actual or anticipated grief. If you can, get massages, Reiki, acupuncture, healing touch, or whatever works for you. Find someone whom you can tell honestly how you are feeling—and who will understand and honor your completely reasonable need to complain.

Ask for prayer support. Even if you yourself are not a believer, ask for prayer from everyone you know for whom it is a vital reality. If you are part of a religious community, tell people—not just the leaders but also the members—that you covet their prayers. Prayer does make a difference. Miracles are rare, which is why they're called miracles. Yet prayer support helps in ways that are hard to explain but real.

Find professional care if needed. Suppose you are taking care of your loved one in your own home. Perhaps you have promised them you will do everything you can so they can die at home. Recognize that no matter how hard you try, this may end up being impossible.

Consider these daunting problems. It is important to prevent bed-sores. But if you are physically unable to do what must be done to prevent them, yet persist in trying, you are likely to hurt yourself—mess up your back, say—and hurt your loved one as well. If they develop complicated symptoms—hard-to-control pain, seizures, agitation, delusions—or if they are too heavy for you to lift or care for in physical ways on your own, you must face reality and get professional help.

It is possible that your situation can be managed by what is called home healthcare, which is help delivered in your loved one's home by people with the necessary physical strength as well as various levels of skill. Finding the right service, and managing it over time, may require considerable effort, attention, and skill on your part. Home healthcare services range from dreadful to excellent.

There may not be good home healthcare in your area; you may be unable to afford it for the number of hours needed; or it may not fully meet your loved one's needs. In such a case, you have no choice but to find an institution to provide the professional care your loved one must have. Ask your physician and your friends for advice about where to go. Check out facilities yourself; ask questions; visit at non-traditional hours as well as traditional ones; and make the move.

Once the move has been made, keep spending as much time as you possibly can in your loved one's new "home." Often, especially at the end of life, you will be able to sleep in your loved one's room or just down the hall.

An *advocate* is essential for someone who is dying in an institution. Be that advocate! Seek and find good and caring people whom you can encourage and who can make a huge difference in your loved one's situation.

Hope. It is only natural, when you are sitting by the side of someone you love who is dying, to ask: "Is this the end?" Many religions teach that life continues after death. But not all of us—irrespective of our official religious beliefs—share that hope, especially when death is near.

I believe that we have reason for significant hope that death is not the end. In my opinion, many of the stories told in this book support that point of view. The choice to hope or not to hope is up to you.

Bibliography

Note: Entries prefaced by an asterisk offer information about the kinds of prayer referred to in this book (silent prayer, contemplative prayer, and/or meditation).

Borg, Marcus. *The Heart of Christianity*. San Francisco: HarperOne, 2004.

*Bourgeault, Cynthia. *The Heart of Centering Prayer: Nondual Christianity in Theory and Practice*. Boulder, CO: Shambhala, 2016.

**The Cloud of Unknowing*. New York: Doubleday, 1996.

Cooper, Diana. *Diana Cooper: Autobiography*. New York: Carroll & Graf, 1985

The Episcopal Church. *The Book of Common Prayer and Administration of the Sacraments and Other Rites and Ceremonies of the Church*. New York: Church Hymnal Corporation and Seabury, 1979.

———. *Ministry with the Sick: Revised and Expanded Edition with rites from The Book of Common Prayer and Enriching our Worship 2*. New York: Church Publishing, 2005

Joseph, Judith C. *A Chaplain's Companion*. Newtown, PA: JCJoseph, Ltd.

*Keating, Thomas. *Open Mind Open Heart: The Contemplative Dimension of the Gospel*. New York: Continuum, 1998.

Kübler-Ross, MD, Elisabeth and Ira Byock, MD *On Death and Dying: What the Dying Have to Teach Doctors, Nurses, Clergy and Their Own Families*. New York: Macmillan, 1969.

*Laird, Martin. *Into the Silent Land: A Guide to the Christian Practice of Contemplation*. New York: Oxford University Press, 2006.

Masci, David. "Scientists and Belief." http://www.pewforum.org/2009/11/05/scientists-and-belief/

Maxwell, Joan Paddock. "Great is Thy Faithfulness." *Journal of Pastoral Care*, 57 (2003) 465–6.

*Merton, Thomas. *Contemplative Prayer*. New York: Doubleday, 1996.

———. *The Seven-Storey Mountain*. Orlando, FL: Harcourt Brace Jovanovich, 1978.

*Nhat Hanh, Thich and Vo-Dihn Mai. *The Miracle of Mindfulness: An Introduction to the Practice of Meditation*. Boston: Beacon, 1987.

*Sardello, Robert et al. *Silence: The Mystery of Wholeness*. Berkeley: Goldenstone, 2006.

Singh, Kathleen Dowling. *The Grace in Dying: A Message of Hope, Comfort, and Spiritual Transformation*. New York: HarperCollins, 1995

Vance, Landis Michaux Fielden. *Spiritual Experiences of Chronic Illness When There Is No Personal God*. PhD diss., Union Institute and University. 2007.

VandeCreek, Larry and Laurel Burton, eds. "Professional Chaplaincy: Its Role and Importance in Healthcare: A White Paper." *The Journal of Pastoral Care* (Spring 2001) 81–97.